Remembering the Reformation

The 500th anniversary of the Reformation in 2017 focuses the mind on the history and significance of Protestant forms of Christianity. It also prompts the question of how the Reformation has been commemorated on past anniversary occasions. In an effort to examine various meanings attributed to Protestantism, this book recounts and analyzes major commemorative occasions, including the famous posting of the 95 Theses in 1517 or the birth and death dates of Martin Luther, respectively 1483 and 1546. Beginning with the first centennial jubilee in 1617, the book makes its way to the 500th anniversary of Martin Luther's birth, internationally marked in 1983. While the book focuses on German-speaking lands, it also looks at Reformation commemorations in other countries, notably in the United States. The central argument is that past commemorations have been heavily shaped by their historical moment, exhibiting confessional, liberal, nationalist, militaristic, Marxist, and ecumenical motifs, among others. Recognizing this reality should make us pause and take stock of exactly what historical conditions and forces underlay the commemoration efforts in 2017. More generally, it should prompt us to reflect on the ethical and interpretative issues at stake in commemorating major religious events and persons.

Thomas Albert Howard is Professor of History and the Humanities and holder of the Phyllis and Richard Duesenberg Chair in Christian Ethics at Valparaiso University.

Remembering the Reformation

An Inquiry into the Meanings of Protestantism

THOMAS ALBERT HOWARD

OXFORD
UNIVERSITY PRESS

Great Clarendon Street, Oxford, OX2 6DP,
United Kingdom

Oxford University Press is a department of the University of Oxford.
It furthers the University's objective of excellence in research, scholarship,
and education by publishing worldwide. Oxford is a registered trade mark of
Oxford University Press in the UK and in certain other countries

First published 2016
First published in paperback 2018

Impression: 1

Published in the United States of America by Oxford University Press
198 Madison Avenue, New York, NY 10016, United States of America

British Library Cataloguing in Publication Data

Data available

Library of Congress Cataloging in Publication Data

Data available

ISBN 978-0-19-875419-0 (Hbk.)
ISBN 978-0-19-880849-7 (Pbk.)

Printed in Great Britain by
Clays Ltd, St Ives plc

To three "Marks," friends and mentors:
Mark A. Noll, Mark L. Sargent, and Mark Schwehn

Acknowledgments

I take great delight in recognizing the individuals and institutions that have enabled me to complete this book.

I have received generous funding from the German Academic Exchange (DAAD), the John Templeton Foundation through its Religion and Innovation in Human Affairs (RIHA) initiative, and the summer scholarship and faculty sabbatical programs at Gordon College. I am also grateful to Valparaiso University and its Provost Mark Biermann for granting me a leave in the spring semester of 2016, which allowed me to bring this project to completion.

A conference panel sponsored by the American Society of Church History, Refo500, the Conference on Faith and History, and the Society of Reformation Research allowed me to present aspects of this book and receive valuable feedback. I am grateful to the Oxford Research Centre in the Humanities at Oxford University for hosting a conference where I presented parts of Chapter 4. Cambridge University's Centre for Research in the Arts, Social Sciences and Humanities hosted me as well and allowed me to present on aspects of Chapter 3.

Some material in this book has previously appeared in other venues; these include "Remembering the Reformation, 1817 and 1883: Commemorating the Past as Agent and Mirror of Social Change," in Donald Yerxa (ed.), *Religion and Innovation: Antagonists or Partners?* (Bloomsbury Academic, 2015); (with Sarah Hinlicky-Wilson) "Repent and Celebrate," *Christian Century*, 132 (2015): 20–3; and (with Mark A. Noll) "The Reformation at Five Hundred," *First Things*, 247 (Nov. 2014): 43–8. I am grateful to be able to reprint material from these sources in this book.

The interlibrary loan staff at Gordon College, and especially Lori Franz, deserve effusive praise and thanks for their many labors on my behalf. I am also thankful for the patience, professionalism, and courtesies of staff members at Harvard University's Widener Library and the Andover-Harvard Theological Library, where much research on this project took place.

I happily sing praises to the highly competent and long-suffering staff members of Gordon College's Center for Faith and Inquiry. These include Ryan Groff, Debbie Drost, Susanne McCarron, and Victoria Quay. Their help was simply first-rate and indispensible. Several of our student aides and "apprentices" at the Center also lent a hand, so many thanks to Elizabeth Baker, Mary Hierholzer, Matthew Reese, Katharine Stephens, Hannah Strauss, and Hilary (Sherratt) Yancey. Elspeth Currie, heroically, procured images and permissions for this book and helped in many other ways.

I would like to say a special word of gratitude to Wolfgang Flügel, Ute Possekel, Zachary Purvis, and Ronald K. Rittgers, all of whom went over the entire manuscript and provided valuable feedback. Other individuals who deserve mention include Mark D. Chapman, Janel Curry, Ernst-Joachim Waschke, Laura Whitney, Martha Crain, Donald Yerxa, Johannes Zachhuber, Herman Selderhuis, and Sarah Hinlicky-Wilson.

Tom Perridge and Karen Raith at Oxford University Press have been extremely helpful, professional, and courteous. I hope that they, too, take satisfaction in the completion of this book.

And once again, let me express gratitude to Agnes R. Howard and delight in the fact that our lives and vocations are deeply intertwined.

This book is dedicated to three "Marks" who have been significant in encouraging, shaping, and ennabling my own scholarly vocation: Mark L. Sargent, Mark Schwehn, and Mark A. Noll.

Thomas Albert Howard

Georgetown, Massachusetts,
March 2016

Contents

List of Figures

Is not the pastness of the past the more profound, the
more legendary, the more immediately it falls before the present?

(Thomas Mann)

He who invokes the past is always secure.
The dead will not rise to witness against him.

(Czesław Miłosz)

Introduction

The Reformation and the Remembered Past

A red-letter date looms: 31 October 2017, the five-hundredth anni-versary of the Reformation, the widely recognized date when Martin Luther putatively nailed his 95 Theses on the Castle Church door in Wittenberg, Saxony, and thereby introduced into the stream of history what came to be called "Protestantism." Many churches, seminaries, educational institutions, and even whole countries are confronted with a formidable task: why and how should one go about marking such a momentous milestone?

Indeed how does one commemorate a historical force of such complexity, diversity, and influence? Protestantism, it merits recalling, has not only been credited for restoring Christian truth or blamed for church divisions, but has been regarded as a cause of modern liber-alism, capitalism, religious wars, tolerance, democracy, individualism, subjectivism, nationalism, pluralism, freedom of conscience, modern science, secularism, and so much else. In the nineteenth century, the philosopher Hegel associated the onward-and-upward course of the "World Spirit" with Protestantism; in the twentieth, Max Weber famously linked it to the rise of capitalism, while H. Richard Niebuhr once called Protestantism simply "the religious phase of modern, western civilization."[1] As the historian Brad S. Gregory, in a much-discussed recent study, has observed: "What transpired five centuries ago continues today profoundly to influence the lives of everyone not only in Europe and North America but all around the world, whether or not they are Christians or indeed religious believers of any kind."[2] The University of Halle-Wittenberg is prepared to recognize in 2017 the Reformation's long-term impact on "social structures, patterns of perception, and customs, as well as legal concepts, economic structures, scopes of artistic expression, and cultural identities."[3]

Of course, Protestantism's historical significance is not restricted to its relationship to "modernity." It has been and remains an enduring, albeit protean *religious* force in its own right, impacting the lives and communities of millions of people in the West and, through missionary endeavors taking off especially in the eighteenth century, across the globe.[4] Today, there are an estimated 500 million Protestants in the world—fractured into thousands of denominations and movements.[5] The dynamics and implications of this reality have been well documented by much recent work on global Christianity by scholars such as Andrew F. Walls, Peter Berger, Dana L. Robert, Philip Jenkins, David Martin, Todd Johnson, among others.[6]

The diverse, far-flung influence of Protestantism could be documented in still other ways, but that might risk belaboring the obvious. In this inquiry, I am not so much interested in tracing the spread and influence of Protestantism per se; rather, with an eye on the quincentenary in 2017, I aim to consider the Reformation as it has been celebrated, interpreted, and remembered on past commemorative occasions, beginning in the early modern period with the first centenary "jubilee" in 1617, but focusing greater attention on anniversary events in the nineteenth and twentieth centuries. My concentration will be primarily on commemorations in German-speaking areas, the cradle of the Reformation. But I shall also offer lingering glances at a number of commemorations in English-speaking countries, particularly those in my native country, the United States, which, as Alexis de Tocqueville and many others have observed, was established, at least in its influential New England parts, on purely Protestant grounds, never having had a "medieval" or "Catholic" past from which to depart.

* * *

An attempt to canvass several hundred years of Protestantism in a single volume understandably raises questions—and likely eyebrows. To define the focus and argument of what follows more precisely, permit me to offer several preliminary reflections and caveats.

First, since this inquiry was occasioned by considering the 500th anniversary of 1517 in 2017, my point of departure will largely be

Luther and the *Lutheran Reformation*, because, at least since the seventeenth century, the Reformation has been associated with Luther's initial condemnation of indulgences—what in German is called Luther's *Thesenanschlag*, which might literally be translated as "the attack of the [95] theses." It is not lost on me that the Reformation has many other personalities and facets: Zwinglian, Calvinist, Anglican, Anabaptist, and so on. And this is to say nothing about the whole topic of the Catholic or Counter-Reformation in the sixteenth century.[7] But what especially fascinates about Lutheran centenary commemorations, whether in 1617 or 1917, is the degree to which they have stirred commemorators to enlist Luther's person and actions in a much broader interpretation of the "significance," "essence," and/ or "influence" of the Reformation or of Protestantism as a whole. The same could be said of commemorations of Luther's birth and death years (1483, 1546), several of which will be treated in this inquiry. Put differently, I am less interested in Luther himself than in how invocatory references to him on major commemorative occasions have served as touchstones for later generations to hazard explanations and/or summaries of the very rhyme and reason of Protestantism.

Second, this inquiry draws material frequently from academic settings, primarily universities but also professional academic societies. The Reformation of course began in such a setting and Luther and his colleagues at the University of Wittenberg (founded in 1502) often appealed to their scholarly credentials to legitimize their actions.[8] Admittedly, there is no such thing as a "pure" academic environment. In German lands and elsewhere, universities have frequently been the sites of messy, competing historical forces and interests, notably political and religious ones. These, too, will also receive significant attention in what follows.

One German academic and ecclesiastical convention in particular merits highlighting at the outset: the jubilee or *Jubiläum*, a term found but employed less commonly in English. "Commemoration," "celebration," or, in some instances, even "anniversary" comes closest to its more frequent German usage. The word is etymologically connected to "celebration" (*Jubel*) and developed its modern usage from an older religious occasion, namely the Catholic jubilee year (*anno iubilaeum*), first proclaimed for the year 1300 by Pope Boniface VIII.[9] The Catholic jubilee stemmed in turn from the still older Jewish jubilee, prescribed for the Israelites in Leviticus 25 of the Hebrew scriptures as a special holy year to be observed every fifty years: "And you shall hallow the fiftieth year, and proclaim liberty throughout the land to all its inhabitants; it shall be a jubilee for you.... [The year] shall be holy to you" (RSV).[10] The original Hebrew term derives from the word used for a ram's horn—made into an instrument and employed sonorously to mark sacred occasions.[11]

Third, examining Reformation commemorations compels one to distinguish sharply between the *past itself* and the *remembered past*. The focus throughout will be on the latter, not the former. In considering this distinction, I have found helpful the work of Jan Assmann, particularly his reflections on "collective memory," "social memory," and/or "mnemohistory"—the latter his neologism for the remembered past. Unlike history proper, he argues, social memory "is concerned not with the past as such but only the past as it is remembered. It surveys the story-lines of tradition, the webs of intertextuality, the diachronic continuities and discontinuities of reading the past." Or, more fully:

> The historical study of the events should be carefully distinguished from the study of their commemoration, tradition, and transformation in the collective memory of the people concerned. Seen as an individual and as a social capacity, memory is not simply the storage of past "facts" but the ongoing work of reconstructive imagination. In other words, the past cannot be stored but always has to be "processed" and mediated. This mediation depends on the semantic frames and needs of a given individual or society within a given present.[12]

Fourth, while this inquiry is concerned about the past as mediated by the present, it is important to keep in mind that the process of mediation or reconstruction is never a purely open-ended one, up to the whim of the collective agency doing the remembering. The actual past (insofar as its relevant contours are more or less known) places boundaries on what can and cannot be remembered and how. That people reconstruct the past to meet the needs of the present is evident enough, as Richard Sennett observes, but this "should not lead to loose talk that suggests it is the whole story. The present shapes our understanding of the past, yes.... [But] the past also shapes the present, even when the most powerful people and classes and institutions least want it to."[13] In what follows, I try to strike a balance, recognizing the selective, sometimes even manipulative, nature inherent in acts of social memory, based on the "needs" and "semantic frames" of a given present. But I also recognize the limits of this process, based on the implacable record of the past itself. Mexico cannot plausibly claim Ronald Reagan as a founding father; Jews cannot insist their faith only started with John Calvin. Not to put too fine a point on it, what, finally, interests me is the act of remembering the past, not the past being remembered: the Reformation as it was understood, say, in 1817, 1883, 1917, or 1983 more than the actual events of 1517—although the former and the latter are of course complexly and inextricably linked.[14]

Furthermore, the fact that different collective bodies in society often compete to remember past events places limits on the possibilities and parameters of social memory. Rivalry over who has the higher ground in remembering—who "gets it right"—frequently leads to disputes and disagreements, and these, in turn, shape the conditions of plausibility for acts of memory. As Michael Schudson writes, "[P]eople's ability to reconstruct the past just as they wish is limited by the crucial social fact that other people within their awareness are trying to do the same thing. Different reconstructions clash. Control over the past is disputed and the past becomes contested terrain.... There is [therefore] a politics of memory that requires study."[15] Although the attempt to convince others of the correctness of one's understanding of the past might motivate acts of remembrance in the first place, it is also true that such competition shapes and places constraints on possible reconstructions. At the same time, competition over historical memory can also amplify differences. It was not lost on early Protestants celebrating the first centennial jubilee in 1617, for example, that their Catholic counterparts possessed a different vantage point; but this usually led to differences being polemically exaggerated, not diminished.[16] In our ecumenical age, of course, this has changed considerably, as shall be made clear in due course, even if the residue of past polemics strongly persists.

Fifth, social memory solicits participation and filiation, and it seeks to stabilize identity, even as it can also modify identities and serve as a measuring rod of previous modifications that have taken place. As Edward Casey writes, "commemoration has everything to do with participation.... [I]ts functional essence is to solicit and sustain participation between commemorators and that to which they pay homage, often by means of co-participation."[17] Or, as John Gillis observes, "The core meaning of any individual or group identity, namely, a sense of sameness over space and time, is sustained by remembering and what is remembered is defined by the assumed identity."[18]

But, again, public remembrance can also reflect and even foster modifications of identity. Prior to the nineteenth century, for example, Reformation commemorations preponderantly sought to sustain religiously loyal identities within the confessional structures of the Holy Roman Empire. After the French Revolution and the collapse of the Empire, commemorations—seen notably during the Reformation's tercentennial in 1817—became imbued with some of the ascendant ideologies of the age, namely liberalism, nationalism, and historicism. In the twentieth century, they reflected Wilsonian idealism (in the United States) and Marxism-Leninism (in the German Democratic Republic), to offer but two more examples. Older religious currents were by no means cast aside in later commemorations, but the act of retrospection presented itself as a vehicle through with more recent ideologies could be amplified and transmitted. To refer to the tercentennial again, the Reformation in 1817 was remembered both as a recovery of religious truth and as the *fons et origo* of modern political freedoms and (German) national identity. Such politicization of the memory and meaning of the Reformation in the modern era is a recurring theme of this book.

In sum, acts of commemoration can serve as agents of both continuity and change. Social memory shores up and stabilizes identity, but it can also "imagine" forgotten or scattered group identities or invest older identity-shaping events—e.g. "the 95 Theses"—with new, often politicized meanings.[19] Identities are strengthened when efforts to achieve "retrospective contemplativeness" bring people together in rituals of memory. Without such efforts, there would be no group identities, or at least they would be fleeting and fragile; and the past that once gave substance and energy to identity formation would become what the memory theorist Maurice Halbwachs once called "dead memory."[20]

With respect to the Reformation and Protestant identity, the *Jubiläum* or special anniversary celebration, I shall argue throughout, has functioned as a crucial ritual of memory, a prophylactic against group forgetfulness and its corollary, the dissipation of identity. At the same time, jubilees have served as a vehicle to modify identity and group consciousness, often through the politicization of memory.

Such politicization—the "uses and abuses" of the past—raises moral questions about the nature of remembrance and commemoration—what we might call an "ethics of memory."[21] Are we obligated to remember people and events in the past? If we are, what is the nature, duration, and scope of this obligation and what are the appropriate means of doing so? How does one define the "we" who ought to be doing the remembering, and how and by what criteria does one distinguish between commemorations that are faithful to the past (and present) versus ones that distort or cajole it to serve dubious causes, legitimize one-sided religious narratives, and/or prop up the interests of powerful actors in society? "The duty of memory," writes Paul Ricoeur, "is the the duty to do justice, through memory, to an other than the self."[22] These deeper moral questions and considerations lurk just under the historical narrative and analysis that follows.

Finally, I should admit that I, the author, am no "detached observer" in this inquiry. As someone shaped and convicted by, although too often a willful underachiever in light of, the Christian Gospel, I have a stake in the moral (and theological) issues at play in this book. Relatedly, I am vexed and saddened by the many unhappy divisions among Christians, especially among Protestants. Remembering the Reformation appropriately and focusing attention on the ignominy of inter-Christian discord and possible remedies thereof, consequently, are some of the desired results of this inquiry. I broach these and the aforementioned ethical matters now, for we shall return to them at greater length in the conclusion.

Since what follows in significant measure is a *tour d'horizon* of past commemorations of the Reformation, permit me candidly to relinquish any claims to exhaustiveness. If I may invoke a metaphor from the natural sciences, what I attempt here might be likened to the sampling of geologic layers. Just as geologists drill into the earth to examine the sediment of remote geologic time, so I drill into layers of the social memory of the Reformation (1617, 1717, 1817...) in an effort to take stock of the circumstances and frameworks of interpretation of the more recent human past. The insights that come from such an exercise of necessity must pass through a rather severe process of selection and abridgement, but it is precisely this process that enables the types of insights that I am eager to pursue.

History does not repeat itself, to be sure. Still, the goal of this endeavor is to situate the 500th anniversary of Luther's actions in 2017 within a broader, meaningful context. What is offered here, finally, is a retrospective foray into acts of retrospection, an inquiry into the significance of commemorations of still older historical events. Such an approach will inevitably be extractive, highly interpretive, and often impressionistic. In the final analysis, then, this study aims to be more suggestive than definitive, more an effort to provoke reflection on memories and meanings of the Reformation than a claim to be the definitive last word on the subject. If one had world enough and time, I suppose more could be done. But as both are chronically in short supply, allow me simply to plead: here I stand; I can do no other.

Notes

1. H. Richard Niebuhr, "Protestantism," *Encyclopedia of the Social Sciences*, xii (New York: Macmillan, 1935), 571.
2. Brad S. Gregory, *The Unintended Reformation: How a Religious Revolution Secularized Society* (Cambridge, MA: Harvard Belknap Press of Harvard University Press, 2012), 1.
3. From conference prospectus, *Kulturelle Wirkungen der Reformation, 2017*. I would like thank professors Ernst-Joachim Waschke and Wolfgang Flügel of the University of Halle-Wittenberg for conversations with them in May of 2013 about past and upcoming Reformation-anniversary events at their singularly important institution for this topic. Flügel's work on Reformation commemorations has been particularly helpful for my own efforts.
4. Stephen Neill, *A History of Christian Missions*, 2nd edn (New York: Penguin, 1986), 187ff.
5. Todd M. Johnson et al. (eds), *The Atlas of Global Christianity, 1910–2010* (Edinburgh: University of Edinburgh Press, 2009), 68.
6. See David Martin: *Tongues of Fire: The Explosion of Protestantism in Latin America* (Oxford: Blackwell, 1990); Philip Jenkins, *The Next Christendom: The Coming of Global Christianity*, 3rd edn (Oxford: OUP, 2011); Peter Berger (ed.), *The Desecularization of the World: Resurgent Religion and World Politics* (Grand Rapids, MI: Eerdmans, 1999); Todd M. Johnson and Cindy M. Wu, *Our Global Families: Christians Embracing Common Identity in a Changing World* (Grand Rapids, MI: Baker Academic, 2015); Andrew F. Walls, *The Missionary Movement in Christian History: Studies in Transmission of Faith* (Maryknoll, NY: Orbis Books, 1996); and Dana Robert, "Shifting Southward: Global Christianity since 1945." *International Bulletin of Missionary Research*, 24(2) (2000): 50–8.

7. We should also not forget reformers prior to Luther, such as John Wycliffe or Jan Hus. See Steven Ozment, *The Age of Reform, 1250–1550: An Intellectual and Religious History of Late Medieval and Reformation Europe* (New Haven: Yale University Press, 1980), 165ff., 397ff.

8. Thomas Albert Howard, *Protestant Theology and the Making of the Modern German University* (Oxford: OUP, 2006), 60ff.

9. Joseph Stricher, "L'Année jubilaire et la tradition catholique," *Foi et Vie*, 99 (2000): 73–86.

10. Leviticus 25: 10–12 (RSV). Biblical passages in this study come from the Revised Standard Version unless otherwise noted.

11. See Calum M. Carmichael, *Illuminating Leviticus: A Study of its Laws and Institutions in the Light of Biblical Narratives* (Baltimore, MD: Johns Hopkins University Press, 2006), 122–35. Cf. Winfried Müller, "Das historische Jubiläum. Zur Geschichtlichkeit einer Zeitkonstruktion," in Winfried Müller (ed.), *Das historische Jubiläum: Genese, Ordungsleistung und Inszenierungsgeschichte eines institutionellen Mechanismus* (Münster: LIT Verlag, 2004), 1–75; J. Blecher and G. Wiemers, "Universitäten und Jubiläen," *Veröffentlichungen des Universitätsarchiv Leipzig*, 4 (2004): 25–33; and Wolfgang Flügel and Stefan Dornheim, "Die Universität als Jubliäumsmultiplikator in der Frühen Neuzeit," *Jahrbuch für Universitätsgeschichte*, 9 (2006): 51–70.

12. Jan Assmann, from *Moses the Egyptian: The Memory of Egypt in Western Monotheism*, excerpted in Jeffrey K. Olick et al. (eds), *The Collective Memory Reader* (Oxford: OUP, 2011), 209–11. Cf. Jan Assmann, "Collective Memory and Cultural Identity," *New German Critique*, 65 (1995): 125–33. Assmann, it bears noting, drew considerably from the earlier works on cultural memory pioneered by Maurice Halbwachs and Aby Warburg.

13. See Michael Schudson, "The Past in the Present versus the Present in the Past," *Communication*, 11 (1989): 105–13.

14. On this distinction, see Allan Megill, *Historical Knowledge, Historical Error: A Contemporary Guide to Practice* (Chicago: University of Chicago Press, 2007), 30.

15. Schudson, "The Past in the Present," 105ff.

16. It bears keeping in mind that both Protestants and Catholics hold in common deeper memories: scripture, the record of early Church Councils, and other memories of the church from antiquity and the Middle Ages. While interpretations of these memories frequently became contested during the 16th century, they have also served in more recent times as grounds for ecumenical rapprochement. See e.g. the use of scripture in the Second Vatican Council's Decree on Ecumenism (*Unitatis Redintegratio*) in Austin Flannery (ed.), *Vatican Council II*, i. *The Conciliar and Post-Conciliar Documents*, rev. edn. (Northport, NY: Costello Publishing Co., 1975), 452–69.

17. From Edward Casey, *Remembering: A Phenomenological Study*; excerpted in Olick et al., *Collective Memory Reader*, 185.

18. John R. Gillis (ed.), *Commemorations: The Politics of National Identity* (Princeton: Princeton University Press, 1994), 3. Cf. Shmuel N. Eisenstadt and Bernhard Giesen, "The Construction of Collective Identity," *Archives Européennes de Sociologie*, 36 (1995): 72–102.

19. Bernard Lewis, *History: Remembered, Recovered, Invented* (Princeton: Princeton University Press, 1975), 10–14. On this point, see also the classic study of Benedict Anderson, *Imagined Communities: Reflections on the Origins and Spread of Nationalism*, rev. edn. (London: Verso, 2006) and Eric Hobsbawm and Terence Ranger (eds), *The Invention of Tradition* (Cambridge: CUP, 2005).

20. Olick et al., *Collective Memory Reader*, 177.

21. Avishai Margalit, *The Ethics of Memory* (Cambridge, MA: Harvard University Press, 2002) and Miroslav Volf, *The End of Memory: Remembering Rightly in a Violent World* (Grand Rapids, MI: Eerdmans, 2006).

22. Paul Ricoeur, *Memory, History, Forgetting*, tr. Kathleen Blamey and David Pellauer (Chicago: University of Chicago Press, 2004), 89.

1

1617, 1717

Commemoration in a Confessional Age

The eternal, all-powerful God has looked upon us graciously and delivered us from the horrible darkness of the papacy and led [us] into the bright light of the Gospel.

(Abraham Scultetus, from a sermon in Heidelberg calling for the first Reformation centenary jubilee, 1617)

And you shall hallow the fiftieth year, and proclaim liberty throughout the land to all its inhabitants; it shall be a jubilee year for you...

(Leviticus 25: 10)

The first centennial of 1617 marks a decisive turning point in the social memory of the Reformation, one that would shape future commemorations, even if later ones also came to evince significant discontinuities. At the time, central Europe was characterized by what historians in recent decades have called "confessionalization," a tight connection between state and faith (whether Lutheran or Catholic), in which the duties of the secular prince and theologians and clergy dovetailed in enforcing religious orthodoxy within their borders. This reality bore testimony to the Peace of Augsburg (1555) and its well-known dictum *cuius regio, eius religio* ("whose land, their religion"), which allowed the prince to determine the confession of his territories.[1]

Not surprisingly, then, matters of religious identity stood at the center of commemorations in 1617: questions of biblical exegesis, theological polemics, and eschatological speculation pervade the events of this year. What is more, in the complex realities of the Holy Roman Empire, the line between religion and politics blurred greatly, and we might do better to think of the events of 1617 as religio-political in character.[2] The commemorations of this year also represent an important moment in the formation of European historical conscious-ness more generally, and, not least, they solidified the view of Martin Luther in the Protestant imagination as the definitive "great man" of the Reformation, the "Moses" or "Noah" of Christianity in his times.

Commemorating the Reformation in 1617 did not take place without precedents. In the late sixteenth century, a patchwork of different dates had been set aside for annual remembrance. The cities of Hamburg, Lübeck, and Braunschweig were among the first to introduce regular commemorations of the Reformation. The first two celebrated it in late spring on Trinity Sunday while the latter marked it on the first Sunday of September. In Eisleben, the town where Luther was born and died, the date of his death, 18 February, had been ceremoniously observed since his passing in 1546. Several other areas observed the date of Luther's birth or baptism each year. Electoral Brandenburg with several other territories singled out for commemoration the acceptance of a new Protestant church order (*Kirchenordnung*) and/or the first Protestant worship service. Still other places annually marked the formal presentation to the Emperor of the Augsburg Confession (25 June 1530).[3] The vast majority of commemorations prior to 1617 either focused on the birth, baptism, or death of Luther or a date marking a territory's embrace of Protestantism. The date of 31 October 1517 and the "posting of the 95 Theses" (*Thesenanschlag*) played virtually no role in the earliest commemorations.[4] In fact, the only known mention in the sixteenth century of the posting of the 95 Theses—which later became the focus of commemorations—came in a brief "vita" of Luther penned shortly after his death (1546) by Philip Melanchthon and published in the first collected edition of Luther's writings.[5]

The circumstances and events of 1617, however, hoisted 1517 into the historical limelight, where it has stayed ever since. Were it not for the occurrences of 1617, in fact, the quincentenary of the Reforma-tion would likely not be designated to occur in 2017.

As the seventeenth century dawned, Protestant territories within the Holy Roman Empire were confronted by several realities that would shape the memory of the Reformation. The first was the threat of an increasingly assertive Tridentine Catholic Church; the second, division in their own ranks between Lutheran and Reformed (Calvinist) areas. Finally, there existed divisions *within* Lutheranism—between stricter traditionalists ("Gneiso-Lutherans") and more moderate ("Philippist") positions. The former cleaved to the Formula of Concord (1577) as the benchmark of Protestant (read: Lutheran) identity; the latter, the Philippists, inspired by the irenic outlook of Phillip Melanchthon, desired greater openness to the thought of the Swiss reformers, Calvin and Zwingli, especially on the topic of the Eucharist. These complex confessional dynamics fundamentally structured the social environment of the commemorations in 1617.[6]

In 1607, with other Catholic territories' nodding approval, Maximillian I of Bavaria reimposed the Catholic faith on the small city of Donauwörth, stirring alarm in many Protestant quarters. This act precipitated in short order the formation in 1608 of the so-called Protestant Union under the (Reformed) leadership of Elector Friedrich V of the Rhineland Palatinate.[7] In the years leading up to 1617, leaders and representatives from several Protestant territories, Lutheran and Reformed, met annually to discuss the Catholic threat along with other matters of common concern.

Among the earliest known calls for a centenary celebration came in 1617 in a new year's sermon given in Heidelberg by the royal chaplain, one Abraham Scultetus (1566–1625), who opined that one hundred years ago "the eternal, all-powerful God has looked upon us graciously and delivered us from the horrible darkness of the papacy (*schrecklichen finsternuß deß Bapstthumbs*) and led [us] into the bright light of the Gospel."[8] In April 1617 at the Protestant Union's annual meeting in Heilbronn, Friedrich V followed up by suggesting that a grand commemoration take place between 31 October and 2 November to mark the beginnings of the Reformation. Signatories to his proposal at the assembly included the territorial princes or their deputies of the Palatinate, Anhalt, Brandenburg, Baden-Durlach, and Württemberg, and the imperial cities of Strasbourg, Nuremberg, and Ulm. For the Elector a driving force behind the initiative was the desire to reduce tensions between Lutheran and Calvinist members of the Union. At this time, the latter were not legally recognized in the Holy Roman Empire and, in light of the Catholic threat, desired to build bridges to their Protestant co-religionists, differences and acrimony notwithstanding.[9] Exactly what commemorative events were to take place was left up to the individual territories, but in a joint resolution from 23 April 1617 the signatories affirmed that during the celebrations all bitterness and personal attacks among Protestants should be suspended and a general thanksgiving offered to God for the recovery and maintenance of the true evangelical faith some 100 years before.[10]

But the Calvinist–Lutheran rupture could not be elided so easily. As the conciliatory plans of the Protestant league and Elector Friedrich V were being hatched, scholars in Saxon Wittenberg had seized upon the moment to assert their own custodial leadership of Lutheran orthodoxy and rally together the "pure" territories—those that had officially accepted the Formula of Concord (1577) as the benchmark of confessional Lutheranism.[11] Already in November of 1616 and again in April of 1617, the dean of the philosophical faculty at Wittenberg, Erasmus Schmidt (1570–1637), made reference to a "jubilee year" (*Jobeljahr*) or "celebratory year" (*Halljahr*) year in 1617, recognizing one hundred years since Luther's initial actions.[12] From the outset, inter-Protestant irenicism was not the goal in Wittenberg. Quite the opposite: the then circulating catchphrase "God's word and Luther's writings are poison to Papists and Calvinists alike" better captures the mood.[13]

On 22 April 1617, Wittenberg's theological faculty wrote to Georg I, Elector of Saxony, requesting that "the first Luther jubilee" (*primus Jubilaeus Lutheranus*) be "celebrated with festive and heartfelt worship."[14] The Elector heartily approved and the decision was supported by the highest church authorities, the Saxon High Consistory (*Oberkonsistorium*) in Dresden, which as a body enjoined all other orthodox Lutheran territories in the Empire to observe the centenary. What is more, the Consistory made know that Saxony's theologians stood ready to provide printed material to all "pure" clergymen to help them correctly celebrate the event.

Wittenberg's theologians also requested that Georg I issue an official "Order and Instruction" to set things in motion. This transpired on 12 August 1617 when the Elector after consulting with church officials in Dresden called for the first centennial "evangelisches Jubel-Fest" and outlined the time and place of the celebrations, including a list of biblical texts on which the sermons over three days (31 October–2 November) were to be based.[15] Deeming many preachers ill-fit to reckon adequately with the significance of the occasion, the Dresden court preacher Matthias Hoë von Hoënegg (1580–1645) contributed exegetical guidelines of the biblical passages.[16] Among the passages-cum-exegeses, two stand out in significance. The first is Daniel 11: 36, interpreted as a prophecy against the papacy: "[H]e [i.e. the Pope] shall exalt himself above every god, and shall speak astonishing things against the God of gods. He shall prosper till the indignation [i.e. the Reformation] is accomplished; for what is determined shall be done." The second passage is Revelation 14: 6, in which Luther is interpreted as an avenging angel of the Apocalypse: "Then I saw another angel [i.e. Luther] flying in mid-heaven, with an eternal gospel to proclaim to those who dwell on earth to every nation and tribe and tongue and people."[17] Practically all exegeses equated devout Lutherans with the faithful remnant, "the elect," and the papacy as the despoiling "Babylon" and/or the seductive Anti-Christ of the Last Days.[18]

Printed copies of Georg's "Order and Instruction" and other directives were sent out to Lutheran territories. Saxony manifestly saw 1617 as an opportunity to shore up its authority both against the Catholic threat and against the perceived dilution of the Protestant faith by Calvinists and by the Lutherans who had rebuffed the Formula of Concord. (The latter, "Philippists" were also sometimes derided as "crypto-Calvinists.") As sermons and pamphlets indicate in the preparation before and during the events between 31 October and 2 November, the first evangelical jubilee was conceived as a commemoration of corrected faith—in contrast to the false and superseded jubilees of the Jews and the Catholics. Rome was the corrupting innovator, it was repeatedly maintained; Luther, heroically, had only returned things to the way they were supposed to be.

Neither Catholic territories within the Empire nor Rome took Protestant developments in 1617 kindly. The Protestant appropriation of the term "jubilee" proved especially vexing. In 1300, as mentioned in the introduction, the first Catholic jubilee had taken place at the instigation of Pope Boniface VIII.[19] Originally, these were to take place every 100 years. Later that was reduced to fifty years (following the biblical example in Leviticus 25), but in 1470, it was officially reduced to every twenty-five years. Prior to 1617, highly triumphalist, Tridentine jubilees had taken place in 1575 and 1600;

the next was scheduled for 1625.[20] But faced with the specter of a
Protestant jubilee, Pope Paul V, indignant, declared on 12 June 1617
that the remainder of the year was going to be observed as a year of
extraordinary jubilee for the Catholic Church. No single period was
set for the holy days, but it was to be a time, as the papal bull indicates,
of prayer and penance, so that God would protect the true faith from
the malice and heresy of its enemies and bring peace and unity to all
true Christian princes.[21] In short, then, because of the actions of
Protestants and retaliation of Catholics, 1617 became a year, we
might say, of "dueling jubilees"; to the political and religious battles
between Protestants and Catholics in the Empire was now added a
symbolic battle over the Christianized meaning of the erstwhile Jewish
"jubilee." The German Jesuit Peter Roest spoke for many of his
co-religionists when he called the Protestant celebrations a "pseudo-
jubilee" fundamentally displeasing to God.[22] A fellow Jesuit, Adam
Contze, derided the Protestant divisions on display in the 1617 jubilee,
comparing them unfavorably to the "constant" nature of the Catholic
Church.[23] Roest, Contze, and others also recycled many earlier Catholic
images of Luther as an antinomian glutton, minion of Satan, corrupter
of the youth, and arch-heresiarch.[24]

Alas, the Catholic "counter jubilee" will have to fall outside of the
scope of this inquiry.[25] But what actually happened in Protestant lands
between 31 October and 2 November 1617? And what is the general
significance of these events for subsequent jubilees and commemorations and for shaping interpretations of the Reformation? A trove of
evidence has been left behind in the form of official ordinances and
reports, sermons, academic addresses, debates, poems, plays, prayers,
pamphlets, broadsheets (*Flugblätter*), woodcuts, pictorial biographies of
Luther's life, and commemorative coins and medals. Such artifacts
made possible what memory theorists call "commemorative rituals"
or "rituals of memory," which have as a key aim "to make the past
emotionally present" to the living.[26] While the ordinances and records
are mostly prescriptive in character, telling us little about how ordin-
ary people experienced the jubilee, they do have much to tell us about
how elites planned and orchestrated the celebrations and what they
hoped to accomplish through them.

The instructions (*Verzeichnus*) for the Lutheran imperial city of
Ulm are representative of the larger phenomenon; these are particularly

important, in fact, as the published version recounts some retrospective details of what actually took place—and these do give at least some hints of the popular experience.[27] As was the case in other areas, the jubilee in Ulm was celebrated over a three-day period, from 31 October to 2 November. A few days prior, however, on 26 October, the ecclesiastical superintendent of Ulm, one Conrad Dieterich (1575–1635), informed the town's citizens that for the coming jubilee they were to comport themselves as virtuous Christians, and not be found drinking, disturbing the peace, or in any other disorderly behavior. Instead, they were to listen to sermons, pray, partake of the Eucharist, and reflect on God's grace for bringing the purified faith to their city. The focal sites of the jubilee were Ulm's main parish cathedral, the Münster, and the Spitalkirche, or the Hospital Church of the Holy Spirit. Because of the expected large number of participants, additional clergy were brought in from the countryside.[28]

The entire period was to be treated as a time of high feast: bells were rung before and after services; a full choir with organ was employed during services. The sermon delivered on 31 October at the city cathedral recalled and derided the indulgence trade, while the one on 1 November proclaimed the proper purpose of worship and inveighed against the papal abuse of the mass. Three sermons were delivered on the day of the celebration proper, Sunday, 2 November. The morning sermon took its biblical cue from Psalm 44: 1–4: "God, we have heard with our own ears, our ancestors have told us of the deeds you performed in their days, in days long ago, by your hand.... You it was my King, my God...through you we trampled down our enemies." This passage served as a touchstone to celebrate Luther and Ulm's embrace of the evangelical faith. The midday sermon had as its text Psalm 79: 1–9: "God, the pagans [read Catholics] have invaded your heritage, they have desecrated your holy temple.... Pour out your anger on the pagans." The evening sermon, based on the passages on jubilee from Leviticus 25, drew a sharp contrast between the evangelical jubilee that Ulm was observing and the misguided jubilees of the Jews and Roman Catholics. On the afternoon of 2 November, the record indicates, children were examined in their knowledge of the catechism, and later they received a special medal with a copy of a jubilee prayer in memory of the occasion.[29]

The official instructions for Ulm indicate that similar services with the same biblical texts took place at the Spitalkirche and in all rural parishes under the supervision of the Ulm church council; children in even the smallest villages were given a commemorative keepsake coin. The jubilee trickled into the week following. On Monday, the rector of the Latin school read a poem on the life of Martin Luther, composed for the occasion. On Tuesday, the rector's assistant delivered an oration on Luther and the Reformation. Later in the week, several orations in Latin were delivered by students, focusing on the topics of Luther's birth, his studies, his conversion to the evangelical cause, praiseworthy deeds during his life, and his death.[30]

The record from Ulm provides a glimpse into what took place in other Protestant territories, although differences in detail and emphasis abounded.[31] Again, most of the records are prescriptive or else homiletic, illustrating more what elites intended for the jubilee than how commoners experienced it. Despite the differences and recognizing the limitations of the evidence, several common themes recur.

First, and not surprisingly, the person of Martin Luther takes center stage in both the written and visual artifacts from 1617; he emerges as the undisputed hero of the Reformation. Like Moses, he was interpreted to be a chosen messenger, God's man or instrument (*Gottesmann, Gotteswerkzeug*), to liberate the faithful from the bondage of "Egypt," i.e. the papalist false church. Luther was also compared to Elijah or Noah, called by God to speak truth to the world and save a believing remnant. Another stock reference likened Luther to Samson slaying a lion. The Reformer's image appeared on broadsheets and commemorative medals and coins, and countless references to him occur in sermons from 1617. Mirroring medieval hagiographies of saints, sermons and images recounted key turning points in Luther's life, such as his decision to become a monk, his anger at indulgences, his burning of Pope Leo X's bull condemning him, his defiant appearance in 1521 before Charles V at the Diet of Worms, his translation of scripture at the Wartburg castle, his marriage to Katherina von Bora, and his death and burial. Much was made of the disparity between Luther's stature—"one little monk"—and the bloated, corrupt papalist system that he attacked. The disparity in fact was regularly seen as *prima facie* evidence that only God could have been behind an occurrence of such implausibility.[32] David had risen up against Goliath, to mention another frequent biblical analogy from 1617.

Second, and related, symbols already associated with Luther in the sixteenth century received wide circulation in the jubilee festivities of 1617, influencing subsequent commemorations and shaping Protestant historical consciousness more generally. Three are particularly noteworthy. The first is the so-called "Luther Rose," an open white rose on a blue field, at the center of which was a red heart emblazoned with a black cross. Luther himself had devised this symbol, adapting it from his family's coat of arms, and had given it a theological interpretation. The black cross signified death and suffering; the red heart, life; the white rose, peace through justification; and the blue field, heavenly joy. Already in wide circulation in the sixteenth century, the Luther Rose appeared on numerous broadsheets, coins, and medals in 1617.[33] The second image is that of a swan. During the heady 1520s and 1530s, the story gained wide currency that the Bohemian reformer Jan Hus from his prison cell had said that, although he might be a weak goose, a more powerful bird would come after him to reform the church. In his funeral sermon for Luther, Wittenberg's Johannes Bugenhagen (1485–1558) made the coming bird a swan and attributed this line to Hus: "You may burn the goose, but in a hundred years will come a swan that you will not be able to burn."[34] The third symbol was the image of a lamp or light derived from Matthew 5: 14–16: "You are the light of the world.... Men do not light a lamp and put it under a bushel, but on a stand, and it gives light and life to all in the house." Frequently, in jubilee artifacts from 1617, the two symbols, swan and light, are joined. In many commemorative medals, for instance, the image of a swan appears on one side, signifying the fulfillment of Hus's prophecy, while on the other side appears a light or an image of Luther removing a lamp from under a bushel, symbolizing the recovery of the true Gospel from centuries of papalist darkness (Figure 1.1).[35]

Third, as one might expect in a confessional age, a firm link between theological and political authority recurred as a motif in 1617. Absent the Catholic hierarchy in Lutheran lands, the prince came to function first as an "emergency bishop" (*Notbischof*) and then as the *summus episcopus*, the titular head of the church and its armed protector.[36] In Saxony, a direct connection was made between the

Figure 1.1. Medals minted for the first centennial jubilee in 1617. Reproduced by permission of the Lutheran School of Theology at Chicago.

past support and protection offered to Luther by Elector Friedrich the Wise and the current protection of the church by the elector in 1617, Georg I. A striking example of this relationship appears in an etching done by Balthasar Schwan, as part of a series of broadsheets published in Nuremberg in 1617 (Figure 1.2). Luther and his key ally, Philip Melanchthon, both stand by an altar with Luther pointing to the open Bible with the phrase, "The Word of God remains forever." The two reformers are flanked by Friedrich the Elector on the left with his sword resting on the altar, a sign of his past protection of the pure faith, and by Georg I on the right, his sword raised in the air, symbolizing his ongoing protection in the present. Variations on this etching were frequently produced for 1617; numerous coins and medals show Friedrich the Wise on one side and Georg I or another Protestant territorial prince on the other.[37] As Charles Zika has summed up, "The *Jubeljahr* [of 1617] links and legitimates the unity of political and religious purpose which is characteristic of the confessional states of the seventeenth century. It is a theme which . . . [became] even more pronounced in the verbal and visual images used in the centenary celebrations of the later seventeenth and eighteenth centuries."[38]

Many of the jubilee's symbols and themes powerfully came together in a widely circulated broadsheet from 1617 titled "The Dream of Friedrich the Elector." The story behind the broadsheet was widely

Figure 1.2. Luther and Melanchthon with the Electors of Saxony. Artist, Balthasar Schwan, broadsheet from Nuremberg in 1617. Reproduced by permission of University of Texas at Austin, Harry Ransom Center, Popular Imagery Collection, image number 301.

believed to go back to actual dreams of the Elector of Saxony just before Luther first challenged the indulgence trade. In the dream, the Elector saw a monk, "a true son of the Apostle Paul" and presumably Luther, who, encouraged by a saintly throng, promised to do wonderful things for souls in purgatory—a pressing concern of Friedrich, as the dream occurred just before All Saints and All Souls (1 and 2 November). The saints asked the Elector if the monk could write a special message on the Castle Church in Wittenberg. Friedrich consented and the monk wrote *Vom Ablass* (Concerning Indulgences). The quill he wrote with was so large that it pierced the ear of a lion (Pope Leo X), tipping the papal tiara from his head—a detail nicely captured in the broadsheet. Various authorities, ecclesiastical and secular, tried to place the tiara back on his head, but to no avail. In a second dream, the Elector saw the lion (Leo X) assembling the estates of the Holy Roman Empire together (upper left in the broadsheet) to plot revenge against the monk. A third dream witnessed many attempts to break the monk's quill, but since it came from a Bohemian goose, this was a fruitless effort. This reference is, of course, to the story of Hus, who is depicted in the broadsheet (bottom right) being martyred at the stake. What is more, the quill had the property of begetting other quills, which the learned of Europe gathered to spread the monk's message.[39]

The story of the dreams had been told many times in the sixteenth century, and in each telling Luther was regarded as the monk of the Elector's dream. It first appeared in written form in a sermon printed in 1604 by the aforementioned Dresden court preacher, Matthias Hoë von Hoënegg. But the jubilee broadsheet of 1617 (Figure 1.3) represents the first time that it was actually illustrated and widely circulated. Significantly, this was also the first visual image of Luther that explicitly made an association between him and the door of the Wittenberg Castle Church—an image that later became and remains iconic.[40] In written or visual form, this image appeared in subsequent jubilees and commemorative occasions and, in the nineteenth century, it "went viral," as we might say today.

* * *

The Reformation jubilee of 1617 set precedents that have enjoyed a long life—and not only with respect to remembering Luther and

Figure 1.3. The Dream of Friedrich the Wise as depicted in 1617. Artist unknown. Leipzig, 1617. © The Trustees of the British Museum.

the Reformation. Historians of public commemoration in general have credited the first centenary jubilee of the Reformation as having helped inaugurate the modern custom of celebrating 100th anniversaries—in German, *Säkularfeier or Säkularfest*—of events and institutions with great fanfare.[41] This was borne out quickly, for following shortly on the heels of 1617 came 1630, when the Augsburg Confession (1530) was festively remembered in Lutheran cities and territories despite the ravaging of the Thirty Years War.[42] In 1639, the Electorate of Brandenburg lavishly commemorated the planting of Protestantism there in 1539; several other territories followed suit. In 1655 the Peace of Augsburg was remembered, whereas a number of areas marked the 150th anniversary of the Reformation in 1667. In all of these jubilees, celebrants often recycled images and motifs from 1617.[43]

At the sesquicentennial in 1667, it bears mentioning, the then Elector of Saxony, Johann Georg II, first decreed an *annual* "Reformation Day" (*Gedenktag der Reformation*) to be observed on 31 October; this became the basis of the annual remembrance—sometimes observed as "Reformation Sunday" on the following Sunday—in many Lutheran countries and churches worldwide.[44]

In 1717, when the 200th anniversary of the Reformation arrived, some patterns of commemoration had begun to have a fixed character. In preparation, many cities and universities, quite literally, dusted off the planning memoranda and records from 1617 and sought to implement similar "rituals of memory" again, albeit with a new cast of characters and under changed historical circumstances. And yet if we glance forward momentarily, the circumstances in 1717, in fact, shared more in common with 1617 than either year did with 1817, the 300th anniversary, which took place after a series of truly watershed events—the European-wide Enlightenment, the French Revolution, and the dissolution of the Holy Roman Empire by Napoleon Bonaparte in 1806.

But before pressing ahead to 1817, it is worth pausing briefly to consider several distinctive aspects of the 200th anniversary.[45] For starters, the 1717 jubilee took place after Calvinism had become a recognized religion in the Empire as a consequence of the Peace of Westphalia in 1648.[46] Although the significance of the year was not altogether lost on Calvinists areas, 1717 was much more a confessional

Lutheran affair than 1617—the idea of a unified Protestantism being largely a thing of the past. What is more, political Catholicism had receded as a force by 1717; Lutheran and Reformed communities, therefore, enjoyed more secure and separate identities than had been the case in 1617 prior to the Thirty Years War—which included among its complex set of causes the Habsburg monarchy's desire to root out all forms of Protestantism from central Europe. More parity between the confessions existed in 1717, in short; the political urgency of commemoration had lessened even if it had by no means subsided.[47]

A medal minted in Nuremberg for the 1717 jubilee nicely illustrates the altered situation of Protestantism. On the side representing the first jubilee of 1617, a female figure symbolizing the (Lutheran) Church stands on the crescent of the moon with twelve stars around her head, looking up anxiously to a sun covered by clouds. On the side representing 1717, by contrast, she sits in serene certainty with palm branches in hand.[48] The relative novelty of Protestant confessions, facing a host of threats, had given way to their taken-for-granted existence. The Lutheran sense of security manifested itself in the popularity of a rhyme: "The Word of God and Luther's Teaching will never pass away" (*Gottes Wort und Luthers Lehr wird vergehen nimmermehr*). At the same time, an entrenched anti-Catholic sentiment threaded the events and rhetoric of 1717 as it had earlier in 1617.[49]

The person of Luther remained at center stage in 1717. While much stayed the same on this score, some things had changed. A particularly intriguing novelty was the prominence of the so-called "incombustible Luther" (*unverbrannter Luther*) motif during the bicentennial jubilee year. In the seventeenth century, a number of stories had arisen of the miraculous survival of images of Luther in fires that had consumed houses and churches. The first of these occurred in 1634, when the study of a pastor near Mansfeld burned to ashes with the exception of an engraved image of Luther. This story was joined by another in 1689 when the house in Eisleben where Luther was born partially burned; a portrait of Luther was found in the debris purportedly wholly untouched by the flames. The accumulation of several similar stories led the Eisleben pastor Justus Schoepffer in 1717 to record them in a book, *The Incombustible Luther: Stories of the Image of Luther Miraculously Preserved from Fire by the Special Providence of God*, first published in Latin; a second, German edition appeared later in the century.[50] Widely attributed to God's miraculous intervention, these occurrences, in the eyes of the faithful, gave ongoing, assuring evidence of Luther's special role in the drama of history and salvation.

In 1717, political absolutism, buttressed intellectually by belief in the so-called "divine right of kings," stood at its apex across Europe. While state power and dynastic ambitions were certainly apparent in 1617, they were arguably even more on display in 1717. On coins, medallions, and other memorabilia from the jubilee, family coats of arms and images of reigning princes positively appear to compete for attention with images of Luther and other religious symbols.[51]

At the same time, the inertial force of confessional divisions placed limits on what a prince could or could not do. The (Reformed) Prussian king and Elector of Brandenburg, Friedrich Wilhelm I (r. 1713–40), for example, did not observe the 200th jubilee at court, but he made allowance for his Lutheran subjects to do so.[52] Even so, some Reformed pastors sought to strike a note of irenicism, at least between Calvinists and Lutherans. One pastor in Berlin, for example, used 1717 to advocate for both "civil peace" and "ecclesiastical peace." "Nothing brings the Church more misfortune," he argued, "than conflict and bickering, while nothing . . . helps spread religion more than harmony and peace."[53]

Astoundingly, the Saxon Elector Friedrich August (r. 1694–1733) had converted to Catholicism in 1697, but cognizant of the fear that this provoked among Lutherans, he had transferred to a government board, the Privy Council, the authority over churches and universities, which until then had been exercised substantially by the sovereign. The Privy Council in turn largely ceded matters to the Lutheran High Consistory in Dresden, which made clear that it planned to mark the occasion in 1717 "just as it had 100 years ago."[54] Oddly then, the vast majority of people in the territorial birthplace of the Reformation, the Electorate of Saxony, robustly observed the 1717 jubilee while an aloof, Catholic ruler—still nominally the head of the church there!—looked on.[55]

The 200th anniversary jubilee stood on the cusp of several major intellectual developments in European thought that would greatly impact future commemorations of the Reformation and interpretations of Protestantism. The early Enlightenment (*Frühaufklärung*) had begun to make its presence felt in some central European universities and cities. Intellectuals such as Gottfried Wilhelm Leibniz (1646–1716) and Christian Thomasius (1655–1728)—figures hardly conceivable from the rigidly confessional standpoint of 1617—had begun to transport ideas from the emergent natural sciences into the domains of theology, politics, and history. In Leibniz, one even finds proto-ecumenical strains of thought. In his outlook, Reformation-era divisions had wounded the universal, "catholic" *mission civilisatrice* that Europe ought to advance.[56] Restoring lost unity, not interminable theological polemics, was for him the imperative of the day.[57]

Equally important, the emergence of the reforming spiritual currents known as Pietism in the late seventeenth and early eighteenth century, notably at the new University of Halle (1694), had begun to call into question, on religious grounds, the strict confessionalism of the times. In the late seventeenth century, two innovative church histories appeared: *Historia Lutheranismi* (1694) by Veit Ludwig von Seckendorf and *History of the Church and Heresy* (1699) by Gottfried Arnold. Evincing both enlightened and Pietist elements, these two works adumbrated a historiographical approach to the Reformation that moved beyond the dogmatic and hagiographical tendencies of earlier works.[58] What is more, both authors—in a different, more explicitly religious key than Leibniz—gave voice to the concern for Christian reunion, striking an irenic tone uncharacteristic of their age.[59] "What could I more desire," Seckendorf wrote, "than [if] . . . foes and persecutors became brothers and fellows, acknowledging with us the pure faith with pure hearts and lips, and in common zeal restoring piety."[60] In a 1717 jubilee sermon, August Hermann Francke, Pietism's leading light, made a sharp distinction between Luther per se and the spiritual message that he had transmitted, encouraging his listeners to concentrate on the latter, not the former.[61]

Such accents of thought made their presence felt in the jubilee events of 1717 (Figure 1.4). But, one hastens to add, they did so only faintly. In the final analysis, neither the Enlightenment nor Pietism ruled the day; older strains of *Lutheran* confessionalism still provided the keynote for the 200th anniversary. The "spirit of the Enlightenment" can be detected here and there in 1717, Hans-Jürgen Schönstädt has concluded, but in its "essential characteristics" 1717 followed dutifully from the script of 1617.[62] From his analysis of the

Figure 1.4. Title-page of Ernst Saloman Cyprian's *Hilaria Evangelica, oder Theologisch-Historischer Bericht vom andern Evangelischen Jubel-Fest* (1719), an overview of all 1717 commemorations in Europe. Photo courtesy of the Andover-Harvard Theological Library.

coins and medals minted in 1717, Hugo Schnell has echoed that "a uniform witness of the uninterrupted dominance of Lutheran orthodoxy, of the traditional categories of interpretation of the Reformation, and of the boundless reverence for the person of Martin Luther" persisted between 1617 and 1717.[63] "Motifs of an enlightened or Pietist provenance found scant entry in the sources from 1717," Harms Cordes has even more firmly concluded; "it is much more the case that ... the attempt was undertaken to ratify the values and ideas understood as orthodox-Lutheran."[64] 1717 demonstrated how firmly precedent had become protocol.

In summary, then, while different historical circumstances were present in 1717, and several new intellectual sensibilities had begun to trickle into view, the jubilee of 1717 by and large was cast in the same mold as 1617.[65]

The 300th anniversary jubilee of 1817 cracked the mold.

Notes

1. On confessionalization in general, see Heinz Schilling, *Konfessionalisierung und Staatsinteressen* (Paderborn: Schöningh, 2007); Joel F. Harrington and Helmut Walser Smith (eds) "Confessionalization, Community, and State Building in Germany, 1555–1870," *Journal of Modern History*, 69 (1997): 77–101. For an evaluation (and criticism) of the so-called "confessionalization thesis," see Hans J. Hillerbrand, "Was there a Reformation in the Sixteenth Century," *Church History*, 71 (2003): 525–53. For confessionalization and German national identity in the modern era, see Wolfgang Altgeld, *Katholizismus, Protestantismus, Judentum: Über religiös begründete Gegensätze und nationalreligiöse Ideen in der Geschichte des deutschen Nationalismus* (Mainz: Matthias-Grünewald, 1992); Helmut Walser Smith, *German Nationalism and Religious Conflict: Culture, Ideology, Politics, 1870–1914* (Princeton: Princeton University Press, 1995); Heinz-Gerhard Haupt and Dieter Langewiesche (eds), *Nation und Religion in der deutschen Geschichte* (Frankfurt a.M.: Campus Verlag, 2001); and Keith H. Pickus "Native Born Strangers: Jews, Catholics and the German Nation," in Michael Geyer and Hartmut Lehmann (eds), *Religion und Nation, Nation und Religion: Beiträge zu einer unbewältigten Geschichte* (Göttingen: Wallstein, 2004), 141–56.

2. R. J. W. Evans et al. (eds), *The Holy Roman Empire, 1495–1806* (Oxford: OUP, 2011), 8–11.

3. The publication of *The Book of Concord* (1580), an authoritative compendium of Lutheran confessional teachings, was intentionally done to coincide with the fiftieth anniversary of the Augsburg Confession (1530). See Paul Timothy McCain et al. (eds), *Concordia: The Lutheran Confessions: A Reader's Edition of the Book of Concord* (St Louis, MO: Concordia Publishing House, 2005), xviii.

4. Hans-Jürgen Schönstadt, "Das Reformationsjubiläum 1617: Geschichtliche Herkunft und geistige Prägung," *Zeitschrift für Kirchengeschichte*, 93 (1982): 5–6.

5. "In hoc cursu cum esset Lutherus, circumferuntur venales indulgentiae in his regionibus a Tecelio Dominicano impudentissimo sycophanta, cuius impiis et nefariis concionibus irritatus Lutherus, studio pietatis ardens, edidit Propositiones de Indulgentiis, quae in primo Tomo monumentorum ipsius extant, Et has publice Templo, quod arci Witebergensi contiguum est, affixit pridie festi omnium Sanctorum anno 1517." See *Philippi Melanchthonis Opera*, ed. C. G. Bretschneider, in *Corpus Reformatorum*, vi (Halle, 1839), 161. In addition, Luther made an indirect reference to the theses (although he mentions nothing about the castle church door) in a letter dated 1 Nov. 1527 to his friend, Nikolaus von Amsdorf, remarking to him that he and some friends had celebrated in his house on 31 Oct. 1527 ten years since the "trampling down of indulgences." See *Luthers Werke: Briefwechsel*, iv 4 (Weimar, 1933), no. 1164, 75.

6. For an overview of the confessional situation in the late sixteenth and early seventeenth century, see Thomas A. Brady, *German Histories in the Age of the Reformation, 1400–1650* (Cambridge: CUP, 2009), 259–318. On the theological arguments that divided Gneiso-Lutherans and Philippists, see Eric W. Gritsch, *A History of Lutheranism*, 2nd edn (Minneapolis: Fortress Press, 2010), 91–106 and R. Kolb, "Dynamics of Party Conflict in the Saxon Reformation Late Reformation: Gnesiolutherans vs. Philippists," *Journal of Modern History*, 49 (1977): 1289–305.

7. Catholic territories founded their own Catholic League in retaliation in 1609. On the founding of the Protestant Union and Catholic League, see Axel Gotthard, "Protestantische 'Union' und katholische 'Liga'—subsidäre Strukturelemente oder Alternativentwürfe," in Volker Press (ed.), *Alternativen zur Reichsverfassung in der Frühen Neuzeit?* (Munich: R. Oldenbourg, 1995), 81–112.

8. Quoted in Gustav Benrath, *Reformierte Kirchengeschichtsschreibung an der Universität Heidelberg im 16. und 17.Jahrhundert* (Speyer: Veröffentlichung des Vereins für Pfälzische Kirchengeschichte, 1963), 37–8.

9. On the origins of the Lutheran split with Swiss Reformed Protestantism, see B. A. Gerrish, "Discerning the Body: Sign and Reality in Luther's Controversy with the Swiss," *Journal of Religion*, 68 (1988): 377–95.

10. Hans-Jürgen Schönstädt, *Antichrist, Weltheilsgeschehen und Gottes Werkzeug: Römische Kirche, Reformation und Luther im Spiegel des Reformationsjubiläum 1617* (Wiesbaden: Steiner, 1978), 13–15.

11. In effect, this meant the desire to exclude not only Reformed territories, but those, such as the cities of Nuremberg and Strasbourg, which had not signed the Book of Concord. See Eric W. Gritsch, *A History of Lutheranism*, 2nd edn (Minneapolis: Fortress Press, 2010), 91ff.

12. Schmidt's utterances are the first known evidence of awareness of the historical significance of 1617. See Schönstädt, *Antichrist*, 12–13.

13. "Gottes Wort und Lutheri Schrift sind des Papst und Calvini Gift," noted Andreas Öhler, "Martinus nach Maß," *Christ & Welt*, 52 (2014).

14. Quoted in Schönstädt, *Antichrist*, 16. Cf. Friedrich Loofs, "Die Jahrhundertfeier der Reformation an den Universitäten Wittenberg und Halle 1617, 1717, 1917," *Zeitschrift des Vereins für Kirchengeschichte in der Provinz Sachsen*, 14 (1917): 5.

15. Quoted in Schönstädt, *Antichrist*, 18. An English translation (with commentary) of this order was made; see W. Jones, *The Duke of Saxonie his iubilee: with a short chronologie of God. Both shewing the goodnesse of God, in blessing the Gospel of Christ, since Luther first oppossed the Popes pardons* (London, 1618).

16. On Hoënegg and his role during 1617, see Wolfgang Sommer, *Die lutherischen Hofprediger in Dresden: Grundzüge ihrer Geschichte und Verkündigung im Kurfürstentum Sachsen* (Stuttgart: Franz Steiner Verlag, 2006), 137–65.

17. In 1617, a broadsheet was printed, depicting Luther as the avenging angel causing terror in the faces of the Pope and clergy. See Wolfgang Harms, *Illustrierte Flugblätter aus den Jahrhunderten der Reformation und der Glaubenkämpfe 24 Juli bis Oktober 1983: Kunstsammlung der Veste Coburg* (Coburg: Kunstsammlung der Veste Coburg, 1983), 86–9.

18. Ibid. 144–5. The association of Luther with the Angel of the Apocalypse can be traced to Luther's funeral sermon delivered by Johannes Bugenhagen. E. W. Zeeden, *Martin Luther und die Reformation im Urteil des deutschen Luthertums: Dokumente zur inneren Entwicklung des deutschen Protestantismus von Luthers Tode bis zum Beginn der Goethezeit*, ii (Freiburg im Bresigau, 1952), 15.

19. Stricher, "L'Année jubilaire et la tradition catholique," *Foi et Vie*, 99 (2000): 73–86. A well-known painting of the proclamation of the 1300 jubilee by Giotto is found in the Basilica San Giovanni in Laterano in Rome.

20. On the first Catholic jubilee after the Council of Trent in 1575, see Barbara Witsch, "The Roman Church Triumphant: Pilgrimage, Penance, and Processions. Celebrating the Holy Year of 1575," in Barbara Witsch and Susan Scott Munshower (eds), *Art and Pageantry in the Renaissance and Baroque* (University Park, PA: Pennsylvania University Press, 1990), 82–117. Cf. Christopher Hibbert, *Rome: Biography of a City* (New York: W. W. Norton, 1985), 165ff. On the Catholic jubilee tradition in general, see Herbert Thurston, *The Holy Year of Jubilee* (New York: AMS Press, 1980). On the biblical roots of the jubilee, see Leonardo De Chirico, "The Biblical Jubilee," *Evangelical Review of Theology*, 23 (1999): 347–62.

21. See Ruth Kastner, *Geistlicher Rauffhandel: Form und Funktion der illustrierten Flugblätter zum Reformationsjubiläum in ihrem historischen und publizistischen Kontext* (Frankfurt a.M.: Peter Lang, 1982), 30–3, and Charles Zika, "The Reformation Jubilee of 1617: Appropriating the Past through Centenary Celebration," in D. E. Kennedy (ed.), *Authorized Pasts: Essays in Official History* (Melbourne, 1995), 84.

22. Peter Roest, *Pseudojubilaeum, anno septimo decimo supra millesimum sexcentesimum, calendis novembribus, insolenti festivitate a Lutheranis tum ob dari coeptas majorum nostrorum religioni in Germania tenebras, tum ob memoriam Martini Lutheri, apostatae selectissimi, celebratum . . .* (Molsheim, 1618); quoted in Kastner, *Geistlicher Rauffhandel*, 236.

23. Adam Contzen, *Iubilum iubilorum iubilaeum: Et pies lacyrmae omnium Romano-Catholicorum ad imperatorem aug. reges, principes, respublicas, populos* (Monguntiae, 1618).

24. There were also several Catholic medals minted in 1617 disparaging Luther and the Reformation. See Frederick J. Schumacher, "Luther's Greatness Reflected in Numismatic Art," *TAMS* [Token and Medal Society] *Journal*, 24 (Oct. 1984): 176–7.

25. The anti-Lutheran activities of the 1617 Catholic jubilee are treated in some detail in Kastner, *Geistlicher Rauffhandel*, 29–33, 226–47. Cf. Joseph Schmidlin, *Die*

katholische Restauration im Elsass am Vorabend des Dreissigjährigen Krieges (Strassbourg: Herder, 1934), 305–30.

26. Jeffrey M. Blustein, *Forgiveness and Remembrance: Remembering Wrongdoing in Personal and Public Life* (Oxford: OUP, 2014), 205. Cf. Paul Connerton, *How Societies Remember* (Cambridge: CUP, 1989). On the fascinating use of drama recounting the life of Luther and shoring up confessional identity, see Detlef Metz, *Das protestantische Drama: Evangelisches geistliches Theater in der Reformationszeit und im konfessionellen Zeitalter* (Cologne: Böhlau Verlag, 2013).

27. Ulm, it should be noted, was firmly in the Gnesio-Lutheran camp and a signatory to the Formula of Concord; different emphases occurred at cities inclined toward "Philippist" currents and in Reformed areas.

28. See the *Verzeichnus wie auf christliche anordnung eines Ersamen Raths das Evangelische Jubelfest allhier zu Ulm 1617.2 Novemb. Freylich begangen,* in Conrad Dieterich, *Zwo Ulmische Jubel und Danckpredigten* (Ulm, 1618). Cf. Schönstädt, *Antichrist*, 64–7.

29. Dieterich, *Zwo Ulmische Jubel und Danckpredigten,* 9ff. Cf. Kastner, *Geistlicher Rauffhandel,* 62–3.

30. Zika, "Reformation Jubilee of 1617," 86.

31. Schönstadt, *Antichrist,* 20–85, and Kastner, *Geistlicher Rauffhandel,* 34–102.

32. Zika, "Reformation Jubilee of 1617," 96.

33. Kastner, *Geistlicher Rauffhandel,* 183.

34. Quoted in Robert Scribner, *Popular Culture and Popular Movements in Reformation Germany* (London: Hambledon Press, 1987), 327. Cf. A. Hauffen, "Husz eine Gans – Luther ein Schwan," in *Untersuchungen und Quellen zu germanischer und romanischer Philologie,* Prager deutsche Studien, 9 (Prague, 1908), 1–28.

35. Heinrich Gottlieb Kreussler, *Luthers Andenken in Jubel-Münzen* (Leipzig, 1818), plate 2, and Scribner, *Popular Culture and Popular Movements,* 342–3. Cf. Schumacher, "Luther's Greatness in Numismatic Art," 171–9.

36. Lewis Spitz, "Luther's Ecclesiology and his Concept of the Prince as *Notbischof,*" *Church History,* 22 (1953): 113–41.

37. John Roger Paas, *The German Political Broadsheet: 1600–1700,* ii (Wiesbaden: O. Harrassowitz, 1986), 111 (plate 302). The imperial city of Nuremberg was not a signatory to the Formula of Concord and hence more open to portraying Melanchthon, whose legacy was then sharply criticized by the Gneiso-Lutherans in Saxony and elsewhere.

38. Zika, "Reformation Jubilee of 1617," 99.

39. Harms and Schilling, *Deutsche Illustrierte Flugblätter,* ii. 222–3. Cf. Hans Volz, "Der Traum Kurfürst des Weisen vom 30./31. Oktober 1517: Eine bibliographisch-ikonographische Untersuchung," *Gutenberg Jahrbuch,* 45 (1970): 174–211.

40. Hartmut Lehmann, *Luthergedächtnis 1817 bis 2017* (Göttingen: Vandenhoeck & Ruprecht, 2012), 17.

41. Zika, "Reformation Jubilee of 1617," 78. Prior to the Reformation jubilee of 1617, there had been a number of centenary anniversaries of the founding of German universities. The custom appears to have migrated from marking a university's 100th anniversary to that of the Reformation at large. On this point, see Flügel and Dornheim, "Die Universität als Jubläumsmultiplikator in der Frühen Neuzeit," *Jahrbuch für Universitätsgeschichte,* 9 (2006): 51ff.

42. Angelika Marsch, *Bilder zur Augsburger Konfession und ihren Jubiläen* (Weißenhorn: Anton H. Konrad, 1980), 55ff., and Alfred Galley, *Die Jahrhundertfeiern der Augsbur-gischen Konfessionen von 1630, 1730 und 1830* (Leipzig: Dörffling & Franke, 1930).

43. Hans-Jürgen Schönstadt, "Das Reformationsjubiläum 1717: Beiträge zur Geschichte seiner Entstehung im Spiegel landesherrlicher Verordnungen," *Zeitschrift für Kirchengeschichte*, 93 (1982): 58–61. Cf. Justus Kutschmann, *Ein Dithmarscher Wandteppich: Biblische Szenen zum Reformationsjubiläum 1667* (Berlin: Verein der Freunde des Museums für Deutsche Volkskunde, 1988).

44. Karl-Heinrich Bieritz, "Reformation Day," in *Religion in Past and Present*, 4th edn, x (Leiden: Brill, 2011), 709. (Hereafter *RPP*.)

45. The events of the 1717 commemoration are well-documented in a large work that appeared in 1719 by the theologian and librarian Ernst Saloman Cyprian, who also served as a Privy Councilor to Duke Friedrich II of Saxony-Gotha. Cyprian was also an influential planner of the 1717 jubilee, commissioned in fact by the Duke to compile various ordinances and instructions from the 1617 jubilee. See his *Hilaria Evangelica, oder Theologisch-Historischer Bericht vom andern Evange-lischen Jubel-Fest. Nebst III. Büchern darzu gehöriger Acten und Materien, deren das erste, die obrigkeitlichen Verordnungen, und, viele historische Nachrichten, das andere, Orationes und Programmata Jvbilaea, das dritte, eine vollständige Beschreibung der Jubel-Medaillen begreiffet* [von Christian Schelgeln] *mit Kupffern, Summarien und einem nützlichen Register* (Gotha: M. G. Weidemann, 1719).

46. Bernd Hey (ed.), *Der westfälische Frieden 1648 und der deutsche Protestantismus* (Bielefeld: Verlag für Regionalgeschichte, 1998).

47. Harm Cordes, *Hilaria evangelica academia: Das Reformationsjubiläum von 1717 an den deutschen lutherischen Universitäten* (Göttingen: Vandenhoeck & Ruprecht, 2006), 13.

48. Hugo Schnell, *Martin Luther und die Reformation auf Münzen und Medaillen* (Munich: Klinkhardt & Biermann, 1983), 65, 181 (image 156).

49. Cyprian, *Hilaria Evangelica*, 47ff. Sometimes anti-Catholic sentiment erupted into intimidation of and even violence against Catholics as demonstrated by an episode from Leipzig in 1717 when a group of rowdy Protestant students roughed up a Catholic priest. See Cordes, *Hilaria evangelica academica*, 66. However, some princes, who had sizeable Catholic minorities in their land or else Catholic neighbors, sought to moderate anti-Catholic polemics. See Ruth Kastner, "The Reformer and the Reformation Anniversaries," *History Today*, 33 (1983): 24.

50. Justus Schoepffer, *Lutherus non combustus sive enarratio de D. M. Luthero eiusque imagine singulari providentia dei T. O. M. duplici vice ab igne miraculosa conservata* (Wittenberg, 1717). The 2nd edn appeared as *Unverbrannter Luther, oder historische Erzählung von D. Martin Lutheri und dessen Feuer erhaltenen Bildnissen* (Wittenberg, 1765–6). See Scribner, *Popular Culture and Popular Movements*, 323–30, and Stephan Horst, "Das evangelisch-Jubelfest in der Vergangenheit," *Deutsch-Evangelisch—Monatsblätter für den gesamten deutschen Protestantismus*, 8 (1917): 10.

51. Schnell, *Martin Luther and die Reformation*, 153–88.

52. Schönstadt, "Das Reformationsjubiläum 1717," 79. On the conversion of the Hohenzollern monarchy from Lutheranism to Calvinism in the early seventeenth century, see Rudolf von Thadden, "Luther in Preussen," *Archiv für Reformations-geschichte*, 79 (1988): 5–26, and Bodo Nischan, *Prince, People, and Confession: The Second*

Reformation in Brandenburg (Philadelphia: University of Pennsylvania Press, 1994), 81–110.

53. *Eine Predigt von der geistlichen Einigkeit und Kirche-Frieden über die Worte Pauli Eph[esian] 4 v. 3.4.5.6 gehalten an dem Reformations-Jubel-Fest den 31. October 1717* (Berlin, 1717). Only the pastor's initials, F. S., are provided.

54. Quoted material taken from Schönstadt, "Das Reformationsjubiläum 1717," 79.

55. The Saxon electors were also traditionally the head of the *corpus evangelicorum* in the Holy Roman Empire. Friedrich August and his Catholic successors remained in this seemingly incongruent role until the dissolution of the Empire in 1806. See Joachim Whaley, *Germany and the Holy Roman Empire*, ii. *From the Peace of Westphalia to the Dissolution of the Reich, 1648–1806* (Oxford: OUP, 2012), 76–7.

56. Ruth Rouse and Stephen Charles Neill (eds), *A History of the Ecumenical Movement, 1517–1948* (Philadelphia: Westminster Press, 1954), 113.

57. Michael J. Murray, "Leibniz's Proposal for Theological Reconciliation among the Protestants," *American Catholic Philosophical Quarterly*, 76 (2002): 623–46.

58. Ernst Walter Zeeden, *The Legacy of Luther*, tr. Ruth Mary Bethell (London: Hollis & Carter, 1954), 55ff., 90ff.

59. An earlier exception to the strict confessionalism can be found in the irenic thought of Georg Calixtus, who taught at the University of Helmstedt. See Thomas Albert Howard, *Protestant Theology and the Making of the Modern German University* (Oxford: OUP, 2006), 79. Cf. E. L. T. Henke, *Georg Calixtus und seine Zeit*, 2 vols. (Halle, 1853, 1860).

60. Quoted in Zeeden, *Legacy of Luther*, 61. Cf. A. G. Dickens and John M. Tonkin, *The Reformation in Historical Thought* (Cambridge, MA: Harvard University Press, 1985), 114ff.

61. Francke, "Der Zuruf Christi: An seine jubilirende Evangelische Gemeine" (31 October 1717), noted in Cordes, *Hilaria evangelica academica*, 44. Cf. Gérald Chaix, "Reformation," in Etienne François and Hagen Schulze (eds), *Deutsche Erinnerungsorte*, ii (Munich: Verlag C. H. Beck, 2001), 13. For a fuller treatment of Francke's views on Luther and Lutheranism, see Erhard Peschke, *Bekehrung und Reform: Ansatz und Wurzeln der Theologie August Hermann Franckes* (Bielefeld: Luther-Verlag, 1977), 136–49.

62. Schönstädt, "Das Reformationsjubiläum 1717," 69, 107–9.

63. Schnell, *Martin Luther und die Reformation*, 71.

64. Cordes, *Hilaria evangelica academica*, 308.

65. Rainer Fuhrmann, *Das Reformationsjubiläum 1817: Martin Luther und die Reformation im Urteil der protestantischen Festpredigt des Jahres 1817* (Bonn: V+V Sofortdruck, 1973), 19.

2

A Turning Point

1817 and the Modern Era

> The spirit of Protestantism necessarily brings the spirit of free-
> dom and the independence of the people; Protestant freedom
> leads necessarily to political freedom.
>
> (Wilhelm Martin Leberecht de Wette, 1817)

While many Reformation anniversaries were marked in the mid- and late eighteenth century—including those of Luther's birth and death dates, respectively in 1746 and 1783—these celebrations paled in comparison to the extravagant commemorations of the nineteenth century—a century that witnessed what one critic has called an "epidemic" of Reformation-related commemorations.[1] While not without continuities with former jubilees, the jubilee of 1817, indeed, bore witness to profoundly altered intellectual and political circumstances. Some of these can be attributed to the revolutionary-Napoleonic watershed years between 1789 and 1815.[2] But others trace their development farther back into the eighteenth century. Four developments, in particular, gaining momentum prior to 1817, merit spotlighting.

First, the trickle of Enlightenment sensibilities evident at the 1717 commemorations had become a gushing stream by 1817, greatly affecting retrospective understandings of the Reformation. While Enlightenment figures (*Aufklärer*) certainly did not speak with one voice, many converged on a stadial view of human history—the view that history was not simply a "vale of tears," the arena of sin, death, and salvation, but a forward-moving enterprise, capable of discernable development and progress.[3] What is more, God himself was sometimes conceived as an "immanent principle," not entirely external to, but steadfastly present within the historical process.[4]

For those who subscribed to such a vision of history, Luther might still be regarded as a restorer of proper religion, but in doing so he also became a catalyzing agent advancing the human story away from superstition and darkness (viz., medieval Catholicism) toward reason and light (viz., modern Protestantism). In figures such as Johann Lorenz von Mosheim (1694–1755) and Johann Salomo Semler (1725–91), moreover, the stirrings of a less confessional, more objective or scientific (*wissenschaftlich*) approach to the Reformation began to come into view.[5]

For such scholars, the creedal correctness of Lutheranism might not be beside the point, but they emphasized the form, not the content, of Luther's challenge to the papacy. Just as Luther had taken on the authorities of his day, so contemporary scholars should challenge authorities—indeed, even orthodox Lutheran ones—if they were beholden to tradition bereft of reason's illumination.[6] The "true Lutheran," as Gotthold Ephraim Lessing put it, "does not take refuge in Luther's writings, but in Luther's spirit," equating it with conscience and reason and pitting it, when necessary, against the "yoke of tradition."[7] In his famous essay, "What is Enlightenment?" Immanuel Kant gave a more expansive expression to this outlook: "Enlightenment is man's release from his self-incurred tutelage. Tutelage is man's inability to make use of his understanding without direction from another.... *Sapere aude!* Have courage to use your own reason!—that is the motto of enlightenment."[8] Popularizers of Kantian and Enlightenment sensibilities soon alighted on the idea that the Reformation remained "unfinished"; Luther and company had begun the task of emancipating reason and enlightening humanity. The job of the present was to carry the torch forward. As the philosopher Karl Leohard Reinhold (1757–1823) quintessentially expressed it:

> As a result of the Reformation, reason has regained the free use of its powers—at least in one half [i.e. among Protestants] of the Christian world—and especially in recent times has recovered quite markedly from the natural consequences of its earlier captivity. Yet however much reason may have accomplished since the Reformation in terms of restoring the unity between religion and morality, the success of its efforts until now has indisputably been more *a preparation for this grand undertaking than a completion of it.*[9]

Such sentiments were echoed in the influential work of the French Kantian Charles Villers, *Essai sur l'ésprit et l'influence de la réformation de Luther* (1804), which went through five editions and was translated into both German and English.[10]

Second, the evangelical renewal movement of Pietism, as already indicated, exerted a significant influence on assessments of the Reformation throughout the eighteenth century and beyond—indeed, it was among Pietists that the word "Reformation" first began to designate a discrete period of church history. While one rightly resists making an overly sharp distinction between Lutheranism and Pietism (as well as between Pietism and *Aufklärung*) in the eighteenth century, Pietists were less inclined to confessional rigidity when interpreting the Reformation and more open to thinking about its ethical and affective dimensions. Figures such as the aforementioned Seckendorf, Arnold, and Francke, along with others like Philipp Jacob Spener or Johann Georg Walch, focused attention on the vital, introspective piety of Luther and often contrasted that against the doctrinal rigidity and bureaucratic control of the Lutheran churches of their times. Many also made distinctions *within* Luther's own life, extolling the young Luther as pious "liberator" and pitting that image against the mature, wizened Luther as "statesman and church builder."[11] Pietist-inflected interpretations and evocations of the Reformation, radiating especially from the university town of Halle, exerted considerable influence in the late eighteenth and nineteenth centuries.[12] Because of Pietists' contacts with Puritans in North America and with John Wesley and the nascent Methodist movement in the Church of England, Pietist thought also played no negligible role in shaping the historical imagination of early Anglo-American evangelicalism and its understanding of the Reformation heritage.[13]

Third, the late eighteenth and early nineteenth century is well known as the crucible period during which historicism (*Historismus*) was born. Historicism is a notoriously difficult concept to get a handle on, in part no doubt because scholars have used it as shorthand to signify such a massive and multifaceted shift in modern German and Western thought—what Friedrich Meinecke famously called "one of the greatest intellectual revolutions that has ever taken place in human thought."[14] Its representative figures such as the philologist Friedrich August Wolf, the statesman and scholar Wilhelm von Humboldt, the jurist Friedrich Carl von Savigny, or the historian Leopold von Ranke looked primarily to the past and to the category of "development" (*Entwicklung*) to understand any human phenomena—not least the French Revolution, which had given practically all Europeans an acute sense of historical rupture and change.[15] To grasp anything relevant about the present, in other words, one must explore the past, try to grasp its manifold contingencies, and seek to divine therein the principal processes of development that had led from "then" to "now." As Maurice Mandelbaum has nicely summed up, "Historicism is the belief that an adequate understanding of the nature of any phenomenon and an adequate assessment of its value are to be gained through considering it in terms of the place it occupied and the role which it played in the process of development."[16] The "turn to history" in early nineteenth-century German thought, it hardly needs under-scoring, brought with it renewed and copious attention to the Refor-mation as a defining transitional era in the not-too-distant past.

Fourth, early German nationalism profoundly influenced assess-ments of the Reformation in the nineteenth century. Incubating in the thought of a few eighteenth-century thinkers and popularized as a result of the French Revolution and Napoleonic wars, nationalism exerted a decisive impact on the jubilee of 1817 and, indeed, on practically all major commemorative events during the century. J. G. Herder (1744–1803) portrayed Luther as a German hero, the repository of a noble past and the herald of a bright future for the German-speaking peoples of central Europe. "Become once more [Luther] the Teacher of thy nation, its Prophet, its Pastor," he wrote.[17] In his famous *Addresses to the German Nation* (1807), the philosopher J. G. Fichte (1762–1814) espied in Luther "proof of German earnestness of soul" and regarded the Reformation as "proof of the characteristic quality of the German people."[18] With others, Herder and Fichte inspired the Idealist-Romantic notion that each nation possessed a "soul" or "spirit" (*Geist*) which at times manifested itself in a "great man," a larger-than-life genius, who embodied the spirit in his very being, albeit while contributing to the spiritual commonweal of humanity at large. For the English, it was Shakespeare; for Italians, Dante; and for Germans, Luther.[19] The image of Luther as the harbinger of the German nation stirred to life toward the end of the eighteenth century, becoming more widely propagated after the Battle of Nations near Leipzig in October of 1813—an event that effectively threw off the Napoleonic yoke and intensified nationalist sentiment, especially among the young and the educated.[20]

* * *

The intertwined fate of Napoleon and the German people provides the crucial, immediate context for understanding the 300th Reformation jubilee of 1817. As Thomas Nipperdey has written, "In the beginning was Napoleon. His influence upon the German people, their lives and experiences was overwhelming at a time when the initial foundations of a modern German state were being laid."[21] In his quest for European mastery, Napoleon's actions had precipitated the massive reorganization of ecclesiastical and political arrangements in central Europe, culminating in the humiliation of Prussia at the Battle of Jena in 1806 and the cessation of the Holy Roman Empire in the same year. Due to the turmoil that Napoleon wrought, the University of Wittenberg was forced to close its doors in 1815 and later merged with Halle as "the united University of Halle-Wittenberg"—an arrangement that has existed until the present.[22]

Under Napoleon's yoke, currents of liberalism and nationalism fanned to life, reaching a feverish crescendo as a consequence of the aforementioned Battle of Nations in 1813, which brought politically fragmented Germans together against a common foe. Regrettably, however, in the view of nationalists, no worthy German state emerged at this time. Instead, the German people had foisted upon them the unwieldy "German Confederation," a sop to nationalist sentiment but in reality an integral part of the reactionary scheme hatched by Count Metternich and other architects of Restoration at the Congress of Vienna (1814–15) in complicity with German princes.[23] (In the territorial outcomes of the Congress, it should be noted, Prussia, in addition to other areas, gained parts of Saxony, including Wittenberg.) In short, the peace settlement at Vienna attempted to put the lid on German nationalism and restore the time-honored principles of throne and altar, crown and church.[24]

But nationalism did not wane. Far from it. It dramatically burst onto the scene in mid-October of 1817 when German students from eleven different universities convened at Wartburg castle near

Eisenach in Thuringia, where Luther had translated the New Testament, to commemorate the fourth anniversary of the Battle of Nations and the 300th anniversary of the Protestant Reformation. This was the first of two defining events of 1817. The other was the establishment of the Prussian Union Church (*Unionskirche*), a government-orchestrated effort to merge the Lutheran and Reformed churches in Hohenzollern lands in an effort to create one harmonious Reformation-heritage (*evangelische*) church—an example imitated by other territorial churches in the Confederation. Examining more closely the "Wartburg rally" and the Union, and then sampling the content of jubilee addresses and sermons (*Festpredigten*) from late October and early November of 1817, will give broader perspective on the 300th anniversary of the Reformation, a landmark event not only for shaping the subsequent memory of the Reformation in German-speaking lands but also for shaping German nationhood itself.

Frustrated by the conservative settlement at Vienna in 1815, nearly 500 young men—all members of university "fraternities" or *Burschenschaften*—met at Wartburg castle on 18 and 19 October 1817 (see Figure 2.1). Most had fought in the wars again Napoleon and they desired to rekindle the exalted pan-German nationalist and liberal sentiment that they had felt in 1813. On the first day, the Allgemeine Deutsche Burschenschaft was founded as an umbrella organization to network German students. In the "Wartburg Rally Declarations," the students summarized their aims: national unity, constitutional freedom, a liberal pan-German government, and the elimination of the vestiges of feudalism.[25] The site where Luther translated scripture into German in 1521–2 seemed an apt symbolic location for such a gathering. Amid the drinking, singing, and nostalgia for the recent past, speeches were given, in which students exhorted one another to long for German nationhood, to love freedom, to transcend particularism, and to defy the reactionary political climate. With explicit reference to Luther setting fire to the papal bull condemning him, students staged a book burning of works deemed "un-German" by their ideological standards. At root, the enthusiasms of the Wartburg rally reflected the students' sense of betrayal; the nationalist-liberal longings of 1813 had been stifled in their view by the political settlement of 1815, and the students desired to use the Reformation's tercentenary of 1817 to bring the spirit of 1813 back to life. "Four

Figure 2.1. The Wartburgfest (1817). Artist unknown (Germany, c.1850). Photo courtesy of Wikimedia Commons.

long years have gone by since the battle," one student exclaimed; "[t]he German people entertained bright hopes, but they have all come to nothing; everything is different from what we expected."[26]

For those who experienced Wartburg, it was an intoxicating event, and, in the judgment of historians, a key moment in shaping German nationalism.[27] A curious blend of nationalist hopes and Protestant conviction threaded the rally. As one popular song put it: "In our own manner, we want / to observe the great festival day. / Today is Doctor Luther's day, / [Thus] above all, everyone must sing / long live doctor Luther!"[28] "By making . . . reference to the Reformation and framing the German national struggle in religious and confessional terms," as the historian Anthony J. Steinhoff has written, "the students did more than just make a powerful political statement. They established a [religious] precedent for nationalist discourse that became especially prominent in later years."[29]

But Luther was not just tied to the "nation." In the judgment of the Wartburg celebrants, the Reformation had produced grand new possibilities for human flourishing in general. It had allowed for a new form of subjective experience or inwardness (*Innerlichkeit*) and an expansive understanding of spiritual or intellectual freedom (*Geistes-freiheit*). Just as the Prussian General Gebhard von Blücher had defeated Napoleon in 1813, so Luther earlier had defeated papal tyranny and superstition, longstanding impediments to progress and freedom. The freedom envisioned by the students, however, was not the anarchic license which was often associated with Western (Anglo-French) liberalism, but a freedom that manifested itself in the progressive unity, solidarity, and statehood of the German people—and this as a beneficent contribution to humanity at large. Surprisingly, even some Catholics and Jews were swept up by this exalted atmosphere, and to a limited degree we may speak of the moment as having an ecumenical or even an interfaith component.[30] As Goethe observed the mood of 1817: "People of all faiths rejoiced and in this sense it was more than a national celebration; it was a celebration of pure humanity."[31] An intriguing oscillation between exalting humanity in the abstract and German unity specifically pervaded the *Jubelfeier* of 1817.[32]

The ruling elite of Prussia envisioned a different sort of unity in 1817: the unity of the two Protestant confessions into one united evangelical church or *Unionskirche*. In part, the drive toward union arose from the King's personal, religious motivations, in which devotion trumped theological subtleties. In the years preceding the union, Friedrich Wilhelm III (r. 1797–1840) had taken an interest in the episcopal structure and liturgies of Anglican, Eastern Orthodox, and Catholic churches. In comparison, his churches in Prussia seemed poorly organized and liturgically too variegated. What is more, the Reformed king's first wife, the popular Louise (d. 1810), was a Lutheran from Mecklenburg, and he had found it frustrating that the two could not share communion together.[33] Yet the decision for union did not emanate from the King's whims alone; other intellectual and political exigencies came into play. To a number of Prussian ministers, the Church Union represented a welcome opportunity to dilute older strains of confessionalism and thus achieve a more progressive understanding of religion, one more in line with the outlook of the Enlightenment and German idealist philosophy. Furthermore, the union was recognized as a matter of *raison d'état*, of bringing religion "into harmony with the direction of the state," as Minister Karl von Altenstein put it.[34] It would help achieve national unity after the Treaty of Vienna (1815), which had greatly increased Prussia's size, population, and religious diversity. In particular, government officials thought that a centrally administered, confessionally united state church would foster greater understanding between Prussia's eastern Lutheran provinces and the newly acquired provinces of the Rhineland and Westphalia, which contained numerous Reformed communities.[35] In turn, a single Protestant church organically connected to the state would present an imposing force in the eyes of the sizeable Catholic minority and the smaller Jewish one.

The dual goals of diminishing intra-Protestant confessionalism and consolidating (Prussian) national unity gained wide support, not least from the likes of the philosopher G. W. F. Hegel, and the theologian Friedrich Schleiermacher, who energetically championed union from the pulpit and university lectern alike.[36] The actual process of church union fully got under way in September of 1817.[37] In anticipation of the tercentenary celebration of the Reformation in late October, the King issued a proclamation on 27 September 1817, in which he deplored Protestant divisions, argued his conviction that only externals still divided the two churches, and commended reunification as an act of deep Christian significance. Regarding "the impending centenary celebration of the Reformation" as the providentially ordained moment to begin the process, he concluded that "such a true religious unification of both [confessions], which really are only divided over external matters, is fitting as the great goal of Christianity; it conforms to the original intentions of the Reformers; it lies in the spirit of Protestantism."[38]

The King indicated that the Reformed did not have to become Lutheran, nor Lutheran Reformed, but that from their separate identities a new "evangelical" church would develop. The King then set an example for his subjects: on 31 October he celebrated the Reformation by attending a service in Potsdam which combined Lutheran and Reformed elements. During the communion, he received the bread from the Reformed court preacher, the cup from a Lutheran pastor.[39] For the occasion, special medals and coins were minted (Figure 2.2): Luther and Calvin's image graced them,

Figure 2.2. Medal of Luther and Calvin made on the occasion of the Prussian Church Union of 1817. Reproduced by permission of the Lutheran School of Theology at Chicago.

accompanied by captions such as "the third jubilee of the Reformation on 31 October 1817" and "the unification of both churches."[40]

The drive toward Protestant union was not limited to Prussia. It was shared by the small Duchy of Nassau and spread to other German states as well, including Baden, the Palatinate, Saxony-Weimar, Hanau, Waldeck-Pyrmont, Anhalt-Brandenburg, Rhine-Hesse, Hildburghausen, and Anhalt-Dessau.[41] A variety of particular circumstances accompanied these unions, but practically all drew inspiration from the lofty rhetoric of the Reformation's tercentenary and the example of Prussia.[42] What is more, in significant measure and although they often enjoyed a measure of popular support, they were "top-down" affairs, influenced and orchestrated by church and state bureaucracies and carried out under the banner of "national interest."

Not everyone was pleased with this development. Many in fact were shocked, given the long history of doctrinal differences between Lutheran and Reformed Christians. In the judgment of more traditional Lutherans, the top-down, coerced unity by the state, was anathema—a betrayal of what Luther desired, not its fulfillment. Arguably, no one evinced greater displeasure than the Kiel pastor Claus Harms (1778–1855), who took it upon himself in 1817 to pen his own 95 Theses against the Prussian Union, publishing them alongside Luther's original 95, which he called the "cradle and diapers in which our Lutheran church lay." A confessional Lutheran of the strict observance, Harms in his exasperation with the direction of events in 1817 provides strong testimony of how this jubilee departed from previous ones. Harms interpreted "unionism" as a worrisome manifestation of various eighteenth-century currents of thought, which he grouped under the catch-all rubric "rationalism." In his judgment, such rationalism had pitted progress, the autonomous conscience, and the drive toward theological conciliation against the time-tested truths of an older, creedal Lutheranism. A sampling of Harms's theses provides a window into his concerns:

> 2. Doctrine in relation to faith and behavior is now construed in such a way so as to conform to the needs of man. This is why protest and reform now have to be repeated.

> 3. With the idea of a progressive reformation (*fortschreitende Reformation*)—as this idea is defined and how it is employed—one reforms Lutheranism into paganism and Christianity out of the world.

> 9. We could call belief in reason our age's pope, our antichrist . . .

> 43. When reason touches upon religion, it throws out the pearls and plays with the husks, the empty words.

> 77. To say that time has abolished the dividing wall between Lutherans and Reformed is nonsense. At issue is: who has fallen away from the faith of their church, the Lutherans or the Reformed? Or perhaps both?[43]

The publication of Harms's theses on 31 October 1817 lit a tinderbox of controversy. Over sixty pamphlets were published, weighing in either for or against Harms. Even the great theologian Friedrich Schleiermacher could not let the matter rest, but came out strongly against Harms's theses in February of 1818.[44] In the ensuing decades, the controversy did not die down. In fact, an attempt by royal officials to impose a new uniform liturgical book throughout Prussia resulted in the further disaffection of large numbers of so-called "Old Lutherans," led by the influential Silesian pastor Johannes G. Scheibel (1783–1843). Their opposition in turn often met retaliation from the state. Under Minister Altenstein in fact some pastors were even imprisioned and coerced "union services" were held in the presence of Prussian troops! The situation seemed so bleak by the 1830s that

many "Old Lutherans" resorted to emigration—to Canada, Austra-
lia, and the United States.[45]

But let us return to 1817. In late October and early November, a
host of customary "rituals of memory" were again enacted in cities
and at schools, churches, and universities. Musical performances,
sermons, academic orations, artwork, processions, publications, the
minting of coins and medals, the dedication of new churches and the
decoration of old ones, acts of philanthropy, and much more went
into the heady mix of this pivotal jubilee. The enthusiastic celebrant
could even purchase porcelain cups and plates with Luther's image,
his sayings, and places important for his life on them.[46] What is more,
the stirrings of a new religious tourism—a Protestant impulse to go on
pilgrimage—can be seen in the number of people in 1817 who visited
"memory sites" significant for Martin Luther's life: above all, Wittenberg, Worms, Eisleben, Erfurt, and, of course, the Wartburg castle.[47]
No less a figure than the Prussian king, Friedrich Wilhelm III, paid a
visit to Wittenberg on 31 October to mark the jubilee there and the
opening in the city of a new pastors' seminary. Organ music and
cannon blasts sounded when the King ceremoniously entered the
Castle Church's "theses door" (*Thesentür*).[48]

In the celebratory sermons and academic addresses of this year,
themes of nationalism and church union, along with those tied to
various "enlightened" intellectual currents of the eighteenth century,
cropped up repeatedly. These did not entirely displace older confessional themes, but the disparity between 1617 and 1717 on the one
hand and 1817 on the other is striking. The 1617 and 1717 jubilees
were "purely religious events (*reine Glaubensfeste*)," according to Rainer
Fuhrmann; "by contrast the centenary festival of 1817 was experienced as a *historical* jubilee."[49]

The Enlightenment-era theme of historical progress in particular
stands out in 1817. The Reformation might have been a religious
event that sought to return Christianity to its sources, but the net effect
of this retrospective vision was to inaugurate a new vision of historical
progress and freedom. The Reformation, thus understood, became a
stepping stone (*Vorstufe*) to the modern world, a premonition (*Vorbote*)
of modern enlightenment. In this vision, Roman Catholicism was less
a false church (though perhaps that too) than a massive historical
impediment to progress, a dungeon of ignorance and superstition

that had long vexed and oppressed the human spirit. Such lines of reasoning helped shape a new, enlightened form of Protestantism (*aufgeklärte Protestantismus*), born from the womb of older, creedal Reformation verities.[50]

Two pastors from Franconia (a Protestant enclave grafted onto Catholic Bavaria after 1815) aptly illustrate such sensibilities in their centenary sermons from 1817. Johann Gottlieb Reuter (1765–1831) from Bayreuth, for example, maintained that the Reformation served all of humanity because it brought with it "enlightenment and morality" (*Aufklärung und Sittlichkeit*). As he elaborated:

> The Christian peoples, who sat enveloped in lamentable darkness, saw in the Reformation a welcomed, bright light, which awakened the spirits to a new active life. The chains that previously held the free development of all thinking minds were loosened. The free spirit of inquiry was aroused and one no longer could be satisfied with holy errors maintained by custom and superstition. People learned to be ashamed of gross ignorance and to pursue knowledge and art with joyful and happy enthusiasm.... Not only did the Reformation bring Enlightenment (*Aufklärung*) to humanity; it also brought a moral vision. The burdens, which fear and superstition... had brought forth and nourished, could no longer stand in the light of a new day.[51]

Valentin Carl Veillodter (1769–1828) of Nuremberg possessed a similar outlook. "The improvement of the church [in the sixteenth century]," he sermonized in 1817,

> stands before us as a world event. That is to say, [the Reformation] had such a massive and far-reaching influence on the entire Christian world, it has brought forth such remarkable alterations in public and private life, it has caused such ineradicable successes, [and] it continues its meaningful work after three hundred years. History, so long as the earth stands, must mention it.[52]

In Berlin, both the pastor August Ludwig Hanstein (1761–1821) and Friedrich Schleiermacher made similar arguments, interpreting the Reformation as humanity's collective step in the right direction. In a series of before-and-after scenarios, Hanstein made his case for the progressive character of the Reformation: "The Reformation brought instead of the word of man, the word of God; instead of constrained interpretation, free inquiry into the Holy Scripture; instead of dark, blind faith, the rational clarity of free conviction; instead of the coercion of conscience under priestly power, the freedom of the spirit and heart under a concience under God's power."[53]

From the pulpit of Berlin's Trinity Church on 1 November 1817, Schleiermacher described the Reformation as the dawning of a "new light," the advent of "true freedom," delivering the faith from the "deep darkness" into which the church had descended. "[W]e live daily in the free enjoyment of the glorious benefits that befall to Christianity on account of the Reformation of the Church," he elaborated,

> [for] all of us can and shall count it a great blessing . . . that God has allowed us to join together in this tercentenary celebration so that we can let ourselves be filled in a more intimate way . . . with the feelings of the great blessings that have come to us from this event [the Reformation], and so that by recalling the divine dispensations and by bringing to mind these cherished instruments [the Reformers] . . . we shall become more actively and joyfully conscious of our relationship to them and with the great energy of their time with all its strains and struggles.[54]

Furthermore, in his office as dean of the University of Berlin's theological faculty, Schleiermacher gave an address, in Latin, on 3 November 1817, in which he praised the Reformation for introducing the critical spirit into theology, without which it would slip back into Catholic dogmatism, itself a species of "Jewish" priestcraft.[55] Luther's acts in the sixteenth century represented for Schleiermacher "the complete overthrow of the superstition of arbitrary works and external merit." While Catholic universities fell prey to papal authority, Protestant universities "were ennobled by freedom of teaching and learning."[56] Schleiermacher also sympathized with the political aspirations of the students who had met at Wartburg castle.[57]

Schleiermacher's future colleague at Berlin, the young Leopold von Ranke, was so stirred by the rhetoric of 1817 that he promptly began writing a biography of Luther. According to the future dean of German historians, Luther was a thoroughly extraordinary individual; the sheer force of his convictions had forever altered human history. "Concerning Luther we need not speak separately of his life and his teaching. . . . [H]e lived in his teaching and his teaching lived in him." "A pure, highly blessed person," Luther sought with singular determination to follow his insights, to follow what he discovered in his "consciousness."[58] While Ranke never completed the biography, this "Ranke Fragment" of his youth paved the way for his mature efforts to interpret the Reformation as a crucial transitional era in European history from the medieval to the modern and as providing the "spiritual" basis for German political nationhood.[59]

Numerous writings, homilies, and orations from the 1817 tercentenary sought to connect the Reformation with the birthpangs of "the modern"—with modern reason, political liberalism, and/or bourgeois society. It was frequently pointed out that all of the major reformers—Luther, Melanchthon, Zwingli, and others—hailed not from aristocratic but middle-class backgrounds.[60] K. H. L. Pölitz of the University of Leipzig captured a broadly felt sentiment in the title of an address he gave on 30 October 1817: "The similarity between the fight for civic and political freedom in our age and the fight for religious and ecclesiastical freedom in the age of the Reformation." Both the religious freedoms sought in the sixteenth century and the civil freedoms sought in the ninteenth, Pölitz opined, first originated as ideals championed by "educated individuals of the third estate."[61] The Berlin theologian and biblical scholar de Wette went further still, contending that the Reformation contained the seeds of practically every sort of modern freedom—and not least the freedoms championed by students at the Wartburg demonstration. "The spirit of Protestantism," de Wette argued, "necessarily brings the spirit of freedom and the independence of the people (*das Volk*); Protestant freedom leads necessarily to political freedom."[62]

But not only did the Reformation anticipate modern political ideals; its influence had improved the material and social circumstances of life. In contrast to Catholicism, which conduced society to accept autocracy, sloth, and social squalor, as many celebrants of 1817 held, Protestantism by contrast encouraged republican civic virtue, domestic manners, and bourgeois respectability. Anticipating Max Weber's famous notion of a "Protestant ethic," Gottfried Erdmann Petri of Zittau, for example, argued that the Reformation by reshaping everyday habits led to overall improved social and moral conditions. "Wherever Protestantism triumphs," he proclaimed, "the conditions of ethics, of the industry of businesses, and domestic life receive a better form."[63] Respect for law and order, industriousness, proper care for the poor, beneficial trade, and better education all coincided with the spread of Protestantism, Petri maintained. The Erlangen pastor Carl Georg Friedrich Goes (1762–1836) reasoned similarly: "A good [Protestant] Christian [is] a good citizen (*Bürger*)." A sense of "vocation and duty" (*Beruf und Pflicht*) followed in the wake of the Reformation; through its influence came "blessing and prosperity to bourgeois life and activity."[64]

The well-ordered Protestant bourgeois life received praise not only in addresses and sermons, but in the many illustrations of Luther's life, which became legion around the time of the tercentennial celebration. Popular artists such as Friedrich Camp, Carl Alexander von Heidel-off, Johann Erdmann Hummel, and Gustav König painted episodes from Luther's life, often in the form of a memory or commemoration panel (*Erinnerungs-Tafel* or *Gedächtnis-Tafel*) (Figure 2.3). Resembling medieval fresco cycles of the lives of saints, these illustrated key turning points of Luther's life—his decision to become a monk, the attack on indulgences, the burning of his letter of condemnation, his appearance at the Diet of Worms, his translation of the Bible at Wartburg castle, and his death. In these, the apocalypticism and polemical confession-alism (hallmarks of earlier illustrations) take a backseat to emphases on bourgeois respectability and a well-mannered society. A popular image in the panels, for example, was that of "Luther as family father," in which the mature Luther played the piano (or engaged in some other domestic activity) in the company of well-behaved, admiring family members (Figure 2.4). A variant on this theme was Luther celebrating Christmas with friends and family. A peaceful deathbed scene of Luther surrounding by adoring friends and family was also popular.

Significantly, it was only at this time that images of the 95 Theses being posted on the Castle Church door in Wittenberg become widespread. This image had several variations. Often the artist depicted a young student proxy posting the theses while Luther and other scholars in the foreground led a discussion as citizens of Witten-berg looked on (Figure 2.5). Sometimes Luther was portrayed posting the theses himself. The now iconic image (the historical veracity of which has been questioned) appears for the first time in print on a cycle of Luther's life done by the artist Georg Paul Buchner

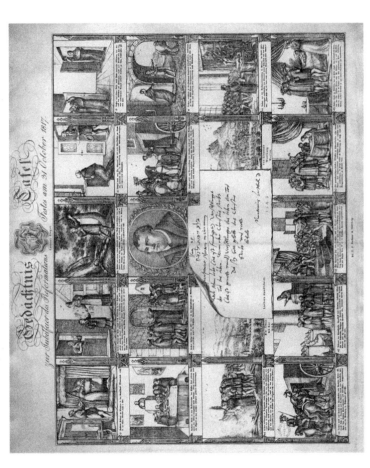

Figure 2.3. *Gedächtnis-Tafel* or Memory Panel of Luther's life (1817). Artist: Georg Paul Buchner, 1817. © The Trustees of the British Museum.

Figure 2.4. Luther as a family man playing the piano (1817). Engraving by Peter Carl Geibler and Fredrich Campe, Nuremberg, 1817. Reproduced by permission from the Germanisches Nationalmuseum.

ANFANG DER REFORMATION.

Luther läßt 95 Sätze gegen den Ablaß an die Schloßkirche zu Wittenberg anschlagen

Figure 2.5. Proxy posting the 95 Theses (1817). Drawing by Wilhelm Baron von Löwenstern. 1817. Reproduced by permission from the Kunstsammlungen der Veste Coburg/Germany.

(1785–1838) (Figure 2.6). Whether wielded by Luther or a proxy, the hammer as the chosen tool for the iconic deed comes into popular circulation at this time.[65]

To say that themes of bourgeois respectability, nationalism, or historical progress coincided with the tercentenary jubilee is not to say that older confessional themes disappeared altogether. As we have already seen, the orthodox pastor Claus Harms took strong exception in 1817 to the "rationalism" and "unionism" that he felt was subverting the religious purity of Luther's message. Harms was not alone, but joined by a chorus of other voices such as Adam Theodor Lehmas of Ansbach, Berlin's Gottfried August Hanstein, and Phillip Friedrich Pöschel of Augsburg.[66] Channeling the stricter orthodoxy of the sixteenth and seventeenth centuries, but also in touch with the awakening movement

Figure 2.6. First printed image of Luther himself posting the 95 Theses (1817). Artist: Georg Paul Buchner, 1817. © The Trustees of the British Museum.

(*Erweckungsbewegung*) and the political conservatism of their day, such figures sought to focus on doctrinal purity above all else—and on Luther's teachings on justification and the Eucharist in particular.[67] They also sought to disassociate the Reformation from the progressive, unionist themes championed by the likes of Schleiermacher. Their historical vision was in fact more one of declension than of progress. The true faith, which Luther had boldly championed, had been modified beyond recognition by the Enlightenment and its adherents.[68] The Protestant churches, as Pöschel lamented, "[have] everywhere [turned] the spiritual into the worldly, the higher things into lower things, the unseen truths into visible ones."[69] Noting the presence of such disaffection does not undermine the claim of the novelty of the 1817 jubilee, but it does provide a necessary qualification.

* * *

While the Continent of Europe witnessed the most extensive outpouring of interest in Luther in 1817, acts of commemoration took place elsewhere as well. This reality provides another contrast between 1817 and the two prior centenary jubilees, which were largely Continental affairs.

In Britain, no elaborate ceremonies took place on the German model, but the memory and menace of "popery" led a handful of clergymen to observe the 300th anniversary of the Reformation in their homilies. Most of these sermons followed a discernable pattern. First, homilists deplored "popery" or, as William Ward put it, that "very essence of Antichristian apostacy [sic], or corruption of Christianity, which the Reformation in a considerable degree removed." Second, they extolled general principles of the Reformation, including, among other points, justification by faith, scripture in the vernacular, and the rights of conscience over "coercion" and "tyranny." Third, they sought to demonstrate the efficacy of Protestantism over Catholicism not only by appeals to scripture, but also by reference to contemporary circumstances. To quote Ward again: "The awful effect of this ['Romish'] system is to be seen in Catholic countries: there ignorance, immorality, and superstition triumph. The state of morals in Italy is peculiarly bad, merely through the effect of Popery; but those nations where the Reformation has been carried the farthest, are most distinguished by science, morality, and good order."[70]

Religious "nonconformists" or "dissenters" in Britain were particularly keen to latch on to the "principles" of the Reformation. They employed them not only to castigate Catholicism, but to condemn putatively "papist" leftovers in the Church of England. After cataloging various tenets of the Reformation, the English Congregationalist Henry Forster Burder, typically, exhorted his congregation as follows:

> These are the grand principles for which the Reformers contended, and these are, permit me to say, the grand principles of Protestant Dissenters. On these principles the Church of England dissents from the Church of Rome, and precisely on these principles we dissent from the Church of England.... We wish only to carry forward the principles of the Reformation to their scriptural and legitimate extent. We only wish the Reformation from popery to be complete; and in this wish we find ourselves associated in sentiment with many of the Reformers themselves. They had accomplished much, but much remained to be accomplished, and still remains.[71]

* * *

If we may briefly cross the Atlantic, mainly Lutheran communities in North America commemorated the 300th anniversary in 1817. Many regarded the occasion as an opportunity to assert their leadership among the diverse and multiplying Protestant bodies that had made their home in the New World.[72] Others saw the moment as a chance to make connections between their Old World past and present situation.[73]

By the summer of 1817, Lutheran synods from New York to North Carolina had set in motion plans to celebrate the beginning of the Reformation by commemorative anniversary services either "on the 31st of October" or the Sunday "nearest to October 31st 1817," as their leaders prescribed. Members of other Protestant churches were sometimes invited to these services, but Lutherans alone had the foresight and intention to make significant arrangements. Often appeal was made to European precedents: "In the year of 1617 and 1717, the commencement of the Reformation was celebrated in Europe," began an account of "the solemnization of the third centurial jubilee" by the Evangelical Lutheran Synod of New York.[74]

While practically all American celebrations shared a baseline anti-Catholicism, many of the same divisions that existed among Old World Lutherans manifested themselves in the New World.[75] Pietist, enlightened, unionist, and confessional accents, therefore, can all be detected in the various events and utterances that took place in 1817 and in resulting publications.

Lutheran commemoration in the New World sometimes provided the occasion for brand-new divisions; the assortment of European Lutheran emigrants led some to emphasize their distinctive ethnic and linguistic identities—German, Danish, or Swedish, et alia—at the expense of their co-religionists. Whether to hold commemorative events in native languages or, as younger generations began to prefer, in English was another issue with which celebrants wrestled.[76]

Confessional emphases came out strongly in an address given by David Frederick Schaeffer, a pastor in Frederickstown, Maryland. While he expressed thanks that the "blessed Reformation" had produced a positive effect on all whom it touched, he lamented that the present-day church looked upon the Reformation "with a degree of ingratitude" which proceeded "from a general ignorance in the history of the church." True Protestants ought, therefore, to return to the purity of sixteenth-century sources if they were to comprehend the gift of having been delivered from "the gross corruption and spiritual tyranny of Rome."[77] Of the many works published in 1817–18 by American Lutherans, among the most popular was a translation made by John Kortz of a biography of Luther written by the superintendent of the Lutheran Church in Saxony, Johann Friedrich Wilhelm Tischer.[78]

In America, pietist and enlightened sentiments jostled with confessional, anti-Catholic ones to produce progressive interpretations of the Reformation as a moment of historical advancement and liberty. Often these accents were jumbled together. The President of the German Lutheran Synod of Pennsylvania, George Lochman, for example, exhorted his co-religionists to mark the jubilee because among "the glorious fruits of the Reformation" were "pure Evangelical doctrine" and "liberty of conscience." "As long as the world exists, this day [31 October 1517] should . . . be held in grateful remembrance," he proclaimed, adding an American embellishment: "What the 4th day of July, 1776, is and must be to our precious political liberty, that the 31st of October of the year 1517, should be, in respect to our religious liberty."[79]

The Enlightenment-leaning Frederick Henry Quitman, similarly, pointed out in a sermon that Luther had "raised the standard of religious liberty . . . and by one bold stroke laid the foundation for the deliverance of his native country from ecclesiastical despotism." The first principle of the Reformation, Quitman held, was that "no man or combination of men has a right to rule over the consciences of others, or to erect a general standard of religious faith and practice." What is more, religious knowledge derived from revelation and reason, not habitual deference to authority, was "the basis by which all religious questions ought to be decided" and that "toleration is an essential characteristic of the Protestant Church."[80] A Lutheran pastor from Harrisburg, Pennsylvania, F. C. Schaeffer, reasoned similarly, eager to make a connection between Luther's defiance of established authority in the sixteenth century and the "liberty of conscience" found in the United States. In Schaeffer's opinion, Luther stood alone among the great men "in the last series of centuries"; the German reformer, therefore, "should not be regarded as a polemic or sectarian, but as a benefactor of the human family."[81]

To summarize: at the tercentennial of the Reformation in 1817, whether in the Old World or the New, older patterns of confessional commemoration had by no means disappeared. But 1817 stands apart from both 1617 and 1717 in that a narrative of general human emancipation, often one laced with nationalist impulses, had begun to rival and in some cases supplant the confessional concern of asserting a direct correspondence between Lutheran teachings and the truth of Christian revelation. Regularly defining itself against Roman Catholic or medieval "superstition" and "tyranny," this emancipatory vision of the tercentenary played no inconsiderable role in helping shape what the historian Herbert Butterfield famously described as "the Whig interpretation of history," a pervasive nineteenth-century "reading" of the Reformation that sought to establish a firm causal link between sixteenth-century church reforms and modern liberalism, the spirit of the modern world.[82] From 1817 onward, this link was repeatedly underscored on both sides of the Atlantic.

In his ruminations on faith, knowledge, and history, Hegel apotheosized this sentiment: "The great form of the [modern] World Spirit . . . is the principle of the North, and, from a religious perspective, Protestantism."[83] The Reformation, as he put it elsewhere, was the "transfiguring sun, the morning dawn that signifies the end of the Middle Ages."[84]

Notes

1. Max L Baeumer, "Lutherfeiern und ihre politische Manipulation," in Reinhold Grimm and Jost Hermand (eds), *Deutsche Feiern* (Wiesbaden: Akademische Verlagsgesellschaft Athenaion, 1977), 48.
2. Wichmann von Meding, *Kirchenverbesserung: Die deutschen Reformationspredigten des Jahres 1817* (Bielefeld: Luther-Verlag, 1986), 201.
3. Jonathan Israel, *A Revolution of the Mind: Radical Enlightenment and the Intellectual Origins of Modern Democracy* (Princeton: Princeton University Press, 2010), 1–36.
4. Karl Barth, *Protestant Theology in the Nineteenth Century: Its Background and History*, tr. John Bowden (London: SCM Press, 1972), 235.
5. John Tonkin, "Reformation Studies," in Hans J. Hillerbrand (ed.), *The Oxford Encyclopedia of the Reformation*, iii (New York: OUP, 1996), 403–5, and Dirk Fleischer, *Zwischen Tradition und Forschritt: Der Strukturwandel der protestantischen Kirchengeschichtsschreibung im deutschprachigen Diskurs der Aufklärung* (Waltrop: H. Spenner, 2006), 517ff.

6. On Semler's views of the Reformation, see Wolfgang Sommer, "Die Stellung Semlers und Schleiermachers zu den reformatorischen Bekenntnisschriften," *Kerygma und Dogma*, 35 (1989): 296–315, and Silke-Petra Bergjan, "'Versuch eines fruchtbares Auszugs aus der Kirchengeschichte': Johann Semler über die Bedeutung und Aufgabe der Geschichte der Alten Kirchen," *Zeitschrift für Kirchengeschichte*, 113 (2002): 51–74. On Mosheim, see Thomas Albert Howard, *Protestant Theology and the Making of the Modern German University* (Oxford: OUP, 2006), 107–14.

7. Quoted in Ernst Walter Zeeden, *The Legacy of Luther*, tr. Ruth Mary Bethell (London: Hollis & Carter, 1954), 137. Cf. Karl Barth's discussion of Lessing in *Protestant Theology in Nineteenth Century America* (London: SCM, 1972), 234–65, and Ernst Schulin, "Luther's Position in German History and Historical Writing," tr. U. Watson, *Australian Journal of Politics and Religion*, 20 (1984): 86.

8. Immanuel Kant, *On History*, ed. Lewis White Beck (Indianapolis, IN: Bobbs-Merrill, 1963), 3.

9. Karl Leonhard Reinhold, *Letters on the Kantian Philosophy*, ed. Karl Ameriks, tr. James Hebbeler (Cambridge: CUP, 2005), 32 (emphasis added).

10. On Villers and his *Essai*, see Michael Printy, "Protestantism and Progress in the Year XII: Charles Villers's Essay on the Spirit and Influence of Luther's Reformation (1804)," *Modern Intellectual History*, 9 (2012): 303–29. Similarly, Heinrich Heine argued that "the philosophical revolution [of Kant] emerged from the religious one, and . . . *is nothing other than the logical conclusion of Protestantism*." See Heinrich Heine, *On the History of Religion and Philosophy in Germany and Other Writings*, ed. Terry Pinkard, tr. Howard Pollack-Milgate (Cambridge: CUP, 2007), 42 (emphasis added).

11. Tonkin, "Reformation Studies," in Hillerbrand, *Oxford Encyclopedia of the Reformation*, 403.

12. A. G. Dickens and John Tonkin, *The Reformation in Historical Thought* (Cambridge, MA: Harvard University Press, 1985), 116ff. Cf. Pentti Laasonen and Johannes Wallmann (eds), *Der Pietismus in seiner europäischen und außereuropäischen Ausstrahlung* (Helsinki: Suomen Kirkkohistoriallinen Seura, 1992). On the influence of the University of Halle in general, see Howard, *Protestant Theology*, 87–104. Interestingly, the Pro-Rector of the University Halle opposed the idea of a jubilee, regarding it as largely a Catholic phenomenon. See Ruth Kastner, "The Reformer and the Reformation Anniversaries," *History Today*, 33 (1983), 25.

13. On this point see Jonathan Strom, Hartmut Lemann, and James Van Horn Melton (eds), *Pietism in Germany and North America, 1680–1820* (Farnham: Ashgate, 2009); Ernest Stoeffer (ed.), *Continental Pietism and Early American Christianity* (Grand Rapids, MI: Eerdmans, 1976); W. R. Ward, *The Protestant Evangelical Awakening* (Cambridge: CUP, 1992); W. R. Ward, *Early Evangelicalism: A Global History, 1670–1789* (Cambridge: CUP, 2006); and Syndey E. Ahlstrom, *A Religious History of the American People* (New Haven: Yale University Press, 1972), 324–5, passim. Cf. Ernst Benz, "Ecumenical Relations between Boston Puritans and German Pietists: Cotton Mather and August Hermann Francke," *Harvard Theological Review*, 54 (1961): 159–93.

14. Friedrich Meinecke, *Historism: The Rise of a New Historical Outlook*, tr. J. E. Anderson (New York: Herder & Herder, 1972), liv.

15. See Thomas Nipperdey's very helpful discussion of the "revolution of historicism," in *Germany from Napoleon to Bismark, 1800–1866*, tr. Daniel Nolan (Princeton: Princeton University Press, 1996), 441–71, and Felix Gilbert, *History: Politics or Culture? Reflections on Ranke and Burckhardt* (Princeton: Princeton University Press, 1990), 3–10. Cf. Georg Iggers, *The German Conception of History: The National Tradition of Historical Thought from Herder to the Present*, rev. edn (Middletown, CT: Wesleyan University Press, 1983).

16. Maurice Mandelbaum, *History, Man, and Reason: A Study in Nineteenth-Century Thought* (Baltimore, MD: Johns Hopkins, 1971), 42. Cf. the helpful article by Georg G. Iggers, "Historicism: The History and Meaning of the Term," *Journal of the History of Ideas,* 56 (Jan. 1995): 129–52.

17. Quoted in Zeeden, *Legacy of Luther*, 172. Cf. the detailed study by Michael Embach, *Das Lutherbild Johann Gottfried Herders* (Frankfurt a.M.: P. Lang, 1987).

18. J. G. Fichte, *Addresses to the German Nation*, tr. R. F. Jones and G. H. Turnbull (Chicago: Open Court Publishing Company, 1922), 95–6.

19. Robert Ergang, *Herder and the Foundations of German Nationalism* (New York: Columbia University Press, 1931). In many respects, the employment of Luther to help "imagine" German nationhood is a classic example of the origins of nationalism; as conceptualized in Benedict Anderson's highly regarded *Imagined Communities*.

20. Arlie J. Hoover, *The Gospel of Nationalism: German Patriotic Preaching from Napoleon to Versailles* (Stuttgart: F. Steiner, 1986), 29ff.

21. Nipperdey, *Germany from Napoleon to Bismarck, 1800–1866*, 1. For more historical context, see Tim Blanning, "Napoleon and German Identity," *History Today,* 48 (1998): 37–43, and George Williamson, "What Killed August von Kotzebue? The Temptation of Virtue and the the Political Theology of German Nationalism, 1789–1819," *Journal of Modern History,* 72 (2000): 890–943.

22. Howard, *Protestant Theology*, 1.

23. On the creation and functioning of the German Confederation, see Roy A. Austenson, "'*Einheit oder Einigkeit*'? Another Look at Metternich's View of the German Dilemma," *German Studies Review,* 6 (1983): 41–87.

24. Nipperdey, *Germany from Napoleon to Bismarck*, 313–16, and Michael Burleigh, *Earthly Powers: The Clash of Religion and Politics in Europe, from the French Revolution to the Great War* (New York: HarperCollins, 2005), 112ff.

25. Nipperdey, *Germany from Napoleon to Bismarck*, 245.

26. Quote taken from H. W. Koch, *A History of Prussia* (London: Longman, 1978), 209.

27. James J. Sheehan, *German History, 1770–1866* (Oxford: Clarendon Press, 1989), 406–7.

28. Robert Keil and Richard Keil, *Die burschenschaftlichen Wartburgfeste von 1817 und 1867* (Jena, 1868), 14.

29. Anthony J. Steinhoff, "Christianity and the Creation of Germany," in Sheridan Gilley and Brian Stanley (eds), *The Cambridge History of Christianity: World Christianities c.1815–c.1914,* viii (Cambridge: CUP, 2006), 283.

30. Stan Landry, *Ecumenism, Memory, and German Nationalism, 1817–1917* (Syracuse, NY: Syracuse University Press, 2014), 17–26.

31. J. W. von Goethe, "Zum Reformationsfest," in Goethe, *Kunsttheoretische Schriften und Übersetzungen*, Berliner Ausgabe, xvii (Berlin: Aufbau-Verlag, 1970), 503. Still, rank confessional polemics were easily apparent. Catholics republished Luther's incendiary *Wider das Papsttum vom Teufel gestiftet* to remind celebrants of Luther's attitude toward Catholics. See Ottmar Friedrich Johannes Hegermann, *Luther im katholischen Urteil: Eine Wanderung durch vier Jahrhunderte* (Munich: J. F. Lehmanns Verlag, 1905), 162.

32. Wichmann von Meding, "Das Wartburgfest im Rahmen des Reformationsjubliäums 1817," *Zeitschrift für Kirchengeschichte*, 96 (1985): 205–7. The focus on "humanity" and "freedom" even elicited the admiration and participation of some Jews in the jubilee events of 1817. See Dorothea Wendebourg, "Jews Commemorating Luther in the Nineteenth Century," *Lutheran Quarterly*, 26 (2012): 249–70.

33. Landry, *Ecumenism*, 9. Cf. W. Wendland, *Die Religiosität und kirchenpolitischen Grundzüge Friedrich Wilhelm des Dritten in ihrer Bedeutung für die Geschichte der kirchlichen Restauration* (Giessen: A. Töpelmann, 1909).

34. Quoted in Howard, *Protestant Theology*, 235.

35. Robert M. Bigler, "The Rise of Political Protestantism in Nineteenth-Century Germany," *Church History*, 34 (1965): 435.

36. Martin Redeker, *Schleiermacher: Life and Thought*, tr. John Wallhausser (Philadelphia: Fortress Press, 1973), 189–91.

37. Walter Elliger (ed.), *Die evangelische Kirche der Union: Ihre Vorgeschichte und Geschichte* (Witten: Luther-Verlag, 1967), 44–5, 195–6. Prior to this, it should be mentioned, a Protestant union took place in the small duchy of Nassau in Aug. 1817. See *RPP* xiii. 194, and Landry, *Ecumenism*, 15.

38. Quoted in Elliger, *Die evangelsiche Kirche der Union*, 44–5. A facsimilie of the original proclamation can be found in J. F. Gerhard Goeters and Rudolf Mau (eds), *Die Geschichte der evangelischen Kirche der Union: Die Anfänge der Union unter landesherrlichem Kirchenregiment (1817–1850)*, i (Leipzig: Evangelische Verlagsanstalt, 1992), 88–90.

39. See J. F. Gerhard and Joachim Rogge (eds), *Die Geschichte der evangelischen Kirche der Union*, i (Leipzig: Evangelische Verlagsanstalt, 1992), 111, and Elliger, *Die evangelische Kirche der Union*, 45–6.

40. Hugo Schnell, *Martin Luther und die Reformation auf Münzen und Medaillen* (Munich: Klinkhardt & Biermann, 1983), 75, 231 (image #273), and Elliger, *Die evangelsiche Kirche der Union*, 176.

41. John E. Groh, *Nineteenth-Century German Protestantism: The Church as Social Model* (Washington, DC: University of America Press, 1982), 41–3, and Franz Schnabel, *Deutsche Geschichte im neunzehnten Jahrhundert: Die protestantischen Kirchen in Deutschland* (Freiburg im Breisgau: Herder, 1965), 104ff. On the implementation of the Union in Prussia, see F. Weichert, "Die Unionsbestrebungen in Berlin und Brandenburg von 1817 bis 1850, Widestände und Motive," *Jahrbuch für Brandenburische Kirchengeschichte*, 54 (1983): 97–155.

42. See G. Friedrich (ed.), *Chronik der dritten Jubelfeier der Reformation in Frankfurt am Main* (Frankfurt a.M., 1817), 135ff.

43. Claus Harms, *Ausgewählte Schriften und Predigten*, ed. G. E. Hofmann, i (Flensburg: Christian Wolff Verlag, 1955), 204–22.

44. Rainer Fuhrmann, *Das Reformationsjubiläum 1817* (Bonn: V+V Sofortdruck, 1973), 35.

45. On the Old Lutheran emigration, see Wilhelm Iwan, *Die altlutherische Auswanderung um die Mitte des 19. Jahrhundert*, 2 vols. (Ludwigsburg: L. Kallenberg, 1943). See also Christopher Clark, "Confessional Policy and the Limits of State Action: Frederick William III and the Prussian Church Union 1817–1840," *Historical Journal*, 39 (1996): 985–1004.

46. Adelheid Mahnert, "Lutherbildnisse und Lutherstätten aud Porzellan," in Hardy Eidam and Gerhard Seib (eds), *"Er fühlt der Zeiten ungeheuren Bruch und fest umklammert er sein Bibelbuch . . . ": Zum Lutherkult im 19. Jahrhundert* (Berlin: Verlag Schelzky and Jeep, 1996), 109–17.

47. Gérald Chaix, "Die Reformation," in Etienne François and Hagen Schluze (eds), *Deutsche Erinnerungsorte* (Munich: C. H. Beck, 2001), ii. 9ff.

48. On the king's visit to Wittenberg, see Otto Dibelius, *Das Königliche Predigerseminar zu Wittenberg, 1817–1917* (Berlin-Lichterfelde: E. Runge, 1918), 43–8. He came there directly after participating in the first Prussian "union" service in Potsdam.

49. Fuhrmann, *Das Reformationsjubiläum 1817,* 19 (emphasis added).

50. Ulrich Barth, *Der aufgeklärte Protestantismus* (Tübingen: Mohr-Siebeck, 2004), 3ff.

51. Johann Gottlieb Reuter, *Fünf Predigten zu und bei der Secularfeier der Kirchenreformation 1817 gehalten* (Bayreuth, 1817), 23–4.

52. V. C. Veillodter, *Zwei Predigten: Am Reformationsfeste im Jahre 1817 gehalten und zur Vorbereitung auf die dritte Säcularfeier herausgegeben von Veillodter und Seidel* (Nuremberg, 1817), 6.

53. August Ludwig Hanstein, *Das Jubeljahr der evangelischen Kirche: Vier vorbereitende Predigten* (Berlin, 1817), 31.

54. Friedrich Schleiermacher, "Am zweiten Tage des Reformations-Jubelfestes 1817," *Sämmtliche Werke*, ii/4 (Berlin, 1835), 67–8.

55. Kurt Nowak, *Schleiermacher: Leben, Werk und Wirkung* (Göttingen: Vandenhoeck & Ruprecht, 2001), 364–5. See also B. A. Gerrish's essay, "Schleiermacher and the Reformation: The Question of Doctrinal Development," in Gerrish, *The Old Protestantism and the New: Essays on the Reformation Heritage* (Chicago: University of Chicago Press, 1982), 179–95. On the Protestant view that Catholicism was contaminated by the retention of many "Jewish" elements, see David Nirenberg, *Anti-Judaism: The Western Tradition* (New York: W. W. Norton, 2013), 246ff.

56. "Oratio in sollemnibus ecclesiae per Lutherem emendatae saecularibus tertiis in Universitate litterarum Berolinensi . . ." in Schleiermacher, *Kritische Gesamtausgabe*, ed. Hans-Joachim Birkner et al., i/10 (Berlin: Walter de Gruyter, 1990), 11. Translations of Schleiermacher's jubilee sermon of 1 Nov. 1817 and his academic address of 3 Nov. 1817 are found in Friedrich Schleiermacher, *On Creeds, Confessions and Church Union: That They May be One*, tr. Iain G. Nicol (Lewiston, NY: Edwin Mellen Press, 2004), 29–63. I have consulted these translations in making my own.

57. For these sympathies, Schleiermacher and several of his colleagues at the University of Berlin were actually monitored by the Prussian government. See Max Lenz, *Geschichte der königlichen Universität zu Berlin*, ii (Halle: Buchhandlung des Waisen-hauses, 1910), 62 and Ernst Staehelin (ed.), *Dewettiana: Forschungen und Texte zu*

Wilhelm Martin Leberecht de Wettes Leben und Werk (Basel: Helbing & Lichtenhahn, 1956), 81ff.

58. Leopold von Ranke, "Fragment über Luther 1817," in Ranke, *Aus Werk und Nachlass: Frühe Schriften*, iii, ed. Walther Peter Fuchs (Munich: R. Oldenbourg Verlag, 1973), 340–2. Cf. Schulin, "Luther's Position in German History and Historical Writing," 87.

59. Ranke's *German History in the Age of the Reformation* was published in 6 vols. in Berlin between 1839 and 1847. Significantly, Ranke listed Thucydides, Barthold Georg Niebuhr, and Luther as "the three spirits to whom I owe the basic elements upon which my later historical studies have been built." See Ilse Mayer-Kulenkampf, "Rankes Lutherverhältnis, dargestellt nach dem Lutherfragment von 1817," *Historische Zeitschrift*, 72 (1951): 65–99, and A. G. Dickens, *Ranke as a Reformation Historian* (Reading: University of Reading, 1980).

60. Fuhrmann, *Das Reformationsjubiläum 1817,* 54ff. and Lutz Winckler, *Martin Luther als Bürger und Patriot: Das Reformationsjubiläum von 1817 und der politische Protestantismus des Wartburgfestes* (Lübeck: Matthiesen Verlag, 1969), 23ff.

61. Karl Heinrich L. Pölitz, "Die Änlichkeit des Kampfes um bürgerliche und politische Freiheit in unserm Zeitalter mit dem Kampfe um die religiöse und kirchliche Freiheit im Zeitalter der Reformation," in Friedrich Keyser (ed.), *Reformations Almanach für Luthers Verehrer auf das evangelische Jubeljahr 1817*, i (Erfurt, 1819), 123.

62. W. M. L. de Wette, "Ueber den sittlichen Geist der Reformation in Beziehung auf unsere Zeit" (1817) in Keyser, *Reformations Almanach*, i. 286–7.

63. Gottfried Erdmann Petri, "Versuch einer Skizze über die Folgen der Reformation," in Keyser, *Reformations Almanach*, i. 170.

64. C. G. F. Goes, *Luthers Kirchenreformation nach ihrer Veranlassung, Eigenthümlichkeit, Beschaffenheit und wohlthätigen Wirksamkeit in einigen Kanzelvorträgen am dritten Säkularfeste nebst kurzem Berichte über die hiesige Festfeyerlichkeit* (Erlangen, 1817), 65ff.

65. See Joachim Kruse, *Luthers Leben in Illustrationen des 18. und 19. Jahrhunderts: Kataloge der Kunstsammlungen der Veste Coburg* (Coburg: Kunstsammlungen der Veste Coburg, 1980), 57ff. An earlier visual representation can be found on a medal minted in Augsburg for the 1717 jubilee. See Schnell, *Martin Luther*, 170 (image 131). Cf. Harmut Lehmann, "Martin Luther und der 31.Oktober," in Lehmann, *Luthergedächtnis 1817 bis 2017* (Göttingen: Vandenhoeck & Ruprecht, 2012), 17–34, and Barry Stephenson, *Performing the Reformation: Public Ritual in the City of Luther* (Oxford: OUP, 2010), 20–1.

66. Fuhrmann, *Das Reformationsjubiläum 1817*, 72.

67. On the awakening movement (*Erweckungsbewegung*) and its influence in the early nineteenth century, see Robert M. Bigler, *The Politics of German Protestantism* (Berkeley, CA: University of California Press, 1972), 128.

68. This reactionary vision of Protestantism took concrete institutional reform when conservative voices convinced the Prussian government to establish the aforementioned seminary in Wittenberg as a counterpoint to the liberal ethos of many universities. See Otto Dibelius, *Das Königliche Predigerseminar zu Wittenberg: 1817–1819* (Berlin-Lichterfelde: E. Runge, 1918).

69. Philipp Friedrich Pöschel, *Zwei Predigten am dritten Saekularfeste der Reformation: Als am 31. October 1817* (Nuremberg, 1817), 34.

70. William Ward, *The Reformation from Popery Commemorated: A Discourse Delivered in the Independent Meeting House, Stowmarket, November 9, 1817* (Stowmarket, 1817), 6, 14.

71. Henry Forster Burder, *The Reformation Commemorated; A Discourse Delivered at the Meeting-House, St. Thomas's Square, Hackney, December 28th, 1817* (London, 1818), 29. On Nonconformity in general in the early nineteenth century, see David Michael Thompson, *Nonconformity in the Nineteenth Century* (London: Routledge & Kegan Paul, 1972) and David Bebbington, *Victorian Nonconformity*, rev. edn (Eugene, OR: Cascade Books, 2011). Such lines of criticism trace their roots back to Puritan perspectives in the seventeenth century; see Preserved Smith, "English Opinion of Luther," *Harvard Theological Review*, 2 (1917): 140–3.

72. On the broader historical context, see Nathan O. Hatch, *The Democratization of American Christianity* (New Haven: Yale University Press, 1989) and Mark A. Noll, *America's God: From Jonathan Edwards to Abraham Lincoln* (Oxford: OUP, 2002).

73. In 1817 Lutherans made up only an estimated 3% of the US population. See Wolfgang Flügel, "Deutsche Lutheraner? Amerikanische Protestanten? Die Selbstdarstellung deutscher Einwanderer im Reformationsjubiläum 1817," in Klaus Tanner and Jörg Ulrich (eds), *Spurenlese: Reformationsvergegenwärtigung als Standortbestimmung, 1717–1983* (Leipzig: Evangelsiche Verlagsanstalt, 2012), 71ff.

74. *The Blessed Reformation* (New York, 1817), 39.

75. On some of the deeper currents of American Protestant anti-Catholicism, see Thomas S. Kidd, *The Protestant Interest: New England After Puritanism* (New Haven: Yale University Press, 2004) and Ray Allen Billington, *The Protestant Crusade, 1800–1860: A Study in the Origins of American Nativism* (New York: Macmillan, 1938).

76. Hartmut Lehmann, *Martin Luther in the American Imagination* (Munich: Wilhelm Fink Verlag, 1988), 75–80. Cf. Carl S. Meyer, "The Process of Americanization," *Concordia Theological Seminary*, 34 (1964): 407–19.

77. D. F. Schaeffer, *Historical Address Commemorative of the Blessed Reformation Commenced by Dr. Martin Luther on the 31st of October A. D. 1517 Delivered in the Lutheran Church at Frederickstown on the 31st of October 1817* (Frederickstown, MD, 1818), 5ff.

78. J. F. W. Tischer, *The Life, Deeds, and Opinions of Dr. Martin Luther*, tr. John Kortz (Hudson, NY, 1818). This translation was to serve as "a monument erected in memory of Luther" in the New World, as the preface puts it. Lehmann, *Martin Luther in the American Imagination*, 80–1.

79. George Lochmann, *A Glimpse of the Beauties of Eternal Truth, contrasted with the Deformity of Popular Error: Intended as a Prelminary to the Grand Centurial Jubilee of the Reformation of the Year 1517* (Philadelphia, 1817), 12–13.

80. F. H. Quitman, *Three Sermons, the First Preached before the Evangelical Lutheran Synod ... and the Second and Third on Reformation of Doctor Martin Luther* (Hudson, NY, 1817), 14, 31, 22, 41.

81. F. C. Schaeffer, *An Address Pronounced at the Laying of the Corner Stone of St. Matthew's Church New York* (New York, 1821), 9–17.

82. Herbert Butterfield, *The Whig Interpretation of History* (London: G. Bell & Sons, 1931).

83. G. W. F. Hegel, "Glauben und Wissen," in *Hauptwerke in sechs Bänden*, i (Darmstadt, 1999), 316.

84. From Hegel's *Vorlesungen über die Philosophie der Geschichte* as noted in Gérald Chaix, "Die Reformation," in François and Schluze, *Deutsche Erinnerungsorte*, ii. 17. Cf. G. R. G. Moore, "Hegel, Luther, and the Owl of Minerva," *Philosophy*, 41 (1966): 127–39, and Constantin Fasolt, "Hegel's Ghost: Europe, the Reformation, and the Middle Ages," *Viator,* 39 (2008): 3345–89. Fasolt summarizes Hegel's understanding of the Reformation succinctly: "The Reformation blazed a trail for a new synthesis of internal spirit with external spirit that would culminate in the Enlightenment, the French Revolution, and the Prussian state" (p. 364). See also Hegel's "Address on the Tercentenary of the Augsburg Confession," in Laurence Dickey (ed.), *G. W. F. Hegel: Political Writings*, tr. H. B. Nisbet (Cambridge: CUP, 1999), 186–96.

3

1883

Luthermania, Germania, and the
Novus Ordo Seclorum

All of Protestant Christianity is to thank God for blessing our
nation with the Reformation.

(Kaiser Wilhelm I, 1883)

If there had been no Luther in Germany, there would have been
no [George] Washington in America. For the invaluable blessing of our civil liberty and free institutions, we thank God for
Luther.

(Emanuel Greenwald, 1883)

The tercentenary celebration of 1817 set in motion a century of
Reformation jubilees, the scale and scope of which had not been
seen before. Leaving aside the birth and death dates of key reformers
besides Luther, mention ought to be made of the 300th anniversary of
the Diet of Worms (1821), the Augsburg Confession (1830), and
Luther's death (1846), the 200th anniversary of the Peace of Westphalia (1848), the 300th anniversary of the Peace of Augsburg (1855),
and the 350th anniversary of the challenge to indulgences (1867),
among others.[1] And this is to say nothing about commemorations of
the publication of important texts, such as Luther's Larger and
Shorter Catechisms, the Book of Concord, or the Heidelberg Catechism. Indeed, the nineteenth century was an age of memory and
retrospection par excellence.[2]

The century also witnessed the design and erection of numerous
monuments (*Denkmäler*) of Luther in Germany—and in the United
States as well, as we shall see.[3] Plans for the first one on German soil

had been hatched prior to the Napoleonic wars, but this only became a reality after 1815. King Friedrich Wilhelm III in fact made it an affair of state of the Prussian monarchy, which, as previously noted, had acquired Wittenberg as a result of the territorial reorganization at the Congress of Vienna. In this storied city of Luther, the foundation stone for a statue of the reformer was laid on the city's square at the time of the 300th anniversary in 1817 and the project was completed by the design of Johann Gottfried Schadows in 1821.[4] As we have seen, around this time, the image of Luther nailing the 95 Theses to the Castle Church door had risen in prominence in depictions of Luther's life. The original church door had burned in a fire in 1760. But this created space for the imagination to do something by way of memorialization. The renovation of the whole church in 1856/7 finally provided the needed opportunity and, again, Prussia, now led by the very pious Friedrich Wilhelm IV (r. 1840–61), provided the impetus and resources for commemoration. In this case, it took the form of casting bronze doors for the church and on them, in Latin, engraving the 95 Theses. Above, the door, to the right and left of the crucified Christ, Luther and his colleague Melanchthon were painted according to depictions of them by Lucas Cranach. Prussia's coat of arms was placed in the door lintel, making clear that the (erstwhile Reformed) Hohenzollern dynasty had become the protector of the Wittenberg Reformation.[5]

In 1867, on the occasion of the 350th anniversary of the Reformation, the grandest of all Reformation monuments neared completion in Worms, the site of Luther's defiance of Charles V. The project had been in the works for nearly a decade. For the official unveiling, which took place on 18 June 1868, thousands of people came by ship, train, and coach for the festive occasion.[6] Among the many dignitaries present, three stood out: the Grand Duke of Hesse, the King of Württemberg, and the German Emperor, Wilhelm I (r. 1861–88). Britain's Queen Victoria sent a telegraph, communicating her heartfelt regards.[7]

The large central statue of Luther was based on the design of Ernst Rietschel. Students of Rietschel and other artists contributed to many figures flanking Luther, such as John Wycliffe, Jan Hus, Johannes Reuchlin, Melanchthon, and others. Allegorized renderings of key Reformation cities, such as Augsburg, Magdeburg, and Speyer also appear around Luther.[8] Along with the (very Calvinist) International Monument of the Reformation in Geneva, dedicated on the 400th anniversary of Calvin's birth in 1909, the Worms monument is today the largest Reformation monument in the world (Figure 3.1).[9]

Although 1867 was certainly significant, pride of place among later nineteenth-century commemorations goes hands-down to 1883, the 400th anniversary of Luther's birth. In both Germany and the United States, Luther's birthday was marked with great pageantry, fanfare, word, and deed, expressive of two different national "civil religions," the emotion-laden blurring of political and religious loyalties.[10]

Times, of course, had changed since 1817. Of capital importance, Germany had recently become unified under the Prussian (Protestant) leadership of Otto von Bismarck—a military-induced national unification with religious dimensions that historians have sometimes not adequately appreciated.[11] After Prussian victories at the Battles of Königgratz and Sedan, the theologian and later imperial chaplain Adolf Stöcker spoke of the coming of the "Holy *Protestant* Empire of the German Nation."[12] In the wake of unification in 1871 came political reprisal against the "unbelieving" Social Democratic Party and against Catholics. The ultramontanism of the latter—quickened by the crusading, beleaguered papacy of Pius IX (r. 1846–78)— collided with Bismarck's anti-Catholic sentiment to produce the well-known *Kulturkampf* of the 1870s, when the new imperial government sought, ultimately unsuccessfully, to blunt the political clout of German Catholics.[13]

The passage of time from 1817 to 1883 had also witnessed the rise of the German research-model university to a position of international fame and emulation. In it, the historical sciences, pioneered by the likes of Leopold von Ranke and his many disciples, had fully come into their own; an air of historicism or "development" permeated many intellectual fields in the human sciences.[14] Begun in England, the Industrial Revolution was also in full swing on the Continent with the new German Empire starting to lead the way. Finally, a Romantic nationalist sentiment, budding at the time of the Wartburg festival as we have seen, had fully flowered into one of the most powerful and fateful forces not just in Germany but across Europe and beyond. Romantic nationalists, according to Thomas Nipperdey, tended to regard institutions of culture and society as "expression[s] of a unitary

Das Lutherdenkmal in Worms.

Reuchlin. Speyer Wiclef (nicht sichtbar) Melanchton.
Augsburg Waldus. Luther. Magdeburg
Friedrich d. Weise Savonarola. Huss Philipp d. Grossmüthige

Christian Herbst, Hofphotogr. Worms 1902

Figure 3.1. The Lutheran Monument in Worms on a postcard from 1902. Photo by Christian Herbst. Worms: 1902. Photo courtesy of Wikimedia Commons.

force which is usually referred to as the soul or mind of nation (or spirit) of a people; the *Volksgeist* or the character of a nation."[15] In 1883, all of these forces churned and jostled for influence, and most manifest themselves in the centenary events of that year.

In the United States, times had changed too. Having avoided national disintegration during the American Civil War, the "new order of the ages" had entered upon a fresh, optimistic phase of its history. Reconstruction was happening in the South, frontier expansion in the West, while industrial production and urbanization took off in the North.[16] The revivalist energies of the Second Great Awakening had long mingled freely with what the historian R. A. Billington has called "the Protestant Crusade" to produce a pan-Protestant, "nativist" sentiment, frequently directed at newly arrived immigrants from Catholic countries.[17] What is more, American scholarship and university development—often borrowing directly from German models—was beginning to enter a phase of extensive growth and institution-building, including the development of the historical sciences.[18] Finally, America's own version of nationalism—less ethnic and cultural than Old-World varieties but political, idealistic, and hazily "Protestant"—had become more prominent and, like its European counterparts, was on the look-out for heroes, harbingers, and prototypes in the recent and distant past.

* * *

In Germany, the tone of the Luther jubilee of 1883 was set from above. The Emperor and *summus episcopus* of the Prussian state church Wilhelm I issued an edict on 21 May 1883, enjoining "all of Protestant (*evangelische*) Christianity to offer thanks to God for blessing our nation with the Reformation." Protestant churches in the Empire eagerly sought to mark the 400th anniversary of Luther's birth, working in cooperation with Prussia's Ministry of Religious and Cultural Affairs and other relevant church councils, synods, and state cultural ministries. The selected dates were 9, 10, and 11 November, a Friday through Sunday. (Luther's actual birthday was 10 November.) On Friday, church bells were to be rung; on Saturday, activities in educational institutions should take place; and on Sunday, special commemorative worship services were to be held. Precise details were left to individual parishes.[19]

In cities and towns across Germany, a flurry of events took place during these dates. These included parades and torch-lit processions; academic orations; the distribution of commemorative coins and medals; exhibitions; the singing of hymns, particularly of course "A Mighty Fortress"; the unveiling of more monuments and busts of Luther; the publication of pamphlets and histories; the printing and dissemination of postcards; encomiums to secular powers for their past protection of Protestantism; the laying of foundation stones for new churches; not to mention countless sermons reflecting on Luther's life and the broader significance of the Reformation.[20]

A hotchpotch of themes and emphases are apparent in these events. Confessional Lutherans in the tradition of Claus Harms remembered Luther as the restorer of true Christianity as expressed in Lutheran creedal documents. More liberal Protestants, amplifying themes also apparent in 1817, saw Luther as the great emancipator from stultifying tradition and authority, the initiator of the modern world. In this vein, Wilhem Möller of Kiel regarded Luther as championing the "free development of thought," someone who had enabled "an extensive and decisive deliverance from the authorities of the Middle Ages."[21] For the influential liberal theologian Albrecht Ritschl, who gave a jubilee lecture on 10 November, Luther had established a beachhead for the possibility of conscience-driven, culture-transforming Christianity. But Luther did not go far enough; Protestantism remained infected with "adolescent sicknesses" (*Kinderkrankheiten*). It was the duty of those living in the present, according to Ritschl, to complete the work of the Reformation by removing "Catholic holdovers" (*katholische Reste*) from Protestant theology. The Catholic Church had possessed a theology of "flight from the world" (*Weltflucht*). By contrast, the task of Protestant theology in 1883 was to achieve "dominion of the world" (*Weltherrschaft*), locating Christian perfection not in monastic-ascetic virtues, but in the very marrow of modern culture, state, and society and in the reconciled heart of the justified Christian.[22]

Among the most conspicuous themes in 1883 arguably was Romantic nationalism: the refrain that Luther was a German hero, a powerful early manifestation of German culture and national identity, which, finally, had rendezvoused with political destiny in 1871. German Protestants in 1883, as Hartmut Lehmann has written, felt that "Luther's heritage demanded . . . nothing less than the completion of

Germany's unification."[23] 1871 made good, in other words, on potentialities unleashed in 1517, which, in turn, were celebrated in 1883.[24] The "Luthermania" of 1883, as the historian Thomas A. Brady once quipped, amounted to a "belated birthday for the new German Reich."[25]

This reality manifested itself in a short work, "Luther and Bismarck," written by one Hermann Hoffmeister, with the subtitle "foundational pillars of our national greatness." Even though they lived in very different times, Hoffmeister argued, Luther and Bismarck were finally cut from the same cloth, sharing both external similarities and an "inner kinship." Although Luther operated in a religious idiom and Bismarck in a political one, both were visionaries, standing together for "Germanness, Christianity, and the principle of monarchy," and standing against "Romanism, atheism, and republicanism." Concerning the latter, Hoffmeister praised the fact that both men respected established political authority: Bismarck did so by opposing Social Democracy in the 1870s, Luther by condemning the Peasant Uprising of 1524/5.[26] It was Luther's gift to the nation to bring about "the rebirth of ancient Christianity enlivening it with genuine Germanic inwardness" (*echt germanischer Innerlichkeit*).[27] It was Bismarck's gift to bring the prior religious and cultural achievements of the German nation to outward political expression.

A similarly triumphalist, nationalist sentiment appeared in an 1883 address, "Luther and the German Nation," given in Darmstadt by the Prussian historian Heinrich von Treitschke and published shortly thereafter. Making overt a xenophobia that had many subtler manifestations in 1883, this work merits a lingering glance.

Pitying German Catholics for their inability to appreciate Luther's legacy, Treitschke identified the Wittenberg reformer as "the pioneer of the whole German nation," as a man possessing "the power of independent thought that typifies the German character," and as someone "with all the native energy and unquenchable fire of German defiance."[28] In throwing off the "foreign [Roman] yoke," Luther had united Germans in a quest for freedom and in the conviction "that no one can sit in judgment over the human conscience but God alone."[29] Luther's impact, as humble in its beginning as extensive in its outcome, had both spiritual and incipiently nationalist aspects: "the actual setting free of Germany was the direct outcome of an internal conflict waged in an honest German conscience."[30]

An untiring champion of German political unification under Prussian leadership, Treitschke praised Luther for liberating the state from "ecclesiastical despotism" and setting in motion the possibility of state sovereignty. Luther's "two kingdoms" political teaching, in particular, merited Treitschke's commendation:

> Luther first smashed into ruins the dictum behind which the Romanists entrench themselves: he denied that "spiritual power is higher than temporal power," and taught that the State is itself ordained of God, and that it is justified in fulfilling and indeed pledged to fulfill the moral purposes of its existence independently of the Church. The State was thus declared to have come of age . . . [A]s the temporal power everywhere received firm support [during the Reformation] from the growing self-realization of the nations, this political emancipation had almost a more powerful and far-reaching influence than the reformation of the Church.[31]

The consequences of this teaching, according to Treitschke, were especially valuable for the future of Germany: "The emancipation of the State from the tyranny of church control nowhere brought with it so rich and lasting a blessing than in Germany, for nowhere had the old Church been more closely interwoven with the State than in the Holy Roman Empire and in the many ecclesiastical princedoms supported by the imperial power."[32]

With many others in 1883, Treitschke traced the achievements of the German language and literature back to the "little monk" of Wittenberg. "Goethe alone has rivaled him in his command over language," Treitschke noted; "but, notwithstanding [Goethe's] eloquence, [Luther] remains the most 'popular' of all our writers." His works "show deep thought, close compression of material, compelling argument, and an immense prodigality of magnificent words, so that the reader seems to hear the heartfelt accents of the preacher himself." In Luther's translations at Wartburg castle, "we received our literary language at a definite moment of time and at the hands of a single man." In taking on this task, Luther rendered it possible "for God to speak German to the German nation."[33]

What was good for language and literature was also good for education. By dignifying the vernacular and allowing for conscience to trump traditional authorities, Luther had set in motion forces salutary for German higher education. These forces bore fruit especially in the eighteenth-century Enlightenment at the Reform university of Halle, epitomized there by the polymath Christian Thomasius (1655–1728), the first scholar to lecture in the vernacular and one keen to appeal to conscience over custom in championing an enlightened cosmopolitanism. But whether at Halle or elsewhere, Treitschke claimed, "all the leaders of this new learning were Protestants. The new [enlightened] ideal of humanity (*neue Ideal der Humanität*) could proceed only from the autonomy of conscience."[34]

In short, the German Empire in 1883 possessed a historical hero worthy of its present-day aspirations. But not only that. Luther in fact towered above other national heroes. There was something primal, commanding, awe-inspiring about this determined monk. In breaking with the church, he had unwitting and incipiently forged "Germania." The nation, the *Volksgeist*, first became personified in his person. In Treitschke's words:

> No other modern nation can boast of a man who was the mouthpiece of his countrymen in quite the same way, and who succeeded as fully in giving expression to the deepest essence of his nation.... "Here speaks our own blood." From the deep eyes of this uncouth son of a German farmer (*urwüchsigen deutschen Bauernsohnes*) flashed the ancient and heroic courage of the Germanic races—a courage that does not flee from the world, but rather seeks to dominate it by strength of its moral purpose. And just because he gave utterance to ideas already living in the soul of his nation, this poor monk...was able to grow and develop very rapidly, until he had become as dangerous to the new [Catholic] Roman universal empire as the assailing Germanic hordes were to the empire of the Caesars.[35]

German Catholics regularly refused to accept the bitter medicine offered them from the likes of Treitschke and preferred to see Luther as a tragic or deluded figure, culpable for splintering the church. The jubilee's widespread conflation of German-ness and Protestantism they saw as a continuation of the policies of the *Kulturkampf* and a "call to arms" against German Catholicism. The retaliatory polemics that they fired back in 1883 lends credence to Olaf Blaschke's characterization of the nineteenth century as a "second

confessional age."[36] Or, as Hans-Volcker Herntrich has put it: there
were many "Luthers" in 1883, but no "ecumenical Luther."[37]

If a pungent imperialist nationalism was one aspect of Treitschke's
address, the Prussian historian also gave indication of the new scholarly historicism of the nineteenth century. Great strides in "historical
science," he observed, had made possible a more penetrating understanding of Luther and the Reformation. Other events and addresses
from 1883 buttress this point. The young Adolf Harnack, for example,
gave an oration on "Martin Luther and his Significance for the
History of Scholarship and Education," in which he argued that
Luther, although no great scholar himself at least by modern standards, had through his defiance of Rome helped conquer medieval
obscurantism and thereby paved the way for the rise of "free
inquiry."[38] Also, in this year, the "Lutherhaus" in Wittenberg and
Luther's cloister in Erfurt were opened as a public museums to
mediate historical knowledge about the Reformer and his times.[39]
Two additional examples from 1883 will underscore the significance
of this anniversary for historical knowledge.[40]

First, the 1883 anniversary witnessed the launch of the monumental
"Weimarer Ausgabe" of Luther's works (Figure 3.2).[41] While there
had been earlier collected editions, the editors deemed these insuffi-
cient with respect to "scholarly research" (*wissenschaftliche Forschung*);
therefore, a genuinely critical collection of Luther's works had become
"an urgent necessity." In light of the "upcoming Luther jubilee," as
recounted in the preface to volume one, the Consistorial Counselor of
Halle, Julius Köstlin, had approached the Prussian Ministry of Culture about the need for such a project. Since his proposal was also
supported by the prestigious Berlin Academy of Science, a "large
sum" was granted by the Emperor "to secure and set in motion the
scholarly preparation of the edition."[42] Printing began in 1883 by the
publisher Hermann Böhlau and, with various twists and turns, continued until 2009! The completed project numbers 121 volumes of
Luther's works in Latin and German—sermons, letters, biblical com-
mentaries, and more—in c.80,000 pages in quarto format. In its early
years, a supervisory commission appointed by the Prussian Ministry of
Culture oversaw the project; this was continued by the Heidelberg
Academy of Science after the demise of Prussia in 1947 as a consequence of the Second World War.[43]

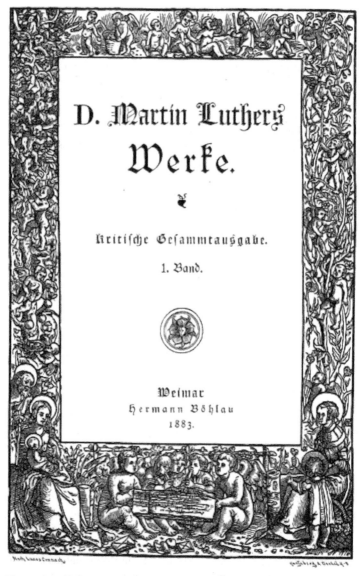

Figure 3.2. Title-page of the first volume of Luther's collected works, the "Weimarer Ausgabe" (1883). *D. Martin Luthers Werke: Kritische Gesamtausgabe.* Weimar: Hermann Böhlau Wiemar, 1883. Photo courtesy of Internet Archive.

Another major scholarly effort tied to the Luther jubilee, launched on 13 February 1883, was the Society for the History of the Reformation (Verein für Reformationsgeschichte). Based at first in Magdeburg and initially directed by the aforementioned Julius Köstlin, it set as its original goal "to spread broadly the results of completed research about the emergence of the Protestant Church, about the personalities and facts of the Reformation, and about [its] effects in all areas of the life of the people." Mainly through conferences and publications, the society pursued its ends, notably launching a series of monographs in 1883 that eventually resulted in 200 volumes. Research impulses, however, sometimes blended freely with religious ones, for the society sought, too, "to solidify and strengthen Protestant consciousness (*evangelische Bewußtsein*) through immediate contact with the history of our church."[44] Such religious objectives mixed worrisomely with nationalist ones in the late nineteenth century through the Nazi period. But since 1945 the Society has sought to reorient itself toward more strictly scholarly aims, and today plays a leading international role in promoting knowledge of the sixteenth century, not least through its well-respected journal *Archiv für Reformationsgeschichte*.

* * *

In the United States, the 400th anniversary of Luther's birth in 1883 was celebrated in a manner that significantly contrasts with 1817. At that time, as we have seen, the Reformation was remembered in the United States mainly by immigrants from Lutheran countries with limited "ecumenical" outreach to other Protestants. By contrast, in 1883, as Hartmut Lehmann has noted, Luther went from being "an acceptable ancestor to one venerated and worshipped" by practically all American Protestants.[45] What is more, the birthday commemoration bore witness to the widespread view that "the American republic was the latest link in the genetic chain of Teutonic liberty": what Luther had first wrought, America had incorporated into its national identity and destiny.[46] A distinctively American "Whig" retrospective vision rivaled and often outshone more specifically religious remembrances in 1883.[47] What wrought the change between 1817 and 1883?

The answer is at least fivefold. First, in the decades after 1817, Unitarians and Transcendentalists in New England had "discovered"

Luther anew, seeing his revolt from Rome as a model of New World liberties and as an example of a "great man" achieving world-historical significance by bending the course of history to his will.[48] Second, in the most influential early history of the United States, penned by George Bancroft, Luther received acclaim, along with Columbus, Gutenberg, and Calvin, as being one of the four fathers of the modern world.[49] Third, the middle decades of the nineteenth century witnessed the rapid growth of American, particularly Protestant, scholars traveling to Germany to study in its world-class universities. There, they absorbed the historicist academic culture that venerated Luther, and many experienced firsthand various commemorations of sixteenth-century events and personalities.[50] Fourth, the revivalist currents known as the Second Great Awakening, while more populist in nature, emphasized many Lutheran theological points pertaining to salvation while also seeing in the Wittenberg reformer an example of the "common man" challenging authority with God on his side. Finally, in part as a reaction to immigration from Catholic countries, anti-Catholicism grew as a pervasive, pan-Protestant, nativist ideology. The sentiment found a political home in the virulently anti-Roman Know-Nothing Party, even as it contributed to a more general association that linked Protestantism with the United States, and both with the emancipatory course of modern history.[51] In this scheme of history, Luther was the fountainhead of progress and democratic civilization, the heroic, distant grandfather of the United States and, by extension, the modern world.

For all these reasons and also for enduringly religious ones, the 400th anniversary of Luther's birth in 1883 was widely celebrated on American soil.[52] As to be expected, Lutheran synods and individual congregations from the Atlantic seaboard states to the Midwest welcomed the centenary, even as its observance often revealed cultural tensions between those beholden to the Old World and those more willing to adapt to the American, English-speaking environment. In 1883, all Lutheran seminaries used the occasion for an impressive array of commemorative endeavors; often, special collections were made, with the money given to build or enlarge facilities or to pay debts on older projects. The Missouri Synod dedicated a number of new buildings at its flagship campus, Condordia, in St Louis.[53] The Lutheran seminary in Philadelphia moved to a spacious new location while Swedish Lutherans in Rock Island, Illinois, built a special "jubilee hall" at their Augustana College.[54] What is more, numerous books on Luther were translated from German and scores of home-grown scholarly and popular books and pamphlets appeared.[55] Journals such as the German-language *Der Lutheraner* and the English-language *Lutheran Quarterly* produced special jubilee editions, featuring titles such as "The Special Fitness of Luther for the Work of the Reformation" and "The Fundamental Principles of the Reformation."[56] In short, American Lutherans in 1883 sought to make a statement: while distinct from their more numerous Calvinist and revivalist peers, they had become time-tested denizens of the New World, building the Kingdom of God on American soil.[57]

But, again, Lutherans were not alone in 1883. This was truly a pan-Protestant moment: practically all Protestant institutions and seminaries held special meetings and various denominational periodicals issued editions devoted to Luther and the early Reformation. To seize upon one example, Charles Dickey, the pastor of Calvary Presbyterian Church in Philadelphia, addressed his congregation and later published a work on the topic "Martin Luther: A Sketch of his Character and Work." "The gladness of this anniversary is a great sign of the life and power in Protestantism," Dickey began. Internecine squabbling among Protestants, therefore, ought to cease, for "by the force of a religious conviction we have gained our civil and religious liberty. Luther opened the Bible and revealed our inheritance. Those who cherish his memory should avoid contention, and, by united effort, defend the truth, which he had the courage to proclaim." The "hammer strokes" against indulgences, Dickey gave voice to a jubilee commonplace, "sent terror to the heart of a corrupt Church . . . and after nearly four hundred years their echoes awaken joy in the whole earth."[58]

Among the many American commemorative efforts, pride of place might well go to that of the American Evangelical Alliance, which held a major meeting on 13 October 1883 in New York. With its roots going back to 1847, the Alliance, a subsidiary of the World Evangelical Alliance begun in Britain, aimed to foster pan-Protestant interests and greater cross-denominational cooperation.[59] Its leaders fixed on 1883 as a momentous occasion to proclaim and solidify its aims.[60] Speakers from Episcopalian, Congregational, Methodist, Presbyterian, and Lutheran churches, among others, were invited to

New York to pay homage to Luther and what he meant for contemporary American religious life. A stalwart of the Alliance, the highly decorated Swiss-German émigré theologian Philip Schaff, "threw all his enthusiasm" into this event, as his son later described. "The occasion aroused scarcely less interest among people of English antecedants than those of German descent," Schaff himself pleasingly recorded.[61] He and others saw in the event the opportunity to lay the groundwork for greater future cooperation and unity among Protestant bodies. What is more, Schaff even reached out to "Old Catholics," who had been in schism with Rome over the declaration of Papal Infallibility at the First Vatican Council (1869–70).[62]

Prior to the celebration, the Evangelical Alliance notified invitees that "the approaching anniversary affords a fit occasion for the American people to contrast the condition of the world before and after the Reformation and to study the instruments and principles by which God promotes the progress of His Kingdom." Alliance members were also enjoined to offer "thanks to God for the blessings of the Reformation, especially for the free circulation of the Word of God and for religious liberty."[63]

On the day of celebration, the Alliance's president, John Jay, expressed gratitude that Luther had delivered the world "from the noxious mists of ignorance and superstition into the pure sunlight of Christianity."[64] "We are [gathered] to think of the one of the greatest men of human history," Phillips Brooks proclaimed in his keynote address:

> [T]his at least is sure, that the great principles of Martin Luther's life must be the principles of every advance of man on to the very end. Always it must be a regeneration of humanity. Always it must be by the power of God filling the soul of man. Always it must be religious. Always it must be God summoning man, man reaching after God. Always it must be the moralist and the mystic, conscience and faith meeting in the single human or in humanity at large, which makes the Reformation. And however it shall come, all human progress must remember Martin Luther.[65]

Other speakers offered similar encomiums, making connections that freely blended the religious and political aspects of the Reformation and associated both with the forward course of (American) history.

Union Theological Seminary in New York City also got into the act, holding its own commemorative symposium on 19 November 1883. There, the Congregationalist minister and church historian Roswell D. Hitchcock proclaimed that Luther had inaugurated "the Teutonic Stadium in history." "Call it what you will," Hitchcock elaborated, "Revolt, Revolution, or Reformation, it was, and is, the individual believer demanding the rights of the Christian organism . . . and the right of way directly to Christ."[66] The greatest hindrance for the future of Protestantism, he argued, lay within, not without, in the Protestant tendency to separate from one another and produce a "sect" mentality. The indefatigable Philip Schaff also gave a speech there, titled "Luther as Reformer." Shortly after the symposium, he described his feelings about the jubilee year to his son: "What a testimony this year is bearing to Luther and the Reformation! There is nothing like it in all church history. So very human and many-sided is he that Luther appeals to universal sympathies more than all the other Reformers combined."[67]

Not only seminaries, but non-religious organizations marked the occasion as well. A particularly interesting case is seen in the Massachusetts Historical Society. Prior to the commemoration, Society member Edward Young had opined: "[Luther] was not merely a prophet; he was a poet, scholar, theologian, preacher, statesman, as well as man of affairs, and he belongs not simply to his fatherland, but to all Protestant Christendom."[68] Already at its meeting on 14 June 1883, the Society resolved that it "is eminently fitting that this Society, the oldest in the country . . . should take not only a leading, but a prompting part, in promoting and securing such a recognition of that birthday [of Luther] as is in perfect harmony with our aims,— secular indeed, but not oblivious of higher interests. It offers us the broadest and most comprehensive themes and aspects, political, intellectual, philosophical, ecclesiastical, and popular." The Society settled on the date, 10 November 1883, Luther's actual birthday, to hold the event (Figure 3.3).[69]

When the day arrived, scholars and statesmen mingled, Lutheran hymns were sung, and several addresses were given, touching upon the religious, cultural, and political aspects of the Reformation. "We are here today to recognize Martin Luther," the judge Robert Winthrop proclaimed, "as, beyond all other men, the instrument of God

COMMEMORATION

OF THE

FOUR HUNDREDTH ANNIVERSARY

OF

THE BIRTH OF MARTIN LUTHER,

BY THE

Massachusetts Historical Society,

NOVEMBER 10, 1883.

BOSTON:
PUBLISHED BY THE SOCIETY.
M.DCCC.LXXXIII.

Figure 3.3. Title-page of commemoration papers on the occasion of Luther's 400th birthday, Massachusetts Historical Society (1883). *Massachusetts Historical Review*, 20 (1883).

in given [sic] the impulse, by thought, word, and act, to that world-wide movement which resulted not merely in the reformation of Europe, but in all that we Americans now enjoy, and that we rejoice in being." This son of a "humble miner" had set in motion a reformation in Europe and, however distant in time and space, "American colonization and the American revolution were among its results."[70]

The keynote address was delivered by the Unitarian minister Frederic H. Hedge (1805–90), among the foremost scholars and translators of German literature and hymnody in America.[71] For Hedge, interpreting Luther strictly as a religious reformer was somewhat beside the point; he was so much more:

> Such significance attaches to the name of Luther, one of that select band of providential men who stand conspicuous among their contemporaries as makers of history. For the Protestant Reformation which he inaugurated is very imperfectly apprehended if construed solely as a schism in the Church, a new departure in religion. In a larger view, it was our modern world, with its social developments, its liberties, its science, its new conditions of being, evolving itself from the old.[72]

Skirting John Calvin's imposing legacy in New England, Hedge pointed to Luther as the primal source of the Society's "inheritance":

> That the dearest goods of our estate—civil independence, spiritual emancipation, individual scope, the large room, the unbound thought, the free pen, whatever is the most characteristic of this New England of our inheritance—we owe to the Saxon reformer in whose name we are here to celebrate.[73]

The United States itself was proof positive of Luther's long-term, salutary influence: "To Martin Luther, above all men, we Anglo-Americans are indebted for national independence and mental freedom."[74]

The veracity of Luther's religious views were of scant concern to the Unitarian Hedge: "As a theologian . . . he taught us little." But in his appeal to conscience and in his actions, and above all in his "spirit," he exposed the "abominations" of papal authority and thereby established a toehold for the modern world to advance: "Honor and everlasting thanks to the man who broke for us the spell of papal autocracy; who rescued a portion, at least, of the Christian world from the paralyzing grasp of a power more to be dreaded than any temporal despotism—a power which rules by seducing the will, by capturing the conscience of its subjects—the bondage of the soul."[75] The principles of the Reformation "shape our life. Modern civilization, liberty, science, progress, attest the world-wide scope of the Protestant reform, whose principles are independent thought, freedom from ecclesiastical thrall, defiance of consecrated wrong." In the final analysis, for Hedge, "[Luther's] theology is outgrown, a thing of the past, but the spirit which he wrought is immortal; that spirit is evermore the renewer and saviour of the world."[76]

In making sweeping connections between Luther and the United States and modern liberty generally, Hedge was by no means alone. The Pennsylvania state senator, A. J. Herr, declared in 1883 that had Luther lived in 1776 "his blood would have stained the snows of Valley Forge, with the rest of those immortal heroes." "Find the birthplace of liberty—Wittenberg. There was the world's 'Declaration of Independence' written, and Martin Luther . . . is the prophet and apostle of human freedom," asserted A. K. Young from Des Moines, Iowa. "If there had been no Luther in Germany," the pastor Emanuel Greenwald gushed, "there would have been no [George] Washington in America. For the invaluable blessing of our civil liberty and free institutions, we thank God for Luther." Such Whiggish sentiments were legion in 1883 as amply borne out in P. C. Croll's *Tributes to the Memory of Luther*, a compilation of encomiums to Luther from the jubilee year.[77]

Perhaps the most interesting and ambitious example of Luther devotion in 1883 in the United States, however, was the proposal and eventual erection of a monument of the Refomer in Washington, DC. The statue was first proposed early in 1883 at the birthday of Dr John G. Butler, pastor of Lutheran Memorial Church in Washington and a former chaplain of the House of Representatives, by Charles A. Shieren, a German-born, New York manufacturer, who later became Mayor of Brooklyn. The idea quickly took hold, receiving funding from both Lutheran and non-Lutheran sources. In April of 1883 a replica of the centerpiece statue of Luther at the Worms monument was cast in Germany. Late in 1883, it was shipped from Hamburg to New York, free of charge, by the North German Lloyd Steamship Company and then from New York to Washington by the

Baltimore and Ohio Railroad Company. Months later it was placed on a massive block of granite.[78]

At a site that was to be dubbed "Luther Place," the official unveiling ceremony took place on 21 May 1884—an event preceded by several orations (in English and German), a procession, and music, including a dutiful singing of "A Mighty Fortress." German and American flags were prominently displayed. Numerous religious and political dignitaries, including Congressmen and members of the Supreme Court, were present. Speakers at the event consistently stressed the close connection between the Reformation and the political ideals of the United States. Senator Omar D. Conger from Michigan, for example, hailed Luther as the founder of modern religious liberty and toleration.[79] "[Luther] brought man face to face with his God without the intervention of priests. . . . Luther is the author of civil liberty that is enjoyed today," the judge William Strong sermonized.[80] A poem dedicated to "The Luther Monument" was penned by Joel Swartz, which includes these lines:

> Come, let us build a monument
> To Luther's mighty fame;
> Let's carve upon it high and deep
> The great Reformer's name.
>
> In this fourth Centennial year,
> Let freemen o'er the earth
> Unite to celebrate with cheer
> His own and Freedom's birth.[81]

The monument was located on a piece of property adjacent to Thomas Circle ceded by the Lutheran Memorial Church to a newly created Luther Statue Association. In 1885 the United States' Congress passed "An Act to incorporate the Luther Statue Association, to erect and maintain a monument or statue in memory of Martin Luther in the District of Columbia." This legislation created an official board of trustees, legally secured 5,000 square feet for the monument, and granted the Luther Statue Association a tax exemption.[82]

Luther, 400 years after his birth, had finally made it big in America.

* * *

In 1883 in both the German Empire and the United States, the Reformer's legacy was implicated in the "civil religion" of two very different national identities. To be sure, images of Luther in Germany possessed more salient ethnic and linguistic aspects than they did in the United States, where the "Whiggish" political implications of the Reformation were more often stressed. Nonetheless, the memory of Luther, *mutatis mutandis*, functioned in each national identity as a powerful legitimizing figure, a pivotal persona in the distant past, who heroically had corrected history's course, making possible, eventually, the symbolically important years of 1776 and 1871. For this reason, on both sides of the Atlantic, gratitude and celebration were regarded as appropriate responses to Luther on his 400th birthday.

To be sure, not all responded in such a manner. But even the critics and detractors in 1883 can help us discern the dominant mood. In Germany, Jews and Catholics, who got caught up in a limited fashion in the post-Wartburgfest euphoria in 1817, were largely silent or critical in 1883. For Jews, the anti-Semitism apparent in lectures like the one of Treitschke did not go unnoticed. For Catholics, the memory the *Kulturkampf* lingered thickly in the air.[83] Faced with the juggernaut of Protestant commemoration, therefore, more than a few Catholics adopted the line of the Society of St Boniface and chose to regard the date of celebration as "a day of general supplication on behalf of our erring brothers, the Protestants." Others regarded it more disparagingly as a "day of lament," a "day of mourning," or even a "day of sin."[84]

In the United States, Catholics were equally taken aback at the widespread association of national identity with Luther and the Reformation. In 1883, the priest and founder of the Paulist Fathers, Isaac Thomas Hecker, for example, contested the pervasive association of the Reformation with freedom, arguing instead that Luther had "played cunningly into the hands of the German potentates."[85] Irritated about the unveiling of the Luther statute in Washington, James Andrew Corcoran, editor of the *American Catholic Quarterly Review*, lambasted what he called the "American glorification of Luther" and sought to refute "the idle boast that our political liberties has any connection with Martin Luther or his Reformation."[86]

Given such contrary sentiments from Catholics, we would do well to conclude that 1883, while a powerful vehicle for more recent political and nationalist attributions of meaning to the Reformation, also continued to bear witness to the enduring confessional fissures of the sixteenth century. The newer meanings did not supplant the old, but were superimposed on them; and indeed drew a measure of their strength from them.

Notes

1. A nice overview of nineteenth-century commemorations is found in Dorothea Wendebourg, "Die Reformationsjubiläen des 19. Jahrhunderts," *Zeitschrift für Theologie und Kirche*, 108 (2011): 270–335.
2. David Lowenthal, *The Past is a Foreign Country* (Cambridge: CUP, 1985), 96ff.
3. Thomas Nipperdey, "Nationalidee und Nationaldenkmal im 19. Jahrhundert in Deutschland," *Historische Zeitschrift*, 206 (1968): 529–85.
4. Petra Roettig, "Hercules Germanicus, Luthers Läuterung zum Nationaldenkmal," in *Deutsche Nationaldenkmale, 1790–1990* (Bielefeld: Verlag für Regionalgeschichte, 1993), 52.
5. Wilhelm Weber, "Luther-Denkmäler: Frühe Projekte und Verwirklichungen," in Hans-Ernst Mittig and Volker Plagemann (eds), *Denkmäler im 19. Jahrhundert: Deutung und Kritik* (Munich: Prestel-Verlag, 1972), 185–200; Cf. Christian Tümpel, "Geschichte der Lutherdenkmäler," in Bernd Moeller (ed.), *Luther in der Neuzeit: Wissenschaftliches Symposion des Vereins für Reformationsgeschichte* (Gütersloh: G. Mohn, 1983), 227–47, and Hartmut Lehmann, *Luthergedächtnis 1817 bis 2017* (Götingen: Vandenhoeck & Ruprecht, 2012), 28–9.
6. Friedrich Eich (ed.), *Gedenkblätter zur Erinnerung und Enthüllungsfeier des Lutherdenkmals in Worms* (Worms, 1868) and Hans Düfel, "Das Luther-Jubiläum 1883," *Zeitschrift für Kirchengeschichte*, 95 (1984): 18.
7. J. Leonard Corning, "The Luther Monument at Worms," *The Manhattan*, 3 (Jan. 1884): 18.
8. W. Weber, "Das Luther-Denkmal in Worms," in F. Reuter (ed.), *Der Reichstag zu Worms von 1521: Reichspolitik und Luthersache* (Worms: Stadtarchiv, 1981), 490–509, and Christiane Theiselmann, *Das Wormser Lutherdenkmal Ernst Rietschels (1856–1868) im Rahmen der Lutherrezeption des 19. Jahrhunderts* (Frankfurt am Main: Europäische Hochschulschriften, 1992). Cf. Wendebourg, "Die Reformationsjubiläen des 19. Jahrhunderts," 273.
9. C. Strohm, "Calvinerinnerung am Beginn des 20.Jahrhundert. Beobachtungen am Beispiel des Genfer Reformationsdenkmals," in Stefan Laube and Karl-Heinz Fix (eds), *Lutherinszenierung und Reformationserinnerung* (Leipzig: Evangelische Verlagsanstalt, 2002), 211–28.
10. On the category "civil religion," see Robert N. Bellah and Phillip E. Hammond, *Varieties of Civil Religion* (San Francisco: Harper & Row, 1980).
11. An exception is Thomas Nipperdey's *Religion im Umbruch, 1870–1914* (Munich: C. H. Beck, 1988). On the tight relationship between Protestantism and "national feeling," see esp. pp. 93ff.

12. Noted in Gérald Chaix, "Die Reformation," in Etienne François and Hagen Schluze (eds), *Deutsche Erinnerungsorte* (Munich: C. H. Beck, 2001), ii. 20. On Stöcker, see D. A. Jeremy Telman, "Adolf Stöcker: Anti-Semite with a Christian Mission," *Jewish History*, 9 (1995): 93–112.

13. Rebecca Ayako Bennette, *Fighting for the Soul of Germany: The Catholic Struggle for Inclusion After Unification* (Cambridge, MA: Harvard University Press, 2012), 15ff.

14. James Turner, *Philology: The Forgotten Origins of the Modern Humanities* (Princeton: Princeton University Press, 2014), 167ff., 197ff. and Thomas Albert Howard, *Protestant Theology and the Making of the Modern German University* (Oxford: OUP, 2006), 12, 29–38.

15. Thomas Nipperdey, "In Search of Identity: Romantic Nationalism, its Intellectual, Political and Social Background," in J. C. Eade (ed.), *Romantic Nationalism in Europe* (Canberra: Humanities Research Centre, 1983), 1.

16. On United States development at this time, see Jürgen Osterhammel, *The Transformation of the World: A Global History of the Nineteenth Century*, tr. Patrick Camiller (Princeton: Princeton University Press, 2014), 331–3.

17. R. A. Billington, *The Protestant Crusade* (New York: Macmillan, 1938).

18. George Marsden, *The Soul of the American University: From Protestant Establishment to Established Nonbelief* (Oxford: OUP, 1994), 101–12.

19. For the royal order, see appendix 8, "Erlaß des Königs von Preußen für die Lutherfeiern 1883," in Düfel, "Das Luther-Jubiläum 1883," 92.

20. Lehmann, *Luthergedächtnis 1817 bis 2017*, 74ff. For a typical program of the "Lutherfeier 1883," see the *Jubelfest-Büchlein zur 400-jährigen Geburtsfeier Dr. Luther's* (Strasbourg, 1884) and Düfel, "Das Luther-Jubiläum 1883," 93. On parades, see Wolfgang Hartmann, *Der historische Festzug: Seine Entstehung und Entwicklung im 19. und 20. Jahrhundert* (Munich: Prestel-Verlag, 1976), 131–2.

21. Wilhelm Möller, *Rede am Luther-Jubiläum den 10. November in der Aula der Christian-Albrechts-Universität* (Kiel, 1883), 3.

22. Ritschl gave this jubilee speech on 10 Nov. 1883 in Göttingen. See Ritschl, *Drei akademische Reden* (Bonn, 1887), 5–29. An English translation appears in the appendix (pp. 187–202) of David Lotz, *Ritschl and Luther: A Fresh Perspective on Albrecht Ritschl's Theology in Light of his Luther Study* (Nashville, YN: Abingdon Press, 1974). Cf. David Lotz, "Albrecht Ritschl and the Unfinished Reformation," *Harvard Theological Review*, 73 (1980): 337–72.

23. Hartmut Lehmann, "Martin Luther as a National Hero," in J. C. Eade (ed.), *Romantic Nationalism in Europe* (Canberra: Australian National University, 1983), 197.

24. In a minor key, some saw the moment as an opportunity to attempt the reunification of the divided confessions in Germany. On this point, see Stan Landry, *Ecumenism, Memory, and German Nationalism* (Syracuse, NY: Syracuse University Press, 2014), 90–1.

25. Thomas A. Brady, *The Protestant Reformation in German History*, Occasional Paper 22 (Washington, DC: German Historical Institute, 1998), 15. On the large literature from this jubilee, see *Zum Luther-Jubiläum: Bibliographie der Luther-Literatur des Jahres 1883* (Frankfurt a.M.: Verlag der Schriften-Niederlage, 1883).

26. Hermann Hoffmeister, *Luther und Bismarck als Grundpfeiler unserer Nationalgröße* (Berlin, 1883), vii, 36.

27. Ibid. 38.

28. Heinrich von Treitschke, *Historische und politische Aufsätze*, iv (Leipzig: Verlag von S. Hirzel, 1897), 378–80, 384. On the *Kulturkampf* as relevant context for this address, see Jonathan Steinberg, *Bismarck: A Life* (Oxford: OUP, 2011), 312ff., and David Blackbourn, *Marpingen: Apparitions of the Virgin Mary in a Nineteenth-Century German Village* (New York: Vintage Books, 1995), 24, 66, passim. With respect to Catholicism, it should be noted that the Catholic historian Johannes Jansen produced his great, multi-volume work, *Geschichte des deutschen Volkes seit dem Ausgang des Mittelalters* (Freiburg im Breisgau, 1880–94) in the context of the *Kulturkampf* and its aftermath. Unlike Ranke and Hegel, Janssen saw the Reformation as a disaster for German political and national development.

29. Treitschke, *Historische und politische Aufsätze*, 383.

30. Ibid. 382.

31. Ibid. 387. On the "Two Kingdoms" teaching, see William John Wright, *Martin Luther's Understanding of God's Two Kingdoms* (Grand Rapids, MI: Baker Academic, 2010).

32. Treitschke, *Historische und politische Aufsätze*, 388.

33. Ibid. 390–2.

34. Ibid. 391.

35. Ibid. 393–4.

36. Landry, *Ecumenism*, 94–5.

37. Hans-Volker Herntrich, "Ein deutsch-nationaler Freiheitsheld: Wie Martin Luther vor hundert Jahren gefeiert wurde," *Lutherische Monatshefte*, 21 (1982): 275.

38. Adolf von Harnack, *Martin Luther in seiner Bedeutung für die Geschichte der Wissenschaft und Bildung* (Giessen, 1911). This short work went through six editions and was translated into Swedish. See Jaroslav Pelikan, "Adolf von Harnack on Luther," in Pelikan (ed.), *Interpreters of the Reformer: Essays in Honor of Wilhelm Paulk* (Philadelphia: Fortress Press, 1968), 253–73.

39. See the site Stiftung Luthergedenkstätten in Sachsen-Anhalt at <http://www.martinluther.de/index.php?option=com_content&view=article&id=36&Itemid=508&lang=de> (accessed May 2015) and Chaix, "Die Reformation," 21.

40. It bears keeping in mind, too, the earlier, major accomplishment of Leopold von Ranke's *Deutsche Geschichte im Zeitalter der Reformation* from the 1830s and 1840s.

41. The "Weimarer Ausgabe" or "WA" is the unofficial title. The actual title is *D. Martin Luthers Werke: Kritische Gesamtausgabe*.

42. *D. Martin Luthers Werke: Kritische Gesammtausgabe*, i (Weimar: Hermann Böhlau, 1883), xv–xvi.

43. See Ulrich Köpf, "Kurze Geschichte der Weimarer Luthersausgabe," in *D. Martin Luthers Werke. Sonderedition der kritischen Weimarerausgabe. Begleitheft zur Deutschen Bibel* (Weimar: Böhlau, 2001), 1–24.

44. From article one of the Society's founding charter. See <http://www.reformationsgeschichte.de> (accessed on Sept. 2013). Cf. Luise Schorn-Schütte (ed.), *125 Jahre Verein Reformationsgeschichte* (Heidelberg: Gütersloh, 2008).

45. Lehmann, "Martin Luther as a National Hero," in Eade, *Romantic Nationalism*, 186–7.

46. Dorothy Ross, "Historical Consciousness in Nineteenth-Century America," *American Historical Review*, 89 (1984): 917. Cf. William R. Hutchison, *The Modernist Impulse in American Protestantism* (Cambridge, MA: Harvard University Press, 1976), 98.

47. A commemoration also took place in Great Britain in 1883. William Ince, canon of Christ Church at Oxford University, remarked that the Church of England "owed more to Lutheran than to any other continental influences." But he also hinted at a diffidence felt by Anglicans concerning the jubilee and alluded to the fact that "Nonconformists" appeared more eager to pay homage to Luther than Anglicans: "But the commemoration [of 1883] is being held among many English-speaking communities . . . notably by many of our Nonconformists. Is there any reason why the Church of England should refuse to take any notice of such a commemoration of a great name in Church History? Can the University of Oxford . . . be content to preserve a cold and dignified silence on such an occasion?" See William Ince, *The Luther Commemoration and the Church of England: A Sermon Preached before the University of Oxford on Sunday November 11, 1883* (London: Rivingtons, 1883), 4–5. A "Nonconformist" opinion of Luther can be seen in a sermon preached by the famous Reformed Baptist C. H. Spurgeon on the jubilee occasion; see Spurgeon, "The Luther Sermon at Exeter Hall, Delivered on the Lord's Day Evening, November 11, 1883," in Henry Davenport Northrop, *Life and Works or Rev. Charles H. Spurgeon* (Chicago, 1890), 244–60. In the sermon, Spurgeon told his audience that "I pray that a Luther may spring from your ranks." For an excellent treatment of the British commemoration of Luther's 400th birthday, see J. M. R. Bennett, "The British Commemoration of 1883–1884 in European Context," *Historical Journal*, 58 (2015): 543–64.

48. Ross, "Historical Consciousness," 917. Cf. E. Emerton, "Martin Luther," *The Unitarian Review and Religious Magazine*, 20 (1883): 435–55.

49. George Bancroft, *History of the United States from the Discovery of the American Continent*, i (Boston, 1834), 266.

50. On American scholars in Germany in the nineteenth century, see Carl Diehl, *Americans and German Scholarship, 1770–1870* (New Haven: Yale University Press, 1978), 49–69, and Howard, *Protestant Theology*, 363–78. Incidentally, George Bancroft was one of the first Americans to study in German universities; he did so at Berlin in 1820–1.

51. Syndey E. Ahlstrom, *A Religious History of the American People* (New Haven: Yale University Press, 1972), 403–28, 555ff.

52. It should be noted that the 1867 jubilee was widely marked by American Lutherans. For a sampling of sermons and publications from that occasion, see John G. Morris, *Bibliotheca Lutherana: A Complete List of the Publications of all the Lutheran Ministers in the United States* (Philadelphia, 1876), 34, 36, passim.

53. Carl S. Meyer, *Log Cabin to Luther Tower: Concordia Seminary during One Hundred and Twenty-Five Years toward a More Excellent Ministry* (St Louis, MO: Concordia Publishing House, 1965), 82–3.

54. One can see older images of "jubilee hall" online at the Upper Mississippi Valley Digital Image Archive at <http://www.umvphotoarchive.org/cdm/search/collection/augsc/searchterm/Augustana%20College%20%28Rock%20Island,%20Ill.%29.%20Jubilee%20Hall/field/all/mode/exact/conn/and/cosuppress> (accessed May 2014).

55. Some examples of publications from the 1883 jubilee include Matthias Sheeleigh, *Luther: A Song-Tribute, on the Four Hundredth Anniversary of his Birth* (Philadelphia, 1883); Enoch Smith, *Martin Luther: A Memorial Volume for Schools and Families* (Allentown, PA, 1883); Joseph Augustus Seiss, *Luther and the Reformation: The Life-Springs of our Liberties* (Philadelphia, 1884); August Lawrence Graebner, *Dr. Martin Luther, Lebensbild des Reformators den Glaubensgenossen in America gezeichnet* (Milwaukee, WI, 1883).

56. See *The Lutheran Quarterly*, 13 (1883) and 14 (1884).

57. Hartmut Lehmann, *Martin Luther in the American Imagination* (Munich: Wilhelm Fink Verlag, 1988), 184–5.

58. Charles A. Dickey, *Martin Luther: A Sketch of his Character and Work* (Philadelphia: Matlack & Harvey, 1884), 5, 16.

59. On the Alliance, see F. L. Cross and E. A. Livingstone (eds), *Oxford Dictionary of the Christian Church*, 3rd edn (Oxford: OUP, 1997), 578–9, and Philip D. Jordon, *The Evangelical Alliance for the United States of America, 1847–1900: Ecumenism, Identity and the Religion of the Republic* (New York: Edwin Mellen Press, 1982).

60. The Alliance also held a meeting in London. See *Evangelical Christendom, Christian Work, and the News of the Churches. Also a Monthly Record of the Transactions of the Evangelical Alliance.* (London, 1883), 287, 361–5.

61. David S. Schaff, *The Life of Philip Schaff in Part Autobiographical* (New York, 1897), 337.

62. On Old Catholicism, see Karl Pruter and J. Gordon Melton, *The Old Catholic Source Book* (New York: Garland Publishing, 1983), 3ff. On Schaff in general, see George H. Shriver, *Philip Schaff: Christian Scholar and Ecumenical Prophet* (Macon, GA: Mercer, 1987).

63. Evangelical Alliance, *Martin Luther: Celebration of the Evangelical Alliance of the United States, of the 400th Anniversary of the Birthday of Martin Luther, October 13th, 1883* (New York, 1883), 4.

64. Ibid. 10.

65. Ibid. 43. On Brooks, see Gillis J. Harp, *Brahmin Prophet: Phillips Brooks and the Path of Liberal Protestantism* (Lanham, MD: Rowman & Littlefield Publishers, 2003).

66. Quoted in Lehmann, *Martin Luther in the American Imagination*, 181.

67. Schaff, *Life of Philip Schaff*, 338.

68. Robert C. Winthrop, Edward J. Young, et al., "November Meeting 1883 . . . ," *Proceedings of the Massachusetts Historical Society*, 20 (1883), 358.

69. *Commemoration of the Four Hundredth Anniversary of the Birth of Martin Luther by the Massachusetts Historical Society, November 10, 1883* (Boston, 1883), 5–6.

70. Ibid. 13–14.

71. On Hedge, see George Huntston Williams, *Rethinking the Unitarian Relationship with Protestantism: An Examination of the Thought of Frederic Henry Hedge* (Boston: Beacon Press, 1949). For additional Unitarian views of Luther and the Reformation in 1883, see Edwin D. Mead, *Martin Luther: A Study of the Reformation* (Boston, 1884) and

Ephraim Emerton, "Martin Luther," *The Unitarian Review and Religious Magazine*, 20 (1883): 435–55.

72. *Commemoration by the Massachusetts Historical Society*, 17.

73. Ibid.

74. Ibid. 19.

75. Ibid. 38.

76. Ibid. 39.

77. Quoted material taken from P. C. Croll (ed.), *Tributes to the Memory of Luther* (Philadelphia, 1884), 225ff. Cf. Lehmann, *Martin Luther in the American Imagination*, 183–5.

78. Lehmann, *Luther in the American Imagination*, 185.

79. Lehmann, *Luthergedächtnis 1817 bis 2017*, 98–100.

80. Croll, *Tributes*, 300.

81. Ibid. 311.

82. Lehmann, *Luthergedächtnis 1817 bis 2017*, 97. One may view a picture of the monument at <http://www.dcmemorials.com/index_indiv0001730.htm> (accessed Oct. 2013).

83. Düfel, "Das Luther-Jubiläum 1883," 19ff., 77–8. On Jewish responses to Treitschke, see Nils H. Roemer, *Jewish Scholarship and Culture in Nineteenth-Century Germany: Between History and Faith* (Madison, WI: University of Wisconsin Press, 2005), 85ff.

84. See Wendebourg, "Die Reformationsjubiläen des 19.Jahrhunderts," 319–20.

85. Isaac Thomas Hecker, "Luther and the Diet of Worms," *The Catholic World*, 38 (1883): 145–61.

86. Corcoran called the statue of Luther erected in Washington "a brazen effigy of the apostate monk." See James Andrew Corcoran, "Martin Luther and his American Worshipers," *American Catholic Quarterly Review*, 9 (1884): 537ff.

4

A Memory Still Mutating

The Twentieth Century

We have gratefully and gladly inherited Martin Luther's...
spirit; and now he is grinding the American intellect and conscience like a sword which shall not return to its scabbard until
democracy is safe everywhere in our world.

> (Frank W. Gunsaulus, Speech at the
> University of Chicago, 1917)

The German Democratic Republic and her people pay homage
to his [Luther's] personality. They pay homage to the historical
achievement he accomplished by initiating the Reformation—
actually being a bourgeois revolution—for the benefit of social
progress and world culture.

> (East German Promotional Book for the
> 500th Anniversary of Luther's Birth, 1983)

Commemorations of the Reformation in the twentieth century witnessed continuities with those of the nineteenth century, but also striking
discontinuities. As one might expect, acts of remembrance were powerfully shaped by the signature geopolitical events and developments of the
century—above all, the two world wars, the Nazi disaster, the partition
of Germany, and the broader Cold War ideological divisions. The
German Democratic Republic (GDR) presents an especially noteworthy
case in its attitude(s) toward the sixteenth century. Further, the ecumenical movement of the early and mid-century, the landmark Second
Vatican Council (1962–5) of the Catholic Church, as well as the creep-
ing secularization of large sectors of Western culture indelibly left their
marks on the cultural frameworks in which Reformation-era church
splits were remembered and assessed in the twentieth century.

Prior to the 400th jubilee in 1917, widely marked despite the ongoing carnage of World War I, several developments were already afoot shaping the modern memory of the Reformation. In the realm of scholarship, Max Weber published in 1904 and 1905 articles that together made up his famous *The Protestant Ethic and the Spirit of Capitalism*, in which he argued for a close link between Calvinist and sectarian manifestations of Protestantism and the emergence of industrial capitalism in the West—particularly in the Anglo-American world. In this landmark work, Weber engendered debates about the significance and influence of the Reformation that have continued until the present.[1] Weber's contemporary, Ernst Troeltsch, also preoccupied himself with the significance of the Reformation. Breaking with nineteenth-century liberal interpreters, Troeltsch saw the Reformation in fundamental continuity with the Middle Ages—"an enormous second bloom" of the Middle Ages in fact—and not as a transition to modernity. For him, it was primarily the Enlightenment of the eighteenth century that contradicted the deeply religious nature of *both* the Middle Ages and the Reformation.[2] Following Troeltsch in some respects, the theologian Karl Holl helped launch the so-called "Luther Renaissance" in modern scholarship by arguing that Luther, historically understood, was no proto-modern man, as the nineteenth-century Whig narrative would have it, but a deeply premodern religious soul whose insights emanated from a tormented conscience and a thoroughly theocentric outlook.[3]

In the realm of public commemoration, the imposing International Monument of the Reformation or the "Reformation Wall" was completed in Geneva on 1909 on the occasion of the 400th anniversary of John Calvin's birth and the 350th anniversary of the founding of the Genevan Academy. The monument pays homage in stone to sixteenth-century Reformed stalwarts such as Guillaume Farel, John Calvin, Theodore Beza, and John Knox. It also calls attention to the political patrons of Calvinism and Reformed Christianity's international influence through statues of Admiral Gaspard de Coligny in France, William the Silent of the Netherlands, Friedrich Wilhelm of Brandenburg (protector of Huguenot refugees in Prussia), Roger Williams in New England, Oliver Cromwell in Britain, and Étienne Bocskay of Hungary. Luther and Zwingli are also peripherally acknowledged by small statues, respectively on the left and right of the main *Reformed* memorial wall. Funding for the project bore witness to an international effort, spearheaded in the United States by none other than the Presbyterian-influenced President Theodore Roosevelt. As mentioned before, along with the Luther-centric monument in Worms, the Genevan monument stands today as the largest Reformation monument in the world.[4]

What Abraham Lincoln said in his *Second Inaugural Address* about the North and South during the American Civil War applies to countries such as the United States and Germany at the 400th anniversary in 1917: "Both read the same Bible, and pray to the same God; and each invokes His aid against the other."[5] Because of the ongoing war, Reformation commemorations in 1917 were neither as numerous nor as lavish as those of 1883, and some anticipated events were either scaled back, canceled, or never proceeded beyond the planning stages. Nonetheless, many institutions marked the milestone in word and deed, in commissioned speeches and books, and, of course, in church services and music. Interpretations varied, to be sure, but commemorators made frequent connections to Reformation ideals and the values that they saw their country fighting for in the ghastly zero-sum game of the Great War.

The jubilee events came at a pivotal moment in the war. On the very day of the celebration, the German Reichstag elected Germany's first *Catholic* Chancellor, the Center Party's Georg von Hertling (1843–1919)—a demoralizing event for many German Protestants.[6] Around the same time, the Bolshevik Revolution toppled the Tsar, soon leading to Russia's exit from the war and the eventual formation of the Soviet Union. After maintaining an isolationist posture at the war's beginning, the United States had entered the fray in April 1917, tilting the balance strongly in favor of the Allied powers. In Germany, the national unity of 1914 (*Burgfrieden*) had ebbed, but strident voices of nationalism and militarism continued apace, symbolized by the founding of the ultra-nationalist "Deutsche Vaterlandspartei" in September of 1917.[7] Not surprisingly, the *Reformationsfeier* of this year became in the words of Philip Jenkins, "a messianic hymning of the German spirit."[8] Significantly, however, anti-Roman polemics were notably quieter than in 1883 as an "ecumenism of the trenches" had drawn German Protestants and Catholics closer together against their respective co-religionists in nations at war against them.[9]

In late October and November of 1917, as tradition now dictated, numerous commemorative events took place in Germany, not the least of which occurred in Wittenberg.[10] Postcards were printed with Luther and the late Otto von Bismarck standing side by side, united in spirit and purpose (Figure 4.1). Speeches and sermons bore such titles as "Luther, Our Comrade in Arms," "Luther and Germany," "Luther and his Beloved Germans," and "Luther and the Essence of German Identity."[11] Popular selections of Luther's writings were printed and distributed en masse throughout Germany and to soldiers on the front. In one of these, the editor Tim Klein included as a preface a hymn to Luther, concluding it with these lines: "Lord Luther, your teaching is good ... / A shining sword in a fair fight— / You remain staunch and despite danger and the ban / Every inch a German man" (*ein deutscher Mann*).[12] "At the end of the day," as the Berlin pastor and Privy Councilor Paul Conrad opined in 1917, "this war is about the German manner, German morality, German science, German conscience, German culture, and German freedom—in a word, [it is] about faith and country (*Heimat*), about the Gospel and German identity (*Evangelium und Deutschtum*), about the legacy of the Reformation."[13]

Ominously, the 1917 jubilee witnessed the overt racializing of theology, which would provide the ideological fundament from which the Nazi-sympathizing "German Christian" (*deutsche Christen*) movement later grew. Four pastors, Friedrich Andersen (Flesenburg), Adolf Bartels (Weimar), Ernst Katzer (Dresden), and Hans Paul Freiherr von Wolzogen (Bayreuth) published in this year a pamphlet calling for a purely Germanic church:

> The newer racial research (*Rassenforschung*) has finally opened our eyes to the pernicious effects of blood mixture between Germanic and un-German peoples and urges us, with all our energies, to strive to keep our people (*Volkstum*) pure and protected. Religion is the inner strength and finest flower in the intellectual life of a people, but it can only be active through expression in popular culture.... An inner bond between Christianity and Germanness can only be achieved when it is released from the unnatural, purely traditional connection it has to the Jewish religion.

According to the authors of this pamphlet, Jewish "menial fear of God" as exhibited in the Old Testament and among Jews in Germany

Figure 4.1. Postcard of Luther and Otto von Bismarck, c.1917. Artist unknown (Oldenburg: Gerhard Stalling Kunstverlag, c.1900). Reproduced by permission of Pictura Paedagogica Online, Universität Hildesheim.

had to be purged to allow for the growth of "child-like confidence in God"—a sentiment, they held, that defined Germany's Reformation heritage. Not doing so risked despoiling Protestant faith by leaving unexpunged a lingering Jewish theology of fear and sacrifice.[14] Several years later, the same authors came together to form the Bund für deutsche Kirche (League for a German Church), the first formal organization within the church to advocate for an ethnically defined German church.[15]

The German professoriate, although less given to such blunt racism, nevertheless reflected the nationalist trends in church and society.[16] In an address from 1917, the Leipzig historian Erich Brandenburg, for instance, saw World War I as nothing less than an epic, international struggle, pitting "the spiritual life according to the inner needs of the German people" against hostile foreign nations. Glancing back at the sixteenth century, he regarded Luther as "[an] early fighter for the German spirit" (*Vorkämpfer deutschen Geistes*): "The Reformation was the first independent creation of German uniqueness (*deutscher Eigenart*), something that had significance for the whole world. It was in its deepest essence a protest of the German conscience and German truthfulness against the ecclesiastical forms of Christianity as they had developed under Roman influence."[17] Invoking Luther's times and trials, the Professor of Church History Walter Köhler, similarly, defended the war effort as a "service of love" and a "just struggle."[18]

In an address in Berlin on 31 October 1917, Adolf von Harnack explicitly connected Luther with German national greatness and the country's wartime efforts. At this time, Harnack was not only a commanding theological mind, but arguably the most prominent "public intellectual" in Wilhelmine Germany. He had been one of several theologians in 1914 who signed the so-called "Manifesto of the 93," a statement by leading scholars justifying "to the civilized world" Germany's war aims and actions.[19] A confidant of the Emperor, Harnack served as professor at the University of Berlin, Director of the Royal Library, Secretary for the Prussian Academy of Science, and co-founder and president of the prestigious Kaiser Wilhelm Society, the forerunner of the present-day Max Planck institutes. He had helped the Emperor draft the speech justifying war, "A Call to the German People," delivered in August 1914.[20] In short, Harnack's words on such a momentous occasion as the 400th anniversary of the Reformation carried great weight.

For Harnack, the Reformation had left behind two vital legacies. First, Luther had made possible an interior spiritual liberty, an "inner freedom" (*innere Freiheit*). The "legalistic religion" of the medieval

Catholic Church, in his view, had egregiously thwarted humanity's religious development; it had produced "bondage" (*Knechtschaft*), from which Luther rightly sought to escape. His escape allowed others to follow. Second, in the Middle Ages, religion inordinately dominated other spheres of human endeavor, whether politics, science, culture, or more. For Harnack, Luther's message amounted to a brief of freedom; released from a religious stranglehold, these areas because of 1517 were able "to develop according to their own law." "The Reformation brought freedom to each [area]," he wrote, "and [in fact] to all important goods and orders of human life." While Luther himself was not free from the taint of "medieval superstition," Harnack conceded, he had nonetheless ably shown posterity the path forward, making him rightfully considered the founder of "the modern age" (*Neuzeit*). "Practically all great men of Germany, whose accomplishments and progress have shaped our development," Harnack argued, "have happily acknowledged their debt to Luther and the Reformation." "Without him Germany would never have had a Leibniz, a Sebastian Bach, a Kant, a Goethe and Schiller, and indeed a Bismarck. . . . Among all genuine and great Germans, he [Luther] is the most genuine and greatest." Therefore, during this "horrible world war," Harnack concluded, all Germans could look to him as an "example to imitate" (*Vorbild*), as someone serenely confident in being "called as an instrument of God" and demonstrating by their life "all the passion of a fighter."[21]

Harnack's sentiments mirrored what others expressed, sometimes in even more stridently nationalist terms. Harnack's colleague, the historian Max Lenz, for instance, gave an address in 1917 on "Luther and the German Spirit." According to Luther, Lenz argued, wars, although horrible, can be both just and necessary. The present war qualified as both in his opinion, for "we are fighting to maintain German identity (*deutsches Wesen*) . . . and [the fact] that we are fighting to the last breath proves itself every day and every hour."[22] In brief, as Martin Greschat has summed up, during the 1917 jubilee "Luther and the Reformation [became] . . . inseparably blended with Germany national identity."[23] Or, to quote Philip Jenkins again, Luther became in 1917 "the human symbol of a nation with a divine mission" and, thus interpreted, beckoned imperial Germany from beyond the grave to "fight to the last."[24]

Not surprisingly, Protestants outside of Germany begged to differ—not least those in the Anglo-American world—and saw widespread abuse of the past in Germany's wartime invocations of Luther. That the German imperial government had set up a POW camp in Wittenberg did not help matters. On the occasion of the 300th anniversary of Shakespeare's death in 1916, for instance, a full-page cartoon ran in the British satirical magazine *Punch*, alluding to the horrors of this camp by having an image of Luther (speaking to Shakespeare) provide commentary: "They have made my Wittenberg—ay, and all of Germany—to stink in my nostrils" (Figure 4.2).[25]

But Luther himself and his legacy also received criticism. In British and American tributes to Luther from 1917, one observes a frequent distinction between the young Luther, a champion of freedom and conscience, and the mature Luther, an ethically compromised mouthpiece of the power interests of German princes. It was this latter spirit, many accused, that had metastasized in the form of "Prussianism" in present-day imperial Germany and had dragged all of Europe into the abyss of war. This form of Lutheranism, according to the Scottish Presbyterian James Stalker, "allies itself too easily with monarchical and aristocratic [powers], being afraid of the freer and more progressive forces in society" and thus "it has not a little to do with the growth of the military power-loving spirit in the Germany which has Prussia for its head." For that reason, as a freedom-loving people, Stalker opined "we [British] claim to be better disciples of Luther than the Germans themselves."[26]

Americans, too, claimed to be abler stewards of Luther's legacy. William Walker Rockwell, for instance, in an address from 31 October 1917 at Union Theological Seminary in New York, argued that the "democratic notion" of the "priesthood of all believers" has been "worked out in practice not so much in the State Churches of Germany, subject to the King of Prussia or to other territorial rulers, but here in the United States."[27] At the University of Chicago, the pastor Frank Wakeley Gunsaulus opined that "we [Americans] have gratefully and gladly inherited Martin Luther's robust and healthful spirit.... [T]he American nation, on this four-hundredth anniversary, follows this nobler German [Luther]" against his present-day homeland "which would Germanize mankind with the help of Krupp guns, poison gases, and liquid fire."[28]

Figure 4.2. Cartoon of Luther and Shakespeare from the British satirical journal *Punch*, 150 (Jan.–June 1916): 265. Cartoon by Bernard Partridge.

Not in every instance did commemorative utterances in 1917 reference wartime realities. The influential new flagship journal of American liberal Protestantism, optimistically titled *The Christian Century*, offered a straightforward Whig understanding of the Reformation with no mention of the war—defining true faith against the old enemy, "the Roman church," instead of Germany. "As we approach the centenary of the posting of the 95 Theses," its editors averred, "there is the need that we understand clearly just what has been the meaning of this history. As we look around our world we observe that the leading nations are for the most part Protestant.... It is clear that the Protestant faith has been favorable to the development of modern civilization." The modern-day goods of democracy, progress, education, and concern for "the welfare of one's neighbors" were several evident fruits of Protestantism, the editors contended. Nonetheless, much more work lay ahead: "The reformation is still going on and is yet to be finished. The so-called modern program in religion carries the work of Luther far beyond where the great reformer expected it to go, but toward greater consistency and power."[29]

During the war, American Lutherans of German descent found themselves in a tough spot. Alarmed by the widespread anti-German sentiment in American society after 1914, they set about making Luther less German and more thoroughly religious in character, as well as casting him as the fountainhead of modern freedoms.[30] "[N]othing can be in more vivid contradiction," wrote the Philadelphia Lutheran pastor Edwin Delk, "than the Prussianism of 1917 and Luther nailing his ninety-five theses to the door of the Castle Church in Wittenberg."[31] The Missouri Synod's organ, the *Lutheran Witness*, defended Luther's crusade against indulgences as "the starting point of the work which still goes, and shall forever go on, that glorious work in which the truth was raised to its original purity, and civil and religious liberty were restored to men."[32] In the same issue, an anonymous writer argued "to be fair to Luther and to Germany we must differentiate between Luther the German and Luther the Protestant," adding further that "the truth which Luther taught was not German truth, but the truth of the Bible."[33] W. H. Rose of New York argued that the Reformation "[had] brought about a separation of Church and State, and established that civil and religious liberty which made possible our American independence, the foundation of our great nation."[34] In the same vein, W. H. T. Dau of Concordia Seminary opined that "under the liberal institutions of the North American republic [in contrast to 'the Reformer's home land'] Lutheran consciousness has been free to exert itself."[35] Such sentiments were commonplace. Frequently in 1917, as Sarah K. Nytroe has nicely summarized, American Lutherans "realigned the Reformation with the course of the history of the United States, rather than German history. In this process Lutherans sought to demonstrate their loyalty to the United States, since some faced the danger of being tainted by association with Germany."[36]

At the same time, some wondered if Protestantism as a whole was tarnished by the war or at least should have provided a greater moral impetus to avert it. To return to the 400th anniversary commemoration at Union Seminary, the theologian Arthur Cushman McGiffert claimed at this event that the "unfinished task" of the Reformation was to blunt national loyalties and strive for "the Christianizing of our international relations" in an effort to bring about "world international brotherhood."[37] What is more, James Stalker wondered aloud if the "Guns of August," at some level, had evinced a massive failure of Protestantism per se:

> When Luther and the Reformation are considered in the light of the War, the sad reflection forces itself on the mind, how little Protestantism at the critical moment affected the decision. It did not delay the outbreak of war even for a day; and this could not be without great guilt on both sides. Germany, Great Britain, and the United States, the three great Protestant Powers, could have not only kept peace among themselves, but imposed peace on the world.[38]

* * *

As is well known, the post-war settlement at Versailles (1919) dealt harshly with Germany, saddling the fragile Weimar Republic with punishing reparations and national humiliation; both, it seems clear in retrospect, became catalysts for economic chaos, political anxieties, and radical movements. Germany's subsequent descent into the abyss from 1933 to 1945, and the fact that worrisomely large segments of German Protestants cast their lot with Hitler affected interpretations of Luther's legacy, inside and outside of Germany.[39] While Nazi top

Figure 4.3. "German Christians" celebrating Luther Day (31 October 1933).
Photo by Georg Pahl, Berlin: 1933. Photo courtesy of Wikimedia Commons.

brass had a diffident relationship with Christianity at best, they found
welcome support in the aforementioned "German Christian Movement," made up of Protestants keen to reconcile their faith with
nationalist and racialist ideologies.[40]

Coincidentally, 1933, the year Hitler came to power, also witnessed
the 450th anniversary year of Luther's birth. Commemoration efforts
tended to be more subdued than in 1883, but many nationalists felt
that it was only fitting that a strong leader take the helm in such an
auspicious year and some felt that the Nazi revolution presented a
"golden opportunity for Christianity."[41] For the jubilee occasion,
"German Christians" staged several major rallies in Berlin in November, proudly displaying flags with a swastika overlaid on a cross with
a red background (Figure 4.3). Threading the rallies was the theme
that a distinctly Germanic church, purged of foreign elements,
represented the culminating logic of the Reformation and reason
to celebrate Luther's legacy. At a conference in the same year, pro-
Nazi Christians drew up the so-called Rengsdorfer Theses, one
of which baldly proclaimed the complementarity between Nazi

ideology and "German Christianity": "For us Germans the Reformation made the gospel accessible in accordance with our national character. History confirms that this proclamation of the gospel of the German race is appropriate."[42] Speaking at a rally in Berlin's Sports Palace, a leader in the movement, Reinhold Krause, asserted that a future German national church (*Volkskirche*) had the responsibility of "freeing itself from all that is un-German in worship and creed, and especially from the Old Testament and its Jewish want of morality (*jüdische Lohnmoral*)."[43] Other German-Christian leaders such as Joachim Hossenfelder and Ludwig Müller made comparable points.

But such rhetoric did not go unchallenged by those identifying with the "Confessing Church," i.e. those who rallied around the Barmen Declaration (1934) in opposition to the racialist agenda of the "German Christians." In 1933, speaking on the jubilee occasion, no less a figure than Karl Barth countered: "The Reformation as renewal of the church based on God's word is 'made accessible' for Germans (*deutsche Menschen*) not in accordance with their character but rather in accordance with the wisdom and will of divine providence. . . . Whoever treats the Reformation as a specifically German phenomenon today interprets it as propaganda and places himself outside of the evangelical Church."[44] Dietrich Bonhoeffer and Hermann Sasse echoed Barth, asserting in a statement from 1933 that

> Martin Luther is for the church of the Reformation the loyal witness of the grace of Jesus Christ. As such he is the "prophet" and "evangelist" to the Germans. But to understand his actions as a breakthrough of the Germanic spirit, or as the origin of the modern feeling for freedom, or as the establishment of a new religion is to completely misunderstand his mission. He fought against [such] modern religiosity in that he demonstrated the fanaticism of people who wished to come to recognition of God based on their own preparation and without the preached word. And he fought against the modern longings for self-sufficiency in that he taught that blind trust on human reason and on human freedom was [itself] blindness.[45]

Sadly, such opposition did not block the advances of "German Christians" in the 1930s; and their critics often went into exile (Barth) or in some cases were executed (Bonhoeffer). Permit three more examples of the employment of Luther from this time. First, on Reformation Day 1935, the "German Christian" Hermann Werdermann gave an address titled "Martin Luther and Adolf Hitler: A Historical Comparison." Hitler speaks, Werdermann asserted, "in the German tongue to German hearts" just as Luther did in the sixteenth century. Hitler is in the present age, he concluded, "as Luther was then, the tutor of the whole German nation" (*der Erzieher der ganzen deutschen Nation*).[46] Second, in May 1939 at Wartburg castle, "the Institute for the Study and Eradication of Jewish Influence on German Church Life" was launched with a speech by the theologian Walter Grundmann. By de-Judaizing the church, this institute, in the words of the historian Alon Confino, sought to "complete the work started by Luther."[47] Finally, shortly following *Kristallnacht*, which took place on 9–10 November 1938 (Luther's birthday), the German Christian regional bishop of Thuringia, Martin Sasse, published *Martin Luther und die Juden: Weg mit ihnen!*, which contained Luther's anti-Semitic screed, "Of the Jews and their Lies" (1543). In the introduction, Sasse voiced approval of the recent violence:

> On Luther's birthday, 10 November 1938, the synagogues burned in Germany. The German people have finally broken the power of the Jews in the economic field and in the new Germany thus completed the divinely blessed struggle of the Führer for the complete liberation of our people. In this hour the voice of the prophet of the sixteenth century must be heard. Out of ignorance he started out as a friend of the Jews, but, driven by conscience and the experience of reality, he became the greatest anti-Semite of his time and the admonisher of his people against the Jews.[48]

Not only "German Christians" but leaders within National Socialism sometimes made favorable references to Luther, often highlighting his exhortations to political obedience and his attitude toward the Jews.[49] In his speeches from the 1920s and 1930s, Hitler himself made several references to Luther as "a great German" and "a great German reformer."[50] The Nazi ideologist Alfred Rosenberg praised Luther for quickening German national identity, interpreting the Reformer's protest against Rome as the assertion of the "Germanic" spirit.[51] On the occasion of 1933 *Lutherfeier*, Julius Streicher, editor of the fiery Nazi journal *Der Stürmer*, exhorted educators to make more of Luther's anti-Semitic legacy:

> Luther stands before us as the warrior against the international power of the Jews. But his stance has been concealed from us. This is a great sin of omission of all responsible educators. For enlightenment about the true power of the Jews is neither an act of hate nor envy but a duty for self-preservation [and] patriotism. We hope that this [jubilee] is the time when Luther will be shown as a warrior to the people. We also want to see the full picture of Luther's life in the church as the most proper place where truth must be honored.[52]

After the war at the Nuremberg Trials, Streicher again made reference to Luther, claiming in his defense that, because of his attitude toward Jews, "Dr. Martin Luther [were he alive] would very probably sit in my place in the defendants' dock today."[53]

In light of such realities, it should perhaps not surprise that Luther's reputation plummeted in the Anglo-American world in the 1930s and 1940s. In 1941 William McGovern, for instance, published *From Luther to Hitler: The History of Fascist-Nazi Philosophy*, in which he argued that Luther's break from Rome led to the "freeing of the state from all ecclesiastical control" and thus "he started the doctrine that all men should be subject to the iron will of their secular lord."[54] In the same year, the former national secretary of the American YMCA, George Sherwood Eddy, argued that "the contribution of Lutheran ethics to German authoritarianism and power politics was one of the root causes of the cleavage between Germany and the West."[55] Similar arguments were presented in *Martin Luther: Hitler's Spiritual Ancestor* (1945), the author of which, Peter Wiener, dispensed with all subtlety, arguing that "the line from Luther to Hitler runs straight."[56]

American and British critics of Luther sometimes received ammunition from German voices. Shortly after the war, for example, the novelist Thomas Mann, renouncing his previous views, prominently pronounced guilt upon Luther. Luther, Mann averred, "is a gigantic incarnation of Germanness. I don't love him, I must freely confess. The purely German, the separatist anti-Roman, the anti-European in Luther I find troubling and alienating—even when it appears in the form of Evangelical liberty and spiritual emancipation.... [Luther] understood nothing of liberty."[57]

1945, "Year Zero" (*Stunde Null*) of modern German history, gave way to 1946, the 400th anniversary of Luther's death. Post-war conditions mitigated against large-scale commemorations, but many German scholars nonetheless made efforts to reclaim Luther's legacy from what they felt were outsiders' unfair readings of the German past. They also faced a formidable, partially "insider," adversary in the Swiss Reformed theologian Karl Barth and his various Reformed allies in and outside of Germany, many of whom were given to believe that deficiencies in Luther's political thought had misdirected Germany's political development.[58] In 1946, therefore, scholars and pastors such as Hans Asmussen, Peter Meinhold, Gerhard Ritter, Heinrich Hermelink, Karl Heim, Paul Althaus, and Hans Preuß, *mutatis mutandis*, sought to disassociate Luther from events in recent German history by arguing that Luther's was a strictly religious mind, interested in salvation not politics, or by suggesting other blameworthy reasons for the rise of Nazism. In doing so, however, many contradicted their own past statements or omitted any reference to Luther's condemnations of Anabaptists or peasants, his excoriating treatment of Zwingli and Erasmus, or his anti-Semitism.[59] "The world-historical accomplishment of the German monk Martin Luther" still speaks, Peter Meinhold averred in 1946, expressing the displeasure of many, even though "we now find ourselves in an ocean of misery."[60]

But it was not just German theologians who were agitated about indictments and caricatures of Luther. In 1946, the Lutheran Bishop of Oslo, Evind Berrgrav, lamented "the attacks on Luther and Lutheranism from the West" and sought to recover "the genuine evangelicalism from which Luther started all later Protestantism." "Hitlerism" should be characterized for what it was, not an as example of "Lutherans' servility to the state and secular authorities." That Luther might have accommodated himself too closely to secular powers, Berrgrav admitted, but the stark contrast between Luther's outlook and that of the Nazis was the relevant and timely point to make: "The Hitlerites put their faith in 'race' and 'Fatherland' and were self-glorified masters. Luther's people were glorious or, in his language, 'justified,' entirely by *grace*. . . . As far as I know, the world till now has not had two more diametrically opposed human contrasts than Adolf Hitler and Martin Luther."[61]

Nevertheless, negative wartime and post-war interpretations of Luther's role in German history could not be dismissed easily; the "Luther to Hitler" canard had sticking power. At the level of popular history, the journalist William Shirer's often simplistic, wildly influential *The Rise and Fall of the Third Reich* (1960) pointedly reaffirmed a connection between Luther and recent history: "The course of German history . . . made blind obedience to temporal rulers the highest virtue of Germanic man and put a premium on servility."[62] Such a political attitude allowed for the ascendancy of Hitler and the Nazis, who were met by the German people "with scarcely a ripple of opposition and defiance."[63] An immediate best-seller and an enduring international sensation, Shirer's book, proclaimed the *New York Times*, was "one of the most important works of history of our time."[64]

Wartime and post-war attitudes towards Luther did not just affect journalists such as Shirer, but professional historians as well. The so-called "Sonderweg Thesis," the idea that Germany had taken a "divergent" or "peculiar" authoritarian route to modernity, instead of the putatively "normal" democratic path trod by its English, French, and American counterparts, because a fixture in post-war historiography of modern Germany, promulgated by some German scholars but especially by German-speaking émigré scholars (many Jewish) who had fled from Nazi rule.[65] And while they recognized that numerous factors had contributed to German authoritarianism, scholars of the Sonderweg Thesis not infrequently claimed or at least intimated that the legacy of Luther and Lutheranism lurked in the background as a subtle and poisonous influence.

Shortly after the war, for instance, Fritz Fischer, best known for his work on the origins of World War I, claimed that the influences of Luther (on Germany) and the influences of Calvin (on Western Europe and America) cut in fundamentally different directions. Calvinist theology contained the principle of the "right of resistance" (*Widerstandsrecht*), indeed the "duty of resistance" (*Widerstandspflicht*), Fritz asserted, whereas Lutheran theology, in the main, promoted "unconditional obedience" (*unbedingten Gehorsam*) to the powers that be.[66] Likewise, Hajo Holborn, concluded, the Lutheran territorial churches of Germany "were, more than any Protestant Church, in the hands of political powers." After 1933, German Protestantism "was [therefore] particularly vulnerable to the National Socialist

onslaught.... [The] cause of the vulnerability of German Protestantism lay in the nationalistic and reactionary spirit that found a home in
these churches."[67] In a similar vein, Leonard Krieger worried that
Luther and his heirs had only sought freedom in a "spiritual plane";
this "spiritualized liberty" in turn inhibited actual political freedom,
thereby contributing to widespread German resignation in the face of
authoritarianism.[68]

While the Sonderweg Thesis has largely been abandoned in recent
decades due to the criticism it has received, particularly from the
historians David Blackbourn and Geoff Eley, its original construction
contains as an ingredient wartime and post-war interpretations of
Luther and the Reformation. But even if largely discarded by professional historians, the thesis powerfully lives on in many other educated
circles and in doing so continues to shape conceptions of the Reformation and its historical influence.[69]

* * *

Cold War geopolitics and ideological struggles, particularly as manifested in the post-war division of Germany, left their impact on the
memory of the Reformation in the second half of the twentieth
century. Following the waves of intra-Protestant ecumenism earlier
in the century, the Second Vatican Council (1962–5) of the Catholic
Church also has immense bearing on our topic, as it heralded an
abrupt, unprecedented warming of relations between Catholics and
Protestants, and particularly between Catholics and Lutherans.[70]
Furthermore, the social and political upheavals of the 1960s alongside
waxing secularism and religious pluralism in Europe and the United
States colored memories, interpretations, and assessments of the
Reformation.[71]

Retrospective attitudes toward Luther in the German Democratic
Republic (GDR) present an especially fascinating case. As fate would
decree, the 50th anniversary of the Bolshevik Revolution coincided
with the 450th anniversary of the Reformation in 1967 while the
500th anniversary of Luther's birth took place in the same year as
the 100th anniversary of Karl Marx's death (1883).[72] Grappling with
these odd coincidences presented a steep challenge for state, church,
and university alike.[73] With respect to official state commemorations,
from the time of the 400th anniversary of Luther's death in 1946 to

the 500th anniversary of his birth in 1983, Luther's official image in the GDR underwent a remarkable metamorphosis. (A time traveler in the GDR from 1946 to 1983 would heartily get the Soviet-era, underground joke that the most difficult thing for a historian in the USSR was not forecasting the future, but predicting the past!) Luther's treatment in the East contrasted strikingly with his treatment in the West, leading one journalist on the occasion of the 1967 anniversary to opine that "Martin Luther appears to be as much a symbol of the division of Germany [today] as he was in his own time."[74]

In the immediate aftermath of the World War, the "problem of German history" loomed as large in the East as it did in the West. Like their Western counterparts, Marxist-oriented scholars rummaged through the German past in search of deep-seated pathologies to help explain the Nazi calamity. A central plank in the Soviet-promoted "Anti-Fascist" ideology, as it took shape in the East, were the twin evils of militaristic "Prussianism" and a German proclivity toward political docility that could be traced all the way back to the Reformation.[75] A leftist journalist and informant to Soviet-occupation authorities, Wolfram von Hanstein published in 1947 *From Luther to Hitler*, criticizing Luther's legacy in ways that mirrored the rebukes found in the Anglo-American world.[76] A year earlier, Alexander Abusch, a future GDR Minister of Culture, had published *The False Path of a Nation* (*Der Irrweg einer Nation*), asserting that the German people had long been corrupted by chauvinistic nationalism that had deep roots in German history and that Luther, in fact, might be considered a distant forerunner of Hitler.[77] A number of similar examples could be adduced.[78] Such large-scale deprecations of Lutheranism and German history found support in the Moscow-encouraged political motivation to dampen all national identities in the emerging "Eastern bloc" and instead promote Marxist-Leninist ideology and admiration for the Soviet Union as the foundation of political unity.[79] The vehicle for such re-education in East Germany was through the Socialist Unity Party (SED) led by the Moscow-trained, German socialist Walter Ulbricht, who once in power consistently pursued a policy of separation (*Abgrenzung*) from the West in the first decades of the GDR.[80]

To achieve a more appropriate political and historical consciousness, the SED could not ignore an era as significant for German history as the Reformation. Accordingly, the sixteenth century received much attention in the early years of the GDR. Yet the spotlight was decisively removed from Luther, who was deemed to present more problems than promise from a Marxist standpoint.[81] The true hero of the Reformation in fact was neither Luther nor any of the "mainstream" reformers. Rather, it was Thomas Müntzer (1489–1525), the fiery, apocalyptic leader of the Peasants' Revolt of 1524/5. Müntzer's revolutionary zeal and his proven ability to translate theology into popular social action received high praise, while Luther's ponderous theologizing and his decision to side with the German princes against the peasants were deplored as reactionary.[82]

This basic interpretive framework of the Reformation was not new. It could be traced back to Friedrich Engels, who, after the failed European-wide revolutions of 1848, had published *The Peasant War in Germany* (1850), in which he praised "the magnificent figure of Thomas Müntzer" and contrasted his actions against Luther's "cowardly servility toward the German princes." To be fair, Luther received a modicum of praise from Engels, for attacking the Catholic Church and translating the Bible into the vernacular. What is more, Luther had stood on the cusp of greatness for helping launch what the Director of the GDR's "German Museum of History," Alfred Meusel, later dubbed an "early bourgeois revolution" (*frühbürgerliche Revolution*)—a key category endlessly debated and discussed in East German historiography and in Western Marxist circles.[83] Sadly, however, in his tract, "Against the Murderous Hordes of Peasants," Luther had "betrayed the popular movement" by siding with the princes and became, in Engels's view, a *Fürstenknecht* (servant of the princes) and a *Bauernschlächter* (slaughterer of peasants)—labels that would stick.[84] Subsequent Marxist scholars such as August Bebel, Franz Mehring, Karl Kautsky, and Ernst Bloch kept alive Engels's interpretation of the sixteenth century.[85] A new edition of *The Peasant War in Germany*, incidentally, was among the first books printed in Soviet-occupied East Berlin at the time of the 400th anniversary of Luther's death in 1946.[86]

The next year, the Soviet historian M. M. Smirin published his extensively researched *The People's Reformation of Thomas Müntzer and the Great Peasants' War*. Soon translated into German, this work, which largely defended and expanded on Engels's conclusions, exerted a tremendous influence on East German views of the Reformation.[87] In 1952, Alfred Meusel reprised arguments of Engels and Smirin in his

Thomas Müntzer and his Time, arguing that the Lutheran "princely" reformation was one of the most tragic "half-accomplishments" in German history.[88] The historian Leo Stern's inquiries led him in the same direction; he asserted that although Luther stood close to enduring greatness, his tract against the peasants rendered him a "traitor" to popular, revolutionary currents in history. "The whole of Luther's tract," Stern wrote, "is written with such an animosity ... that it will forever form a blot on Luther's character; it shows that if he began his career as a man of the people, he was now entirely in the service of the oppressors."[89]

To be sure, some East German historians made guarded defenses of Luther, praising his catalytic role and his assertion of conscience against established power. And he did receive some public recognition in the early years of the GDR. Take for instance the decision to rename the University of Halle-Wittenberg in his honor.[90] Even so, from the war's end until the mid-1960s, Luther's legacy in the GDR by and large stood in the shadow of Thomas Müntzer—the latter regarded as an indisputable historical hero and the clearer harbinger of socialism. This slant on the sixteenth century became the sanctioned view of the SED, presented in public documents and taught in school curricula.[91] A major film on Müntzer's life and times was produced and released in 1956.[92] More than a few streets in the GDR were renamed "Thomas Müntzer Strasse," and the leader of the Peasants' Revolt even appeared on the GDR's five-mark bill (Figure 4.4).[93] On the occasion of the 450th anniversary of the Peasants' War in 1974/5, a massive panorama painting of the Battle of Frankenhausen (1525), where the peasants were defeated, was commissioned in the city of Bad Frankenhausen.[94] As late as 1977, the East German Foreign Press Service printed a colorful set of pamphlets (in English), featuring Müntzer as a great, liberating figure in German history, making no mention of Luther.[95]

But this interpretation presented problems, and by the eve of the 1967 jubilee modifications of it were already under way. A key issue was that it failed to garner the support of the Protestant churches, which not only remained intent on recognizing Luther as a laudable, if flawed, figure, but who desired to commemorate 1967 alongside their fellow Christians in the Federal Republic, with whom they were still statutorily partnered.[96] What is more, in the GDR's efforts to solidify

Figure 4.4. GDR five-mark bill with image of Thomas Münzter, leader of the Peasants' Revolt. Artist unknown, German Democratic Republic, 1975. Photo courtesy of Wikimedia Commons.

a specifically East German, socialist national identity (an acute political concern in light of disaffection caused by the erection of the Berlin Wall in 1961), a figure as immense as Luther in German history could not simply be shoved aside. Efforts commenced, therefore, to downplay the notion that Luther had "betrayed" progressive currents of the Reformation. Rather, he and Müntzer began to be hailed together as early signposts of history's appropriate course.

GDR historians contributed to this partial rehabilitation of Luther. In light of the impending 1967 jubilee, several conferences and publications in the early 1960s set the stage for a revision of the Reformer's image. In 1967, Herbert Trebs published *Martin Luther heute*, in which he questioned the assumption of an early, progressive Luther and a mature, reactionary Luther. For Trebs, the important thing remained that Luther had defied both Pope and Emperor, and that this, despite relying on the power base of the German princes, remained truly revolutionary and of world-historical importance. This view gained wider currency and became a frequent refrain expressed shortly before and during the 1967 commemorations. "Whoever affirms one [Luther or Müntzer] need not damn the other," as Gerhard Brendler summed up in 1967:

> Marxist historical research has, on the contrary, through the exposition of the legitimate interrelationship of the Reformation and the Peasants'

War as [joint] phases of the bourgeois revolution, uncovered the progressive meaning of the Lutheran Reformation and with it has created the scientific basis of the national jubilee marking the passing of 450 years since the Reformation, which appreciated Martin Luther as belonging to the good traditions of our republic.[97]

This more positive assessment of Luther made its ways into the GDR's planning phases for the Reformation jubilee of 1967, which began in 1965, the same year as the church began its own plans for the year's activities.[98] In 1966 party leaders established "the committee of the GDR's central administration to mark the 450th anniversary of the Reformation," chaired by Gerald Götting.[99] In addition to connecting the jubilee to the Bolshevik Revolution, officials sought to tie it to other events of ideological and national importance—in particular, the 900th anniversary of Wartburg castle and the 150th anniversary of the previously discussed Wartburgfest of 1817.[100]

Although the committee secured the participation of a few church leaders, many became vexed by the persistent linking of the *Reformationsfeier* with the Bolshevik Revolution's fiftieth anniversary. Several high-level church officials, including Bishop Johannes Jänicke of Magdeburg, resigned in protest. While the churches largely sought a *modus vivendi* with the government—being a church not for or against but a "church in socialism" (*Kirche im Sozialismus*)—their leaders could not suppress discomfort at the political instrumentalization of the Reformation.[101]

The focal point of official commemoration in late October 1967 was not surprisingly in Wittenberg. Here a week-long spate of activities climaxed in events on 31 October, the date of the "Thesenanschlag." As fireworks filled the evening skies, images of Luther, Müntzer, Lenin, and Walter Ulbricht all jostled for attention on the city's streets.[102] The GDR's director of the jubilee Gerald Götting sized up the historical occasion as follows:

The fact that our celebration of the Reformation directly follows the fiftieth anniversary of the great socialist October Revolution affords us the occasion to reflect on the relationship between revolution and reformation, between social transformation and ecclesiastical renewal. In point of fact, one can only rightly understand the Reformation if it is seen as a part of a more comprehensive revolutionary process between the years 1517 and 1525 [including the Peasants' War], a time one must characterize as the high point of the early bourgeois Revolution (*frühbürgerliche Revolution*) in Germany.[103]

A symposium took place from 24 to 26 October, the proceedings of which were later edited by Max Steinmetz and Gerhard Brendler and published as *Weltwirkung der Reformation* (The Reformation's Global Influence).[104] In its epilogue, Steinmetz gave explicit expression to the deeper politics informing the 1967 jubilee: "The 450th anniversary of the Reformation is a matter of basic confrontation . . . with the view of Luther and the Reformation of imperialist [i.e. Western] historians. . . . [T]he historical lessons of the Reformation are relevant in the GDR, for they cannot be appreciated in the West German state."[105]

West Germans hardly had the chance to get the message. Of the hundreds of West Germans invited to jubilee events in 1967 by the churches, only thirty-nine were granted visas.[106] Similar obstacles were encountered by invitees from other nationalities.[107] Those who succeeded in gaining entry were expressly forbidden to travel outside of the county (*Bezirk*) where Wittenberg was seated. What is more, they could read in the official program that it was the GDR (viz., not the FRG) that was "the heir and protector of all progressive, humanitarian, and revolutionary traditions in German history."[108] To enhance Luther's image next to that of Müntzer, the government had printed commemorative stamps with Luther's image and those of historic sites in Wittenberg.

And yet. Although the 1967 jubilee brought a halt to the earlier stark dichotomy between the Reformation and the Peasants' War, Luther and Müntzer, they were rarely discussed apart from one another. The main justification for rehabilitating Luther, in fact, had been to note that he had paved the way for Müntzer and "the revolutionary process" in modern history. A more forthright celebration of Luther per se and the Reformation per se in the GDR awaited the quincentenary jubilee of Luther's birth in 1983: *Lutherjahr 1983*.

Several developments help explain this. The Social Democrat Willy Brandt, who became Chancellor of the FRG in 1969, pursued a new policy of openness (*Ostpolitik*) toward the GDR. This allowed for more Western influences in East Germany.[109] Scholarly conferences and exchanges involving Western historians at the time of the 450th anniversary of the Peasants' War in 1974/5 exposed GDR scholars to the criticism that their views of Müntzer were ideologically laden and unable to stand up to closer historical scrutiny. Simmering discontent among clergy with the regime, already apparent in 1967, led to open, official dialogues in 1978 between the churches and SED leaders, resulting in a less constricted role for religion in society.[110] What is more, to assist a sputtering economy, the impending 500th anniversary promised the hard currency of Western tourists coming to visit the East's many Reformation sites—something that was not a concern in 1967. Finally, there remained the ongoing Cold War imperative for the GDR to legitimize its power internally and burnish its confidence and prestige on the international stage.[111]

For all these reasons and more, SED party leaders well before 1983 set about a rehabilitation of Luther, albeit even if still interpreting him under the aegis of Marxist-Leninist thought. Preparations got under way in the late 1970s. State officials expressed a strong desire to differentiate their "honoring of Luther" from what was taking place in West Germany and from GDR church organs, which in 1975 had already begun their own plans for 1983 in the form of seven scheduled church conferences (*Kirchentage*).[112] "For the further development and intensification of the Marxist-Leninist conception of history in a developed socialist society," as one early governmental planning memorandum put it, "[we must] wrestle against the modern bourgeois-reactionary conception of history." Therefore, it must be proven "that the onset of the Reformation movement was not only an ecclesiastical-religious phenomenon, but a comprehensive, and in essence bourgeois-revolutionary one, more or less oriented to the deep-seated transformation of social relations."[113]

With echoes of the Kaiser's involvement in 1883, SED Party Chairman Erich Honecker became personally engaged, even honorifically chairing the 100-member "Martin Luther Committee of the GDR" to make preparations for 1983 as a special year of "Honoring Martin Luther by the German Democratic Republic." In a speech from 1980, he hailed Luther as "one of the greatest sons of the German people" and made clear that the GDR planned to recognize "the historical achievement he [Luther] accomplished by ushering in the Reformation (which represented a bourgeois revolution), and which contributed to social progress and world culture." With his "famous 95 Theses on the church door in Wittenberg," Honecker claimed, Luther had introduced "the decisive impulse for liberation" into the stream of modern history.[114]

In September 1981, "15 Theses on Martin Luther" were officially released, published in the SED party organ *Einheit* and as a separate brochure. The theses make clear that Luther ranks "among the great personalities in German history." What is more, the GDR, as a "socialist German state," was conceived as the "result of centuries-long striving of all the progressive forces of the German people." In this sense, the GDR sought to celebrate "the historical accomplishments of Martin Luther . . . [and] steward the progressive legacy that he left behind." No mention was made in the theses of Luther as a servant of the princes or a murderer of peasants, and no sharp distinction was drawn between him and Müntzer.[115]

When 1983 arrived, predictably enough, numerous activities and events took place: academic conferences, visits to key Reformation cities (where many Luther sites had been refurbished), conferences and colloquia, the publication of books and articles, exhibitions, drama, a major celebration at Wartburg castle, and even the release of a five-part television series on the life of Luther.[116] The desired ethos of the year is nicely captured in a large booklet, an accompaniment to a museum exhibition in East Berlin.[117] "November 10, 1983," the title page (Figure 4.5), quoting Hoenecker, proclaims,

> will be the 500th anniversary of Martin Luther's birthday, a man who is among the greatest sons of the German people. The German Democratic Republic and her people pay homage to his personality. They pay homage to the historical achievement he accomplished by initiating the Reformation . . . for the benefit of social progress and world culture. It is just the deep changes at our time that call for the support of historical progress, of reason and humanism.

The booklet concludes with another quote from Honecker, suggesting that the memory of the Reformation will help GDR citizens take "responsibility for the world":

> We live in a time when it is more than ever imperative to determinedly defend peace as the greatest good of mankind. On all continents of our globe there are taking place deepgoing transformations. The peoples are looking for new ways of life, and we ourselves create our socialist order. May the homage on the occasion of the 500th anniversary of

1483 · 1983

Am 10. November 1983 jährt sich
zum 500. Mal der Tag,
an dem Martin Luther, einer der
größten Söhne des deutschen Volkes,
geboren wurde.
Unsere Deutsche Demokratische
Republik und ihre Bürger
würdigen seine Persönlichkeit.
Sie würdigen die historische
Leistung, die er durch die
Einleitung der Reformation,
die eine bürgerliche Revolution
darstellt, für den gesellschaftlichen
Fortschritt und die Weltkultur
vollbracht hat.
Gerade die umfassenden
Wandlungen unserer Zeit
fordern Parteinahme
für das historisch
Fortschrittliche, das
Vernünftige und Menschliche.

Erich Honecker
Vorsitzender des Staatsrates der DDR
und des Martin-Luther-Komitees

Martin Luther
Ehrung 1983
der Deutschen
Demokratischen
Republik

Luther

Figure 4.5. Cover page of GDR booklet on the occasion of Luther's birthday in 1983. German Democratic Republic, 1983.

Martin Luther's birthday worldwide—as it is due to the worldwide
influence of the Reformer—benefit the struggle for the preservation of
peace and the peaceful co-existence of the people and states.[118]

Ironically, at the same time that the GDR was burnishing its image of
Luther, its own image was worsening in the eyes of many Christians.
The Soviet arming of the GDR with short-range missiles (prompted
by the US's intention to put Pershing II missiles in the FRG) under the
mantle of "peace must be defended" had awakened a powerful
opposition movement (directed at Moscow, Berlin, and Washington)
among the churches, which countered with their own mantra, "swords
into plow shares." Many in the churches, moreover, felt that the
GDR's use of Luther was unconscionably selective and self-serving.
Such opinions, although voiced with circumspection, were regularly
expressed at the seven-church orchestrated *Kirchentage* that took place
in 1983. As one critic intrepidly put it: "Luther does not belong to
the GDR, but rather he really belongs . . . to the worldwide community of churches."[119] The official church motto for the year—"Fear,
trust, and love God above all things" (*über alle Dinge*)—amounted to a
not-too-subtle critique of the all-demanding loyalty desired by the
regime.[120]

Finally, there was the awkward matter of the 500th anniversary of
Luther's birth taking place in the same year as the 100th anniversary
of Marx's death. While Honecker had declared Luther as "one of the
greatest sons" of Germany, Marx garnered "the greatest." This odd
coincidence led to many humorous quips. "Martin Luther [can]
celebrate his 500th birthday in our time, but Karl Marx is 100 years
dead" was one line that regularly made the rounds. An artist ably
captured both the historical dissonance of the two anniversaries and
the oppressive nature of the GDR regime when he painted two "Joker
cards" with the images of Luther and Marx on each. The inscriptions
under them, in a gently mocking tone, read: "Marx's teaching and
Luther's word will last forever" and "grin and bear it; the end is never
certain" (Figure 4.6).

In the final analysis, the curiosity and puzzlement caused by a
repressive regime committed philosophically to historical materialism
celebrating a fundamentally religious thinker could be neither avoided
nor contained. No one in 1983 could have anticipated the events of

Figure 4.6. "Joker '83," Rendering of Luther and Karl Marx (1983). From *Deutsches Blatt* (1983). Artwork from Wittenberg: Luther Haus Museum. Photo courtesy of M. Ryan Groff.

1989, of course. But given the well-documented role of religious voices leading up to the Fall of the Wall, perhaps in retrospect we might be permitted to glimpse at least a premonition of things to come in the celebratory confusions and contradictions of 1983.[121] Hands down, the line of the year in 1983 goes to one exasperated parishioner in the East, weary of commemoration, who sighed: "Here we stand in the GDR. And we can do nothing else. God help us, Amen."[122]

* * *

On the western side of Europe's "Iron Curtain" and in the United States, post-war commemorations also reflected much about the times. In the West, liberal democracy meant pluralism in society and this translated into pluralism, if not infrequently cacophony, in interpreting the Reformation—even if a Whiggish undercurrent (i.e. the Reformation sowed the seeds of liberal democracy, tolerance, and the modern age) remained irrepressible. What is more, many commemorative lectures and sermons took stock of waxing secularism in Western societies. *Time* magazine, it merits noting, famously asked on its cover "Is God Dead"? just a year before the 450th anniversary of the Reformation in 1967—even if it must be added that Luther himself made the cover of the magazine's issue of 24 March 1967![123]

Two minor commotions from earlier in the 1960s left a mark on the 1967 jubilee. The first stemmed from a book published by the Catholic scholar Erwin Iserloh, *Luther between Reform and Reformation: The Posting of the [95] Theses Did Not Occur*, in which the author claimed— not without considerable scholarly efforts of documentation—that Luther had never posted 95 Theses, but merely circulated them to the relevant church authorities; the iconic moment at the Castle Church door was simply a long, self-perpetuating myth.[124] Second, in 1963 members of the Lutheran World Federation (an umbrella organization founded in 1947) had met in Helsinki, Finland, for their fourth assembly.[125] They sought to produce an agreed-upon statement on justification, the signature theological issue of the Reformation, but the various Lutheran bodies failed to reach consensus.[126] Both Iserloh's publication and the "failure of Helsinki" persisted as nettlesome points of discussion into 1967.[127]

But these issues were overshadowed by the theological earthquake of the Second Vatican Council (1962–5). While the ecumenical movement among Protestants dates to the early twentieth century, Vatican II brought a sea change of new possibilities to Protestant–Catholic relations.[128] This was the first ecumenical council of the Catholic Church since the papacy of Pius IX (r. 1846–78), who in the footsteps of his predecessors since the sixteenth century had condemned Protestantism root and branch. In 1928, in the encyclical *Mortalium animos*, Pope Pius XI (r. 1922–39) had scorned (Protestant) ecumenism, forbidding Catholics "to take part in the assemblies of the non-Catholics: union of Christians can only be promoted by promoting the return to the one true Church of Christ of those who are separated from it, for in the past they have unhappily left it."[129]

Vatican II controverted such sentiments. Prior to the Council, Pope John XXIII (r. 1958–63) presided over the establishment of a Secretariat for Promoting Christian Unity (1960), led by the German Jesuit and pioneer ecumenist, Augustin Bea.[130] In an unprecedented development, many Protestant theologians were actually invited to Vatican II's sessions as observers, and their insights—conveyed in informal conversations with the gathered bishops and theologians as they, the Protestants, were not permitted to speak in the assemblies—played no small role in shaping the Council's conciliatory direction.[131] Of particular significance was the Council's "Decree on Ecumenism" (*Unitatis Redintegratio*), which included among its key lines:

> The restoration of unity among all Christians is one of the principal concerns of the Second Vatican Council. Christ the Lord founded one Church and one Church only.... Even in the beginnings of this one and only Church of God there arose certain rifts, which the Apostle strongly condemned. But in subsequent centuries much more serious dissensions made their appearance and quite large communities came to be separated from full communion with the Catholic Church—for which, often enough, men of *both sides were to blame.* The children who are born into these Communities and who grow up believing in Christ cannot be accused of the sin involved in the separation, and the Catholic Church *embraces them as brothers, with respect and affection....* The ecumenical movement is striving to overcome these obstacles. But even in spite of them it remains true that *all who have been justified by faith in Baptism are members of Christ's body, and have a right to be called Christian, and so are correctly accepted as brothers by the children of the Catholic Church.*[132]

Alongside this Decree, significance should also be accorded to the Council's Dogmatic Constitution on the Church (*Lumen Gentium*), which, departing from custom, did not claim the Catholic Church as the exclusive repository of Christian truth. Instead, the bishops maintained that "[the] Church, constituted and organized in the world as a society, subsists in (*subsistit in*) the Catholic Church, which is governed by the successor of Peter and by the Bishops in communion with him, although many elements of sanctification and of truth are found *outside of its visible structure*. These elements, as gifts belonging to the Church of Christ, are *forces impelling toward catholic unity*."[133] Together these two irenic documents, *Unitatis Redintegratio* and *Lumen Gentium*, represented nothing less than a revolution in Catholic theology, providing a basis for ecumenical communication and outreach impossible prior to the Council.[134]

The 450th anniversary of the Reformation in 1967 followed directly on the heels of Vatican II. As expected, scores of conferences, symposia, concerts, exhibitions, and lectures, took place in academic, seminary, and ecclesiastical settings. In Germany, the Protestant Church of West Germany (EKD) held its principal celebration at Worms where Luther had defied Charles V and the site of the massive Reformation monument.[135] The Lutheran World Federation observed the occasion (and its own twentieth anniversary) with a meeting in Lund, Sweden. There, unprecedentedly, the Catholic Cardinal Jan Willebrands, soon to replace Augustin Bea as the head of the Secretariat for Promoting Christian Unity, was not only invited but actually gave one of the keynote addresses. In it, he called the occasion "a gift of God": the fact that in "rediscovered brotherhood" Catholic and Lutherans could "come together after a long history of conflict and inquire into the past and present meaning of the Reformation."[136] In a greeting sent to Lund, Cardinal Bea himself echoed Willebrand's sentiment: "We do not want to shove the blame for this horrible division at one another; rather, we want together to seek a way to restore the lost unity."[137]

Ecumenism was not the only novelty in 1967. One notices strenuous efforts, particularly in Germany, to denationalize the Reformation, regarding it no longer as a "German" event but as a pan-Christian and pan-European one and, indeed, a phenomenon of world-historical significance. New academic approaches to the sixteenth century also added to the mix. Experimentation with new, "post-confessional" methodologies, such as psycho-biography and social history, as well as attention to the categories of class, race, and gender, had begun to open up whole new areas for Reformation scholarship, and these novelties made their presence felt in 1967.[138]

Indeed, the sheer accretion of divergent interpretations, and the overt politicization of Luther's legacy under the Nazis and in the GDR, gave an impetus for many commentators to castigate simplistic attribution of meaning to the Reformation. The theologian Helmut Gollwitzer spoke for many when he exclaimed that "[Luther] has remained concealed behind the illusion of acquaintance.... [T]he real Luther has become invisible on account of the many distorted images [of him]." In an article for the newspaper *Die Zeit*, Heinz Zahrnt observed that in 1967 Luther's legacy had become fundamentally "controversial," adding: "The 450th anniversary of the Reformation is anything but a day of hero worship. Much more it poses a self-critical question to us: how are we going to deal with Luther's legacy?"[139] Marginalized or omitted altogether in past commemorations, Luther's attitudes toward Jews, Muslims, women, and peasants became inviting items for discussion in 1967. Much past scholarship was dismissed by critics as residually confessionalist and/or Protestant hagiography.[140]

If interpreting Luther often confounded Protestants in 1967, many post-conciliar Catholics made efforts to re-evaluate the Reformation in a more positive light—something that only could have happened after the Second Vatican Council.[141] Catholic historiography since mid-century had witnessed a shift from viewing Luther primarily as a heretic (as well as a neurotic) to regarding him as an earnest *homo religiosus* deserving more open-minded evaluation.[142] In an address at Fordham University in New York, the American Jesuit Robert E. McNally remarked that "[i]n 1967 it is no easy matter to discover the 'culprit' of 1517, whether he be pope, emperor, bishop, prince or friar.... Out of the ninety-five theses grew schism and disunity; but nothing that happens to the Church...happens by chance. Everything has purpose and meaning, even though its full significance and relevance may be revealed only centuries later, when the dust of history settled. So it is with the Reformation."[143] In two weighty volumes, *The Theology of Justification in Martin Luther and Thomas Aquinas* and *The Doctrine of Justification in Catholic Perspective*, the Dominican Otto Hermann Pesch argued in 1967 that starkly different emphases, not irreconcilable differences, produced church division. Accordingly, he suggested that "polemics between Protestants and Catholics...has perhaps been only a big misunderstanding."[144]

While most Catholics would not go that far, the 1967 jubilee did mark the beginning of official dialogue between the Catholic Church and the Lutheran World Federation for the purpose of overcoming misunderstandings and clarifying differences. Acknowledging the significance of the 450th anniversary, Cardinal Bea on behalf of Pope Paul VI sent greetings to Frederik Schiotz, the Federation's president, remarking that "[w]ith all of you we deeply regret that 450 years ago the unity of Western Christianity was broken."[145] Brought to life by such sentiments, warmly reciprocated by Lutherans, the first official meeting between the two camps took place in Zurich on 26–30 November 1967.[146] This led to several subsequent meetings and eventually to the signing in Malta of the joint statement, "The Gospel and the Church" (sometimes called the "Malta Report") in 1972. While abiding differences were articulated in the document, both sides testified to a "truly brotherly encounter" and "sense[d] even more deeply our profound community and joint responsibility for our common Christian heritage."[147]

This encounter paved the way for additional meetings and eventually to far-reaching agreement on a number of contested topics. On a practical level, the ecumenical ethos that such conversations generated brought institutions of different confessional backgrounds together in symbolic if not always in substantive ways. In the United States, to offer but one example, Lutheran Valparaiso University in Indiana as part of its 1967 festivities conferred an honorary doctorate on Father Theodore Hesburgh, president of nearby Notre Dame University.[148]

Ecumenical developments were not limited to Lutherans. The postconciliar climate allowed the Catholic Church for the first time to join arms more robustly with the work of the World Council of Churches.[149] Pope Paul VI had ordered and published in 1967 an "Ecumenical Directory" to offer guidance to dioceses worldwide on the parameters of ecumenical engagement.[150] In the United States, a number of institutes of higher education sponsored ecumenically focused academic conferences in 1967, such as one on "A Reappraisal of the Reformation," sponsored jointly by Fordham University, a Jesuit school, and Union Theological Seminary, arguably the nation's flagship Protestant seminary.[151] In 1967, the Presbyterian Church in America produced a new confession—the so-called Confession of 1967—that, while not focused on Catholics alone, made reconciliation of various sorts its leitmotif.[152] Princeton University, historically in the Reformed tradition, held its first joint Protestant–Catholic service in its 221-year history.[153]

Of course, anti-Catholicism as an integral part of Protestant identity did not simply vanish in 1967. Far from it. In an essay on "The Abiding Validity of the Reformation," the theologian John H. Tietjen of the North American Lutheran Missouri Synod acknowledged the winds of change at Vatican II, but concluded that many things in Roman Catholicism still "obscure and contradict the Gospel" and that Protestants were duty-bound to "call Roman Catholics to further and continuing reform."[154] What is more, at a more popular level in the United States, the message of Vatican II had been partially muddied by an earlier controversy surrounding the election of John F. Kennedy as the nation's first Catholic president—a development lamented by many evangelical Christians.[155] Throughout most of the 1960s, whether from lingering "nativist" reasons or more high-minded theological ones, American evangelicals largely viewed Vatican II with skepticism.[156] "Ecumenicity" in fact was regularly seen as a seductive theological dead-end that only *liberal* Protestants pursued.[157] At the same time, as the historian Mark A. Noll has demonstrated, this period also witnessed the beginnings of a "minor revolution" in the improvement of evangelical–Catholic relations that has continued until the present.[158]

In West Germany, the jubilee of 1967 met varied responses. The intellectual resources of Catholic social thought and the long tenure of the post-war Catholic chancellor Konrad Adenauer, the steely leader of the Christian Democratic Union (CDU), had contributed significantly to post-war rebuilding and stability. Anti-Catholicism, while not absent from the FRG, therefore faced headwinds in the years following the Vatican Council. To counter the heavily Marxist reading of the Reformation in the GDR, many West German politicians contended that the legacy of the Reformation should be something that brought the two Germanies together, not drove a wedge between them. At the same time, in the Federal Republic no small number of intellectuals and activists were attracted to Marxism and sought, too, to enlist Luther in radical leftist politics. The notion of *ecclesia semper reformanda*, according to the radical student activist-pastor Martin Stöhr of Darmstadt, should be expanded to all of society: "The Word of God concerning human freedom, as Luther understood it, implies political and social revolution."[159]

* * *

The 500th anniversary of Luther's birth, 10 November 1983, brought yet another round of Reformation celebrations and commemorations. Not to be outdone by the GDR, West Germany witnessed its own outpouring of exhibitions, conferences, minted coins and medals, books, symposia, and more—planned and supported by a wide range of organizations whether governmental, academic, or ecclesiastical. As the jubilee's centerpiece, the German National Museum in Nuremberg organized a major exhibition in collaboration with the Society for the History of the Reformation.[160] The Society had organized earlier an international conference on Luther at Heidelberg, while the city of Hamburg put on a massive exhibition dedicated to Luther's implications for the arts.[161] Another international research congress of 300 participants met in Erfurt, where Luther had become an Augustinian friar.[162] Meanwhile, the EKD celebrated Luther's birth in Worms and paid tribute to Luther's lasting legacy at a major conference in Bad Tutzing. Numerous universities, seminaries, and individual parishes also marked the occasion with special events. Books, essays, and articles on Luther and the Reformation proliferated.[163]

Political leaders in the Federal Republic of Germany (FRG) faced a delicate balancing act. As before in 1967, they felt the imperative to claim Luther's legacy for both Germanies, while distancing themselves from Marxist interpretations in the East—and also, of course, from past nationalist interpretations. The large Catholic population in the West also had to be taken into consideration and not gratuitously offended. The fact that the FRG did not put out anything like the GDR's centrally released "15 Theses on Luther" itself speaks volumes about the nature of the two regimes.[164]

Even so, key leaders weighed in on the Reformer's legacy, most notably at the EKD's celebration at Worms and at the opening of the Luther exhibition at the national museum in Nuremberg. The chairman of the SPD, Willy Brandt, emphasized that "Luther belongs to all Germans. His legacy should not be divided into a western and an eastern part. Luther offers orientation and is a model in society that is experiencing a crisis of purpose."[165] The head of the CSU, Franz Joseph Strauß, inveighed against misinterpretations of Luther's "two kingdoms" teaching. The doctrine created the imperative, Strauß held, for the recognition of the political realm, not as an "ethical no-man's land" but as a secular domain of value and independence, to which Christians and all people of good will were called to serve and protect.[166] Speaking at the opening of the exhibition in Nuremberg, the FRG's President Karl Carstens struck a pious note: "All that Luther did and accomplished is a strong sign of what a person can do, acting in the freedom of God. . . . We treat Luther correctly when, learning from his example, we do not trust in ourselves and in our own strength, but in God."[167]

West German's Chancellor, Helmut Kohl, arguably gave one of the more memorable addresses of 1983, notable for its candid recognition of the past abuses of Luther's legacy, even if it displayed its own Whiggish mien. Speaking at Nuremberg, he recognized that "running like a red thread throughout [past] centenary anniversaries was the temptation for contemporaries to instrumentalize Luther." Elaborating on this point, he indicated that "for some Luther was a revolutionary and for others a reformer, he is regarded as a pioneer of the Enlightenment and as a mastermind of the German nation-state. . . . But primarily Luther was a man of the church who wanted to improve it. That's what he was about—not revolution, politics, worldly power and earthly strife." At the same time, Kohl could not help but attribute many of the goods of liberal democracy to the Wittenberg reformer—including freedom of conscience, toleration, the dignity of the individual, an orderly state, and even the right to education. While Kohl rued the fact that the Reformation had caused the division of Europe into confessional states, he nonetheless felt that from the discord and conflicts of the early-modern era the praiseworthy principles of "pluralism," "diversity," and "federalism" had gradually emerged. These should be preserved, he believed, for

German history offered lessons about what happens when they are forfeited: "No dictatorship of the twentieth century can call on Luther as a source of legitimacy"—presumably a gibe not only at Germany's Nazi past but also at the GDR.[168]

Of course, the two Germanies were not alone in remembering Luther in 1983. Other Lutheran and Protestant communities behind the "Iron Curtain" joined in, such as the Lutheran churches in Slovakia and Hungary. In the latter, a statute of Luther was finally raised at the Lutheran Theological Seminary in Zugló; it had been partially completed before the war in the 1930s, and first proposed in 1917![169] In the West, practically every country touched by the Reformation witnessed commemorative events and activities. The Scandinavian countries, not surprisingly, were especially active. Sweden's Uppsala was the site of a major academic conference on 10 November, an evening ecumenical worship service in the city's cathedral, and a special exhibition in the University's library.[170] In Britain, a new film, *Martin Luther, Heretic*, was released on 8 November, just two days before Luther's actual birthday.

While different in tone than 1883, Luther's birthday was widely marked in the United States in 1983. A pluralism of viewpoints, critiques of past abuses, and displays of new methodologies characterized the academic conferences, sponsored by organizations such as the Sixteenth Century Studies Conference, the American Society of Church History, and the American Society of Reformation Research. A major conference was held between 31 May and 4 June at Concordia Seminary in St Louis, the seat of the Missouri Synod. The evangelical Wheaton College held a "Lutherfest" throughout the fall semester of 1983 with a host of activities, lectures, and worship services. Major research universities such as the University of Michigan also got into the act, holding a conference between 26 and 29 September. Countless speakers contributed to these conferences, but some usual suspects such Lewis Spitz (Stanford), Jaroslav Pelikan (Yale), Steven Ozment (Harvard), and Heiko A. Obermann (flown in often from Tübingen) regularly appeared in the roster of speakers. Creativity often accompanied academic rigor; at the University of Michigan, for instance, an English version of the sixteenth-century Protestant satirical play, "The Indulgence Peddler" (*Der Ablasskrämer*) was staged to well-attended audiences.[171]

Publications on Luther and the Reformation abounded. A number of journals devoted whole issues to mark the centenary year; others ran lengthy, single articles. An array of new publications appeared alongside translations of well-regarded books from European languages. *National Geographic Magazine* commissioned a major essay, "The World of Martin Luther," which appeared in its October issue.[172] Prominent news venues such as the *New York Times* covered events and added their own commentary. "By the time the year is over," one journalist wryly observed, "Martin Luther will have had an extraordinary birthday. He has been feted, lauded, and celebrated, and his writings and life have been pored over."[173]

Much attention in 1983 focused on a series of events held the first week in November in Washington, DC, where earlier the United States Postal Service had issued a stamp with Luther's picture (Figure 4.7). Supported by the Lutheran Council in the USA, the Folger Shakespeare Library, and the University of Maryland, several days of festivities included academic lectures and discussions, musical performances, artwork, and exhibitions. A play written for the occasion brought figures from the sixteenth century, such as Luther and Calvin, into conversation with twentieth-century figures such as Martin Luther King Jr. The Folger Shakespeare Library put on a special exhibition of its considerable collection of Luther memorabilia.[174] For many, the highlight was an ecumenical worship service that took place in the (Catholic) Basilica of the National Shrine of the Immaculate Conception. One journalist summed up the service: "Many in the overflow congregation of 2,500 noted with awe that the event symbolized ecumenical progress in a stunning way".[175]

Indeed, 1983 was an auspicious year for Lutheran–Catholic relations and for the cause of Christian unity more generally. While not without their detractors, the ecumenical seeds sown at the Second Vatican Council, germinating in the jubilee of 1967, developed considerably in 1983. Three aspects of this anniversary year concerning ecumenism merit highlighting.

First, 1983 witnessed the ongoing softening of the image of Luther among Catholic scholars. Building on the work of past figures such as Augustin Bea and the Dominican ecumenist Yves Congar, Catholic authors, sometimes collaborating with Protestants, published a spate of irenic articles and books just before, during, or after 1983 in an

Figure 4.7. US commemorative stamp of Luther (1983). Artist: Lucas Cranach the Elder.

effort to re-evaluate Luther.[176] Lutheran and other Protestant creedal documents also received new Catholic attention. The German scholar Martin Brecht published *Martin Luther: Sein Weg zur Reformation* and the American Jesuit Jared Wicks published *Luther and his Spiritual Legacy* (1983); both works received considerable attention. Peter Manns and Harding Meyer's edited volume, *Luther's Ecumenical Significance*, also deserves mention—the work grew out of an international ecumenical conference at the (Lutheran) Institute for Ecumenical Research in Strasbourg, France. George H. Tavard (Catholic) and Mark Edwards (Lutheran) published *Luther: Reformer for the*

Churches—An Ecumenical Study Guide (1983) in an effort to portray Luther as a reformer who could be embraced by both Catholics and Protestants. Many similar works could be mentioned. "One of the more intriguing aspects of [1983] . . . ," as Kenneth Strand observed, "[was] the effort to see Luther as an 'ecumenical person' . . . to be claimed, in a certain sense, by Catholics as well as Protestants."[177]

Second, in May 1983, the Lutheran–Catholic Dialogue Commission, which had met regularly since the 1960s, published a joint statement titled *Martin Luther: Witness to Truth*. While recognizing that "historical events cannot be reversed or undone," the document extolled numerous areas of Luther's theological legacy that could and should be embraced by both Catholics and Protestants, many of which were realized on the Catholic side at the Second Vatican Council. "The 500th anniversary of the birth of Martin Luther" provided the right occasion to look back and see that recent decades had "paved the way toward a more positive Catholic attitude to Luther. We see on both sides a lessening of outdated, polemically colored images of Luther. He is beginning to be honored in common as a witness to the Gospel, a teacher in the faith and herald of spiritual renewal."[178]

Finally, Pope John Paul II threw the dignity of his high office—once denounced as the very seat of Anti-Christ by Luther—behind the ecumenical cause. In a letter (dated 31 October 1983, no less) addressed to Cardinal Johannes Willebrands, president of the Pontifical Council for Promoting Christian Unity, the Pope recognized Luther's "great impact on history" and noted with gratitude that numerous Protestant churches had declared the anniversary year an occasion to promote "a genuine ecumenical spirit." The Pope called for ongoing research "that does not take sides, motivated only by the search for truth," in order to provide a "true image" of Luther and the Reformation, adding that "guilt, wherever it exists, must be recognized on whichever side it is found." The Pope concluded by saying that the anniversary provided "an occasion to meditate, in Christian truth and charity, on that event engraved in history that was the epoch of the Reformation." Actions followed words: on 11 December 1983 the Pope made a historic visit (the first ever by the Roman Pontiff) to the Lutheran Church in Rome.[179] "From afar," he told the congregants, "there seems to arise like a dawn on the 500th anniversary of the birth of Martin Luther, the advent of a restoration of our unity and community."[180]

The net effect of these developments, alongside others, played no small role in making conceivable two subsequent ones: John Paul II's 1995 encyclical on ecumenism *Ut unum sint* ("that they all may be one," John 17: 21), in which he proclaimed the Catholic Church's "irreversible" commitment to the ecumenical enterprise, and the Lutheran–Catholic Dialogue Commission's epochal *Joint Declaration on the Doctrine of Justification* (1999), which affirmed Catholic–Lutheran agreement on the central doctrinal controversy of the sixteenth century. While the latter did not necessarily mean that the "Reformation was over," as some in the media hyperbolically proclaimed, and although both documents were then and remain now not without thoughtful critics, they nonetheless represent a sea change in attitude when compared to past polemics—say, in 1617 or 1717 or, for that matter, 1817 or 1917.

They merit more reflection and discussion in 2017 and beyond.

Notes

1. See William H. Swatos and Lutz Kaelber (eds), *The Protestant Ethics Turns 100: Essays on the Centenary of the Weber Thesis* (Boulder, CO: Paradigm Publishers, 2005).
2. See Ernst Troeltsch, *Die Bedeutung des Protestantismus für die Entstehung der modernen Welt* (Munich: R. Oldenbourg, 1906) and *Die Soziallehre der christlichen Kirchen und Gruppen, Gesammelte Schriften* 6 (Tübingen: J. C. B. Mohr, 1912). Cf. Klaus Penzel, "Ernst Troeltsch on Luther," in J. Pelikan (ed.), *Interpreters of the Reformer* (Philadelphia: Fortress Press, 1968), 275–303.
3. A. G. Dickens and John Tonkin, *The Reformation in Historical Thought* (Cambridge, MA: Harvard University Press, 1985), 202–3, 265–9. Cf. Johannes Wallmann, "Karl Holl und seine Schule," *Zeitschrift für Theologie und Kirche,* 4 (1978): 1–33. For an overview of early twentieth-century interpretations of the Reformation, see Thomas McNeill, "The Interpretation of Protestantism during the Past Quarter-Century," *Journal of Religion,* 6 (1926): 504–25.
4. Daniel Buscarlet, *International Monument of the Reformation* (Geneva: Éditions l'Eau Vive, 1966).
5. On this theme in World War I, see Doris Bergen (ed.), *The Sword of the Lord: Military Chaplains from the First to the Twenty-First Century* (Notre Dame, IN: Notre Dame University Press, 2004), 200–21. On comparisons and contrasts with the American Civil War, see Mark A. Noll, *The Civil War as a Theological Crisis* (Chapel Hill, NC: University of North Carolina Press, 2006).
6. Wolfgang Flügel, "'Ein feste Burg ist unser Gott': Luther im Weltkrieg des Reformationsjubiläum 1917," *Dresdner Hefte,* 1919 (2014): 60.

7. Martin Greschat, "Reformationsjubiläum 1917: Exempel einer fragwürdigen Symbiose von Politik und Theologie," *Wissenschaft und Praxis in Kirche und Gesellschaft*, 61 (1972): 420–1.

8. Philip Jenkins, *The Great and Holy War: How World War I Became a Religious Crusade* (New York: HarperOne, 2014), 175.

9. Stan Landry, *Ecumenism, Memory, and German Nationalism* (Syracuse, NY: Syracuse University Press, 2014), 102–12. The Jesuit Hartmann Grisar noted that German Catholics observed a "dignified reticence" in the face of 1917 commemorations, motivated in part from a desire to serve "the interest of peace during wartime." Grisar, "Die Literatur des Lutherjubiläums 1917: Ein Bild des heutigen Protestantismus," *Zeitschrift für katholische Theologie*, 42 (1918): 810.

10. A much grander, national event at Wittenberg, however, had been cancelled; it had been planned since 1914. See Silvio Reichelt, *Der Erlebnisraum Wittenberg: Genese, Entwicklung und Bestand eines protestantischen Erinnerungsortes* (Göttingen: Vandenhoeck & Ruprecht, 2013), 117–21. Cf. *Die Reformationsfeier zu Wittenberg 1917* (Wittenberg: Max Senf, 1918).

11. Quoted in Greschat, "Reformationsjubiläumjahr 1917," 421–3. On the large literature from 1917, see Gottfried Maron, "Luther 1917: Beobachtungen zur Literatur des 400. Reformationsjubiläums," *Zeitschrift für Kirchengeschichte*, 93 (1982): 177–221.

12. Tim Klein, *Luther: Deutsche Briefe, Schriften, Lieder, Tischreden* (Munich: Langewiesche-Brandt, 1917), 6.

13. Paul Conrad, *Die Reformation und das deutsche Volk: Festschrift zur Jahrhundertfeier der Reformation* (Berlin: E. S. Mittler & Sohn, 1917), 3.

14. Friedrich Andersen et al., *Deutschchristentum auf rein-evangelischer Grundlage: 95 Lehrsätze zum Reformationsfest* (Leipzig: Theodor Weicher, 1917), 6.

15. Susannah Heschel, *The Aryan Jesus: Christian Theologians and the Bible in Nazi Germany* (Princeton: Princeton University Press, 2008), 45.

16. Fritz K. Ringer, *The Decline of the German Mandarins: The German Academic Community, 1890–1933* (Cambridge, MA: Harvard University Press, 1969), 180.

17. Erich Brandenburg, *Martin Luther als Vorkämpfer deutschen Geistes: eine Rede zur 400-jährigen Jubelfeier der Reformation* (Leipzig, 1917), 6.

18. Quoted in Ruth Kastner, "The Reformer and Reformation Anniversaries," *History Today*, 33 (1983): 24.

19. Jürgen von Ungern-Sternberg and Wolfgang von Ungern-Sternberg, *Der Aufruf "an die Kulturwelt": Das Manifest der 93 und die Anfänge der Kriegspropaganda im Ersten Weltkrieg* (Stuttgart: Franz Steiner Verlag, 1996), 145–7, and Karl Hammer, "Adolf von Harnack und der erste Weltkrieg," *Zeitschrift für evangelische Ethik*, 16 (1972): 85–101.

20. On Harnack's involvement in the war's initial stages, see J. C. O'Neill, "Adolf von Harnack and the Entry of the German State into War, July–August 1914," *Scottish Journal of Theology*, 55 (2002): 1–18.

21. Adolf von Harnack, *Martin Luther und die Grundlegung der Reformation* (Berlin: Wiedmannsche Buchhandlung, 1917), 63–4.

22. Max Lenz, *Luther und der deutsche Geist: Rede zur Reformationsfeier 1917 in Hamburg* (Hamburg: Broschek, 1917), 31.

23. Greschat, "Reformationsjubiläumjahr 1917," 421.

24. Jenkins, *The Great and Holy War*, 176. There were a few—very few—exceptions to this line of thinking. One of them was the liberal theologian Martin Rade, editor of the Protestant weekly *Das Christliche Welt*. In 1917, Rade diverged conspicuously from the mainstream opinion of imperial Protestant triumphalism, arguing that "Luther's center of gravity lay not in his German manner, his German sensibility or his actions, but solely in his faith, in his Christianity." From *Das Christliche Welt*, 31 (1917) as cited in Heiko Oberman, "The Nationalist Conscription of Martin Luther," in Oberman (ed.), *The Impact of the Reformation: Essays* (Grand Rapids, MI: Eerdmans, 1994), 66–7. But Rade, Oberman notes, was "hardly . . . a representative voice." Cf. Günter Brakelmann, *Protestantische Kriegstheologie im Ersten Weltkrieg* (Bielefeld: Luther-Verlag, 1974) and Günter Brakelmann (ed.), *Der Deutsche Protestantismus im Epochenjahr 1917* (Wittenberg: Luther-Verlag, 1974) and Frank J. Gordon, "Liberal German Churchmen and the First World War," *German Studies Review*, 4 (1981): 39–62.

25. *Punch* (19 Apr. 1916); noted in Preserved Smith, "English Opinion of Luther," *Harvard Theological Review*, 2 (1917), 157. See also *The Horrors of Wittenberg: Official Report to the British Government* (London, 1916), as discussed in Heather Jones, *Violence against Prisoners: Britain, France, and Germany, 1914–1920* (Cambridge: CUP, 2011), 94–5, 405.

26. Stalker, *Luther Celebrations of 1917* (New York: George H. Doran, 1917), 15–16.

27. William Walker Rockwell, "Luther and the Catholic Church," in *Three Addresses Delivered in the Chapel of the Union Theological Seminary in the Commemoration of the Four Hundredth Anniversary of the Reformation* (New York, 1917), 9.

28. Frank Wakeley Gunsaulus, *Martin Luther and the Morning Hour in Europe: Two Lectures Delivered at the University of Chicago, October 16 and 17, 1917* (Chicago: University of Chicago Press, 1917), 45–6.

29. "What has Protestantism Accomplished," *Christian Century* (25 Oct. 1917): 5.

30. On anti-German sentiment in the US during the war, see Leslie V. Tischauser, *The Burden of Ethnicity: The German Question in Chicago, 1914–1941* (New York: Garland, 1990), 6–63.

31. Delk, as quoted in Hartmut Lehmann, *Martin Luther in the American Imagination* (Munich: Wilhelm Fink Verlag, 1988), 282.

32. Lehmann, *Martin Luther in the American Imagination*, 283.

33. Quoted material from Lehmann, *Martin Luther in the American Imagination*, 283.

34. Rose as quoted in Sarah K. Nytroe, "The American Reformation Quadricentennial, 1917," *Lutheran Quarterly*, 26 (2012): 73.

35. W. H. T. Dau, "Luther's Relation to Lutheranism and the American Lutheran Church," *American Journal of Theology*, 21 (Oct. 1917): 524, 526.

36. Nytroe, "The American Reformation Quadricentennial, 1917," 73. Scandinavian-American Lutherans were also eager to sever the relationship between Luther and Germany. See Enok Mortensen, *The Danish Lutheran Church in America: The History and Heritage of the American Evangelical Lutheran Church* (Philadelphia: Board of Publication, Lutheran Church in America, 1967), 172–84.

37. Arthur Cushman McGiffert, "Luther and the Unfinished Reformation," in *Three Addresses Delivered in the Chapel of the Union Theological Seminary*, 26.

38. Stalker, *Luther Celebrations of 1917*, 14–15. Cf. Adolf Keller, *Protestant Europe: Its Crisis and Outlook* (New York: George H. Doran, 1927).

39. On Protestant electoral support for National Socialism, see Slvia Wasmeier, *Wer wählte Hitler? Erklärungsansätze der historischen Wahlverhaltensforschung* (Wiesbaden: Drewipunkt, 2009).

40. On the "Glaubensbewegung Deutsche Christen," see Doris Bergen, *Twisted Cross: The German Christian Movement in the Third Reich* (Chapel Hill, NC: North Carolina Press, 1996).

41. Ibid. 1 and Siegfried Brauer, "Das Lutherjubiläum 1933 und die deutschen Universitäten," *Theologische Literaturzeitung*, 108 (1983): 641–62.

42. Quoted in Dean G. Stroud (ed.), *Preaching in Hitler's Shadow: Sermons of Resistance in the Third Reich* (Grand Rapids, MI: Eerdmans, 2013), 24.

43. Quoted at "Die Lutherfeier," at <http://www.emmaus.de/chronik/lutherfeier. html> (accessed May 2015). This so-called "Sport's Palace Affair" scandalized many, because Krause also vilified both the Apostle Paul and many aspects of Christianity for retaining unacceptable Jewish holdovers. See Doris Bergen, "Storm Troopers of Christ," in Robert P. Ericksen and Susannah Heschel (eds), *Betrayal: German Churches and the Holocaust* (Minneapolis: Augsburg Fortress Publishers, 1999), 43–4. For the Nazi response, see Georg Kretschmar (ed.), *Dokumente zur Kirchenpolitik des Dritten Reiches: Das Jahr 1933*, i (Munich: Chr. Kaiser Verlag, 1971), 170–5.

44. Karl Barth, *Lutherfeier 1933* (Munich: C. Kaiser, 1933), 18. Cf. Hartmut Lehmann, *Luthergedächtnis, 1817 bis 2017* (Göttingen: Vandenhoeck & Ruprecht, 2012), 138–75, and Stroud, *Preaching in Hitler's Shadow*, 24–5.

45. Quoted in Stroud, *Preaching in Hitler's Shadow*, 25. For a fuller treatment of the uses and abuses of Luther by churchmen during the Nazi years, see Christopher J. Probst, *Demonizing the Jews: Luther and the Protestant Church in Nazi Germany* (Bloomington, IN: Indiana University Press, 2012). On this period in Bonhoeffer's life, see Charles Marsh, *Strange Glory: A Life of Dieterich Bonhoeffer* (New York: Vintage, 2015), 162ff.

46. Hermann Werdermann, *Martin Luther und Adolf Hitler: Ein geschichtlicher Vergleich* (Gnadenfrei in Schlesien, 1935, 2nd edn 1937), 9, 12.

47. Alon Confino, *A World without Jews: The Nazi Imagination from Persecution to Genocide* (New Haven: Yale University Press, 2014), 146. The Institute was headquartered in Eisenach in a building provided rent-free by the Evangelical Church of Thuringia. On the operations of this institute, see Heschel, *Aryan Jesus*.

48. Martin Sasse, *Martin Luther und die Juden: Weg mi ihnen!* (Freiburg im Bresigau: Sturmhut Verlag, 1938), quoted in Raphael Gross, *1938. Die Katastrophe vor der Katastrophe* (Munich: C. H. Beck, 2013), 79.

49. For an overview of the uses of Luther during the Nazi period, see Lehmann, *Luthergedächtnis, 1817 bis 2017*, 138–75. For a response of American Lutherans (and other American Protestants) to "Luther Year 1933" in Germany, see Robert P. Ericksen, "The Luther Anniversary and the Year 1933 in the Mirror of U. S. Church Press Reports," *Kirchliche Zeitgeschichte*, 26 (2013): 319–34.

50. See Adolf Hitler, *The Speeches of Adolf Hitler, April 1922 to August, 1939*, i, ed., Norman H. Baynes (New York: H. Ferig, 1969), 440.

51. Alfred Rosenberg, *Protestantische Rompilger: Der Verrat an Luther und der Mythus des 20. Jahrhunderts* (Munich: Hoheneichen-Verlag, 1937), 17.

52. Quoted in Johannes Brosseder, *Luthers Stellung zu den Juden* (Munich: H. Hueber, 1972), 185.

53. Streicher's words at greater length from 29 Apr. 1946: "Anti-Semitic publications have existed in Germany for centuries. A book I had, written by Dr. Martin Luther, was, for example, confiscated. Dr. Martin Luther would very probably sit in my place in the defendants' dock today, if this book had been taken into consideration by the prosecution. In this book *The Jews and Their Lies*, Dr. Martin Luther writes that the Jews are a serpent's brood and one should burn down their synagogues and destroy them." See *Trial of the Major War Criminals before the International Military Tribunal, Nuremberg, 14 November 1945 to 1 October 1946* (Nuremberg: International Military Tribunal, 1947–9), xii. 318. Cf. Raul Hilberg, *The Destruction of the European Jews*, 3rd edn (New Haven: Yale University Press, 2003), 689–90; Oberman, "Nationalist Conscription of Luther," 71; and Hans Asmussen, "Muss Luther nach Nürnberg?" *Nordwestdeutsche Hefte*, 11 (1947): 31–7. It bears noting that in 1938 Kristallnacht took place on the night of 9 November and into 10 November, Luther's 455th birthday. See Sibylle Biermann-Rau, *An Luthers Geburtstag brannten die Synogogen* (Stuttgart: Calwer Verlag, 2012), 141ff.

54. William McGovern, *From Luther to Hitler: The History of Fascist-Nazi Philosophy* (Boston: Houghton Mifflin, 1941), 27–35.

55. Eddy as quoted in Lehmann, *Martin Luther in the American Imagination*, 295.

56. Peter F. Wiener, *Martin Luther: Hitler's Spiritual Ancestor* (London: Hutchinson & Co., 1945), 21. For an impassioned critique of Wiener, see Gordon Rupp, *Martin Luther: Hitler's Cause or Cure?* (London: Lutterworth Press, 1945).

57. Thomas Mann, *Politische Schriften und Reden*, iii (Frankfurt am Main: Fischer Bücherei, 1968), 166.

58. Eberhard Busch, *Karl Barth: His Life from Letters and Autobiographical Texts*, tr. John Bowden (Philadelphia: Fortress Press, 1976), 350. Cf. Jan Herman Brinks, "Luther and the German State," *Heythrop Journal*, 39 (1998): 1ff.; Donald D. Wall, "Karl Barth and National Socialism, 1921–1946," *Fides et Historia*, 15 (1983): 80–95; and Arne Ramusson, "'Deprive them of their Pathos': Karl Barth and the Nazi Revolution Revisited," *Modern Theology*, 23 (2007): 369–71.

59. Lehmann, *Luthergedächtnis, 1817–2017*, 176ff. It is indisputable that some theologians who supported Hitler cited Luther's anti-Semitism as a rationale for their own. See Heschel, *Aryan Jesus*, 144–5.

60. Peter Meinhold, *Martin Luther: Der Mann und das Werk: Rede zum vierhundertjährigen Todestag Martin Luthers gehalten bei der Gedächtnisfeier der Universität Kiel am 18. Februar 1946* (Hamburg: Nölke, 1946), 7, 23. Cf. Theodor Brandt, *Zwei Vorträge im Lutherjahr 1946* (Bad Salzuflen: MBK-Verlag, 1946). Turning to Luther, according to Brandt, was an important aspect of "the reconstruction of our nation" and bulwark against "Anti-Christianity [i.e. the USSR] that threatens us from the East" and from "worldliness that seeks to flood us from the West" (8, 16).

61. See *Luther Speaks: Essays for the Fourth Centenary of Martin Luther's Death Written by a Group of Lutheran Ministers from North and Central Europe at Present in Great Britain*, with a foreword by the Bishop of Oslo (London: Lutterworth, 1947), 5–7, 12–13. American Lutherans, especially those of German descent, often adopted a similar line of argument. See Lehmann, *Martin Luther in the American Imagination*, 292–3.
62. William Shirer, *The Rise and Fall of the Third Reich: A History of Nazi Germany* (New York: Simon & Schuster, 1960), 1080.
63. Ibid. 95.
64. "Books of the Times," *New York Times* (17 Oct. 1969): 27. On the reception of Shirer's work, see Martin Broszat, "William Shirer und die Geschichte des Dritten Reiches," *Historische Zeitschrift*, 196 (1963): 112–23, and Gavriel D. Rosenfeld, "The Reception of William L. Shirer's *The Rise and Fall of the Third Reich* in the United States and West Germany, 1960–62," *Journal of Contemporary History*, 29 (Jan. 1994): 95–128. For a more recent critical evaluation of the book and of the "Luther to Hitler" canard in general, see Uwe Siemon-Netto, *The Fabricated Luther: Refuting Nazi Connections and Other Modern Myths*, 2nd edn (St Louis, MO: Concordia, 2007), 21–41, passim. Cf. Peter Clarkson Matheson, "Luther and Hitler: A Controversy Reviewed," *Journal of Ecumenical Studies*, 17 (1980): 445–53.
65. On the important role of émigré historians shaping post-war German historiography, see Hartmut Lehmann and James Sheehan (eds), *German-Speaking Refugee Historians in the United States After 1933* (Washington, DC: German Historical Institute; Cambridge: CUP, 1991).
66. Fritz Fischer, "Die Auswirkungen der Reformation auf das deutsche und westeuropäisch-amerikanische politische Leben," in Fischer (ed.), *Der Erste Weltkrieg und das deutsche Geschichtsbild: Beiträge zur Bewältigung eines historischens Tabus: Aufsätze und Vorträge aus drei Jahzehnten* (Düsseldorf: Droste Verlag, 1977), 38, 41. Also see his essay in the same volume titled "Der deutsche Protestantismus und die Politik im 19. Jahrhundert."
67. Holborn, *A History of Modern Germany, 1840–1945* (Princeton: Princeton University Press, 1969), 374, 739–40. For a brief overview of the "Sonderweg debate," see Jürgen Kocka, "German History Before Hitler: The Debate about the German Sonderweg," *Journal of Contemporary History*, 23 (1988): 3–16.
68. Leonard Krieger, *The German Conception of Liberty* (Boston: Beacon Hill, 1957), 61.
69. David Blackbourn and Geoff Eley, *The Peculiarities of German History* (Oxford: OUP, 1984).
70. Edward Idris Cassidy, *Ecumenism and Interreligious Dialogue: Unitatis redintegratio, Nostra aetate* (New York: Paulist Press, 2005), 3ff. Mauro Velati, "Il secolo dell'ecumenismo cristiano," *Christianesimo nella Storia*, 22 (2001): 605–31.
71. On the broad background of what follows, see Owen Chadwick, *The Christian Church in the Cold War* (New York: Penguin Books, 1992) and Tony Judt, *Postwar: A History of Europe since 1945* (New York: Penguin, 2005).
72. Hermann Weber, *Die DDR, 1945–1990* (Munich: Oldenbourg Wissenschaftsverlag, 1993), 100.
73. The post-war Protestant Church of Germany (EKD) was created in 1948. Because of the politics of estrangement (*Abgrenzungspolitik*) of the GDR, the churches of East

and West were essentially separated but not formally disconnected at the time of the 1967 jubilee. The official break came in 1969. On the history of the EKD from the post-war era through the Fall of the Wall and Reunification, see Claudia Lepp and Kurt Novak (eds), *Evangelische Kirche im geteilten Deutschland, 1945–1989/90* (Göttingen: Vandenhoeck & Ruprecht, 2001).

74. David Bender, "East Germans Limit their Luther Observance," *New York Times* (29 Oct. 1967).

75. On Anti-Fascism generally, see Robert Erlinghagen, *Die Diskussion um den Begriff des Antifaschismus seit 1989/90* (Berlin, Argument, 1997). On the early years of the GDR, see Mary Fulbrook, *The People's State: East German Society from Hitler to Honecker* (New Haven: Yale University Press, 2005), 23–48. On early GDR historiography, see Ilko-Sascha Kowalczuk, *Legitimation eines neuen Staates. Parteiarbeiter an der historischen Front: Geschichtswissenschaftler in der SBZ/DDR, 1945–1961* (Berlin: Links, 1997).

76. Wolfram von Hanstein, *Von Luther bis Hitler* (Dresden: Voco Verlag, 1947).

77. Alexander Abusch, *Der Irrweg einer Nation* (Berlin: Aufbau-Verlag, 1946).

78. See Stephen P. Hoffmann, "The GDR, Luther, and the German Question," *Review of Politics*, 48 (1986): 250ff.

79. Mary Fulbrook, *Anatomy of a Dictatorship: Inside the GDR, 1949–1989* (Oxford: OUP, 1995), 22–30.

80. Lothar Kettenacker, *Germany since 1945* (Oxford: OUP, 1997), 37ff.

81. Siegfried Bräuer, *Martin Luther in marxistischer Sicht von 1945 bis zum Beginn der achtziger Jahre* (Berlin: Evangelische Verlagsanstalt, 1983), 4–12.

82. Heinrich Bornkamm, *Luther im Spiegel der deutschen Geistesgeschichte: Mit ausgewählten Texten von Lessing bis zur Gegenwart* (Heidelberg: Quelle & Meyer, 1955), 176–8.

83. Thomas Meusel, *Thomas Müntzer und seine Zeit* (Berlin: Aufbau Verlag, 1952), 41. Cf. Lehmann, *Luthergedächtnis 1817 bis 2017*, 273; Bornkamm, *Luther im Spiegel der deutschen Geistesgeschichte*, 176; and Gerhard Brendler, *Die frühbürgerliche Revolution in Deutschland: Referat und Diskussion zum Thema Probleme der frühbürgerliche Revolution in Deutschland* (Berlin: Akademie-Verlag, 1961).

84. See Engels, *The Peasant War in Germany*, in Leonard Krieger (ed.), *The German Revolutions* (Chicago: Chicago University Press, 1967), 33ff. Cf. Lehmann, *Luthergedächtnis 1817 bis 2017*, 272.

85. Cf. e.g. Karl Kautsky, *Vorläufer des Neueren Sozialismus II: Der Kommunismus in der Deutschen Reformation* (Berlin: Dietz, 1947) and Ernst Bloch, *Thomas Müntzer als Theologe der Revolution* (Frankfurt a.M.: Suhrkamp, 1969).

86. Gordon R. Mork, "Martin Luther's Left Turn: The Changing Picture of Luther in East German Historiography," *History Teacher*, 16 (1983): 586.

87. M. M. Smirin, *Die Volksreformation des Thomas Müntzer und der grosse Bauernkrieg*, tr. Hans Nichtweiss (Berlin, 1952; 2nd edn 1956).

88. Meusel, *Thomas Müntzer und seine Zeit* (Berlin: Aufbau-Verlag, 1952), 118.

89. Leo Stern; quoted in Mork, "Martin Luther's Left Turn," 586.

90. Gunnar Berg and Hans-Hermann Hartwich (eds), *Martin-Luther Universität von der Gründung bis zur Neugestaltung nach zwei Diktaturen* (Opladen: Leske & Budrich, 1994), 400–1.

91. On history and school textbooks, see John Rodden, *Textbook Reds: Schoolbooks, Ideology, and Eastern German Identity* (University Park, PA: Penn State University Press, 2006), 119–20; Douglas C. Stange, "A Marxist De-Lutheranization of the German Reformation," *Concordia Theological Monthly*, 38 (1967): 598; and Angela Broch, "Producing the 'Socialist Personality'? Socialisation, Education, and the Emergence of New Patterns of Behavior," in Mary Fulbrook (ed.), *Power and Society in the GDR, 1961–1979: The "Normalisation of Rule"?* (New York: Berghahn Books, 2009), 220–52.

92. Robert Walinski-Kiehl, "History, Politics, and East German Film: The Thomas Müntzer (1956) Socialist Epic," *Central European History*, 39 (2006): 30–55.

93. Lehmann, *Luthergedächtnis 1817 bis 2017*, 274 and Johanna Sänger, "Geduldet und geehrt: Martin Luther und Thomas Müntzer in Straßen- und Ehrennamen der DDR," in Jan Scheunemann (ed.), *Reformation und Bauerkrieg: Erinnerungskultur und Geschichtspolitik im geteilten Deutschland* (Leipzig: Evangelische Verlagsanstalt, 2010), 87–100.

94. Eckhart Gillen, "Werner Tübke's Apocalyptic Panorama in Bad Frankenhausen and the End of the German Democratic Republic," *Getty Research Journal*, 3 (2011): 99–116.

95. Mork, "Martin Luther's Left Turn," 588. Cf. Walter Elliger, "Zum Thema Luther und Thomas Müntzer," *Luther Jahrbuch*, 34 (1967): 90–116.

96. Gerhard Ringshausen, "Das 450. Reformationsjubiläum 1967 in West und Ost," *Kirchliche Zeitsgeschichte*, 26 (2013): 383 and Frédéric Hartweg (ed.), *SED und Kirche: Eine Dokumentation ihrer Beziehungen*, i (Neukirchen-Vlyun: Neukirchener, 1995), 277ff.

97. Brendler, "Reformation und Forschritt" and Brendler, "Frühbürgerliche Revolution und Tradition," in Leo Stern and Max Steinmetz (eds), *450 Jahre Reformation* (Berlin: Deutscher Verlag der Wissenschaften, 1967), 67, 184. Cf. the biography by Gerhard Zschäbitz, *Martin Luther: Grösse und Grenze* (Berlin: Verlag der Wissenschaften, 1967).

98. Wolfgang Flügel, "Konkurrenz um Reformation und Luther: Die Konfessionjubiläen der Kirchen und der SED in den Jahren 1967 und 1983," in Klaus Tanner and Jörg Ulrich (eds), *Spurenlese: Reformationsvergegenwärtigung als Standortbestimmung, 1717–1983* (Leipzig: Evangelische Verlagsanstalt, 2012), 246ff.

99. Flügel, "Konkurrenz um Reformation und Luther," 248, and Peter Maser, "*Mit Luther alles in Butter?*": *Das Lutherjahr 1983 im Spiegel ausgewählter Akten* (Berlin: Metropol Verlag, 2013), 50–4.

100. Martin Roy, *Luther in der DDR: Zum Wandel des Lutherbildes in der DDR-Geschichtsschreibung: Mit einer dokumentarischen Reproduktion* (Bochum: Verlag Dieter Winkler, 2000), 311–16. 1967 was also the 150th anniversary of the merged university of Halle-Wittenberg. See Joachim Dietz (ed.), *Hallesche Universitäts-Festage 1967: Festwoche anläßlich des 150. Jahrestages der Vereinigung der Universitäten Halle und Wittenberg, 1817–1967: Bericht-Reden-Ansprachen* (Halle, 1967).

101. Flügel, "Konkurrenz um Reformation und Luther," 255.

102. "Church Bells Vie with Red Flags," *The Times* (31 Oct. 1967): 5, and Max L. Baeumer, "Lutherfeiern und ihre politische Manipulation," in Reinhold

Grimm and Jost Hermand (eds), *Deutsche Feiern* (Wiesbaden: Akademische Verlagsgesellschaft Athenaion, 1977), 59–60.

103. Gerald Götting, "450 Jahre Reformation," in Stern and Steinmetz, *450 Jahre Reformation*, 11.

104. Max Steinmetz and Gerhard Brendler (eds), *Weltwirkung der Reformation: Internationales Symposium anläßlich der 450-Jahr-Feier der Reformation in Wittenberg vom 24. Bis 26. Oktober 1967* (Berlin: Deutscher Verlag der Wissenschaften, 1969).

105. See Steinmetz's "Schlusswort" (epilogue) in *Weltwirkung der Reformation*, 496.

106. Gerhard Ringhausen, "Das 450. Reformationsjubiläum in West und Ost," *Kirchliche Zeitgeschichte*, 26 (2013): 383, and Robert F. Groeckel, "The Luther Anniversary in East Germany," *World Politics*, 37 (1984): 117.

107. "Interchurch Services Raise Doubts," *The Times* (26 Oct. 1867).

108. Ringhausen, "Das 450. Reformationsjubiläum in West und Ost," 384.

109. Judt, *Postwar*, 496–500, 526, 570, and Fulbrook, *People's State*, 2, 37–8, 82, 242, 278.

110. Hartweg, *SED und Kirche*, 99–101 and Chadwick, *Church in the Cold War*, 43–5.

111. On the broader historical context of 1983, see Peter Maser, *"Mit Luther alles in Butter?,"* 25–77.

112. Rudolf Mau, "Luthers 500. Geburtstag: Feiern ohne zu Rühmen: Beobachtungen zum Lutherjubiläum 1983 in der DDR," *Theologische Literaturzeitung*, 138 (Oct. 2013): 1047, and Irmgard Lent, "Kirchentage in der DDR im Lutherjahr 1983," *Kirchliches Jahrbuc,h* 110 (1983): 179–93.

113. Planning memoranda and other documents are located in the Akten des Zentralinstituts für Geschichte der Wissenschaften der DDR, now in the Archives of the Berlin-Brandenburgischen Akademie der Wissenschaften, Bestand ZIG 709, 1–4. Many of these documents were published in *Martin Luther und unsere Zeit: Konstituierung des Martin-Luthers-Komitees der DDR am 13 Juni 1980 in Berlin* (Berlin, 1980).

114. The speech of Honecker's was published as "In der DDR wird die historische Leistung Martin Luthers bewahrt," *Zeitschrift für Geschichtswissenschaft*, 10 (1980): 927–8. On the international reaction to this revised view of Luther, see Elizabeth Pond, "Martin Luther Lauded by East Germany," *Christian Science Monitor* (17 June 1980).

115. Horst Bartel et al., "Thesen über Martin Luther. Zum 500. Geburtstag," *Zeitschrift für Geschichtswissenschaft*, 11 (1982): 879ff.

116. See Stewart Anderson, "Martin Luther in Primetime: Television Fiction and Cultural Memory Construction in Cold War Germany," *View: Journal of European Television, History, and Culture*, 3 (2012): 22–6, and Host Dähn and Joachim Heise, *Luther und die DDR: Der Reformator und das DDR Fernsehen 1983* (Berlin: Edition Ost, 1996), 104ff.

117. For more context on this, see David E. Marshall, *Das Museum für deutsche Geschichte: A Study of the Presentation of History in the Former German Democratic Republic* (New York: Peter Lang, 2010).

118. *Luther, 1483–1983* (Martin Luther Ehrung 1983 der Deutschen Demokratischen Republik, 1983). The book is multilingual. I use here the English renderings provided.

119. Quoted without attribution in Groeckel, "Luther Anniversary in East Germany," 121.

120. "Gott über alle Dinge fürchten, lieben, und vertrauen" is taken from Luther's Smaller Catechism. In the public relations and at the actual Kirchentage, sometimes the theme was expressed as "Vertrauen wagen" (Wager on Trust) On the church celebrations of 1983, see *Gott über alle Dinge: Begegnungen mit Martin Luther 1983* (Berlin: Evangelische Verlagsanstalt, 1984); "Kurzberichte über die 7 Kirchentage," *Glaube und Heimat*, 21 (1981): 183–93; and Maser, *"Mit Luther alles in Butter?,"* 338–87.

121. John Moses, "The Church's Role in the Collapse of Communism in East Germany, 1989–1990," *Colloquium*, 23 (1991): 122–34. Cf. Richard Crouter and Barbara Crouter, "Traveling with Luther and Marx: On and Off the Luther Trail in the GDR," *Dialog*, 23 (1984): 218–22.

122. Quoted without attribution in Groeckel, "Luther Anniversary in East Germany," 118.

123. "Obedient Rebel," *Time*, 89/12 (1967): 90–8.

124. Erwin Iserloh, "Luthers Thesenanschlag—Tatsache oder Legende?" *Trierer Theologische Zeitschrift*, 70 (1961): 303–12, and *Luther zwischen Reform und Reformation: der Thesenanschlag fand nicht statt* (Münster: Aschendorff, 1962).

125. On the establishment of the Lutheran World Federation, see Eric W. Gritsch, *A History of Lutheranism*, 2nd edn (Minneapolis: Fortress Press, 2010), 230–4, 243, 257.

126. *Proceedings of the Fourth Assembly of the Lutheran World Federation, Helsinki, July 30–August 11, 1963* (Berlin: Lutherisches Verlagshaus, 1965).

127. Franz Lau, "Die gegenwärtige Diskussion um Luthers Thesenanschlag," *Luther-Jahrbuch*, 34 (1967): 11–59.

128. Martin E. Marty, "Never the Same Again: Post-Vatican II Catholic–Protestant Interactions," *Sociological Analysis*, 52 (1991): 13–26, and Mark A. Noll and Carol Nystrom, *Is the Reformation over?* (Grand Rapids, MI: Baker Academic, 2005), 60–3.

129. *Mortalium animos*: On Religious Unity: Encyclical of Pius XI, 6 Jan. 1928; see Claudia Carlen (ed.), *The Papal Encyclicals, 1903–1939*, iii (Raleigh, NC: Pieran Press, 1990), 313–19.

130. On its founding, see Jerome-Michael Vereb, *"Because he was a German": Cardinal Bea and the Origins of the Roman Catholic Engagement with the Ecumenical Movement* (Grand Rapids, MI: Eerdmans, 2006), 3–4, 19, passim.

131. On the importance of the decision to invite non-Catholic observers, see Giuseppe Alberigo (ed.), *History of Vatican II*, i. *Announcing and Preparing Vatican Council II: Toward a New Era in Catholicism* [English version ed. Joseph A. Komonchak] (Maryknoll, NY: Orbis, 1995), 318–26, and Yves Congar, "Le Rôle des 'Observateurs' dans l'avancée oecuménique," in *Le Concile Vatican II: Son Eglise, Peuple de Dieu et Corps du Christ* (Paris: Beauchesne, 1984), 90–8. For an account of a non-Catholic observer, see John Moorman (Anglican Bishop of Ripon), *Vatican Observed: An Anglican Impression of Vatican II* (London: Darton, Longman & Todd, 1967).

132. Austin Flannery (ed.), *Vatican Council II*, i. *The Conciliar and Post-Conciliar Documents*, rev. edn (Northport, NY: Costello Publishing Co., 1975), 455 (emphasis added).

133. Flannery, *Vatican Council II*, i. 357 (emphasis added).

134. John O'Malley, *What Happened at Vatican II* (Cambridge, MA: Belknap Press of Harvard University Press, 2008), 7, 162–4, 194–8, passim.

135. Flügel, "Konkurrenz um Reformation und Luther," 254.

136. See Johannes Cardinal Willebrands, "Reformation und Reform heute," in Willebrands (ed.), *Mandatum unitatis: Beiträge zur Ökumene* (Paderborn: Bonifatius, 1989), 29.

137. Quoted in Ringshausen, "Das 450. Reformationsjubiläum 1967 in West und Ost," 380.

138. For instance, Erik H. Erikson's much-discussed *Young Man Luther: A Study in Psychoanalysis and History* (New York: Norton, 1958) had appeared in 1958. For historiographical shifts in the post-war period, see Lewis Spitz, "The State of Reformation Research," *Concordia Journal*, 4 (1978): 6–15, and Christoph Burger, "Theologiegeschichtliche Darstellungen zur Reformation seit dem Zweiten Weltkrieg," *Archiv für Reformationsgeschichte*, 100 (2009): 326–49.

139. Heinz Zahrnt, "Was its geblieben von Martin Luther?" *Die Zeit* (27 Oct. 1967).

140. Phillip Benedict, "What is Post-Confessional History," *Archiv für Reformationsgeschichte*, 97 (2006): 277ff.

141. A more positive Catholic view of Luther had been developing well prior to Vatican II. See Franz-Peter Sonntag, "Luther in katholischer Sicht," in Alfons Skowronek (ed.), *Martin Luther in ökumenischer Reflexion* (Warsaw: Akademia Teologii Katholickiej, 1984), 178–90.

142. Jos E. Vercruysse, "Katholische Lutherforschung im 20. Jahrhundert," in Rainer Vinke (ed.), *Lutherforschung im 20. Jahrhundert: Rückblick, Bilanz, Ausblick* (Mainz: Verlag Philipp von Zabern, 2004), 191–212.

143. Robert E. McNally, "The Ninety-Five Theses of Martin Luther, 1517–1967," *Theological Studies*, 28 (1967): 480. Cf. Yves Congar, "Church Reform and Luther's Reformation, 1517–1967," *Lutheran World*, 14 (1967): 351–9.

144. Pesch, as quoted in Johann Heinz, "Martin Luther and his Theology in German Catholic Interpretation Before and After Vatican II," *Andrews University Seminary Studies*, 26 (1988): 261.

145. Quoted in Ringshausen, "Das 450. Reformationsjubiläum in West und Ost," 379.

146. Earlier, unofficial meetings preceded the one in 1967. On these, see John A. Radano, *Lutheran and Catholic Reconciliation on Justification: A Chronology of the Holy See's Contributions, 1961–1999, to a New Relationship between Lutherans and Catholics and to Steps Leading to the Joint Declaration on the Doctrine of Justification* (Grand Rapids, MI: Eerdmans, 2009), 16ff.

147. See the "The Gospel and the Church: The Malta Report" (1972) at <http://www.prounione.urbe.it/dia-int/l-rc/doc/e_l-rc_malta.htmlMalta> (accessed June 2014).

148. Letter of Richard Baepler to Theodore Schwan (27 Mar. 1967), Papers of the Committee on the Observance of the 450th Anniversary of the Reformation in 1967, Box 275, Valparaiso University Archives.

149. John J. McDonnell, *The World Council of Churches and the Catholic Church* (New York: Edwin Mellen Press, 1985), 197ff.

150. See Secretariat for Promoting Christian Unity, *Directory for the Applications of the Decisions of the Second Ecumenical Council of the Vatican Concerning Ecumenical Matters* (Washington, DC: United States Catholic Conference, 1967).

151. Edward B. Fiske, "The Reformation Gets Reappraisal," *New York Times* (22 Oct. 1967).

152. See Edward A. Dowey, *A Commentary on the Confession of 1967 and an Introduction to the Book of Confessions* (Philadelphia: Westminster Press, 1968) and, for a more critical response, Cornelius van Til, *The Confession of 1967: Its Theological Background and Ecumenical Significance* (Philadelphia: Presbyterian and Reformed Publishing Co., 1967).

153. "Princeton Marks Reformation at Catholic–Lutheran Service," *New York Times* (6 Nov. 1967).

154. John H. Tietjen, "The Abiding Validity of the Reformation," in Heino O. Kadai (ed.), *Accents in Luther's Theology: Essays in Commemoration of the 450th Anniversary of the Reformation* (St Louis, MO: Concordia Publishing House, 1967), 41.

155. John McGreevy, *Catholicism and American Freedom: A History* (New York: W. W. Norton, 2003), 213–14. Cf. Richard Kim, "A Roman Catholic President in the American Scheme," *Journal of Church and State*, 3 (1961): 33–40.

156. Henry A. Buchanan and Bob W. Brown, "The Ecumenical Movement Threatens Protestantism," *Christianity Today* (20 Nov. 1964): 21–2, and Neil J. Young, "'A Saga of Sacrilege': Evangelicals Respond to the Second Vatican Council," in Alex Schäfer (ed.), *American Evangelicals and the 1960s* (Madison, WI: University of Wisconsin Press, 2013), 255–79.

157. David A. Hollinger, *After Cloven Tongues of Fire: Protestant Liberalism in Modern American History* (Princeton: Princeton University Press, 2013), 17–24.

158. Mark A. Noll, *American Evangelicalism: An Introduction* (Oxford: Blackwell, 2001), 112.

159. Quoted in Ringhausen, "Das Reformationsjubiläum in West und Ost," 388.

160. See *Martin Luther und die Reformation in Deutschland: Ausstellung zum 500. Geburtstag Martin Luthers veranstaltet vom Germanischen Nationalmuseum Nürnberg in Zusammenarbeit mit dem Verein für Reformationsgeschichte* (Frankfurt a.M.: Insel Verlag, 1983) and Kurt Löcher, *Martin Luther und die Reformation in Deutschland: Vorträge zur Ausstellung im Germanischen Nationalmuseum Nürnberg 1983* (Schweinfurt: Weppert, 1987).

161. The proceedings of the conference at Heidelberg were published as Bernd Moeller (ed.), *Luther in der Neuzeit: Wissenschaftliches Symposion des Vereins für Reformationsgeschichte* (Gütersloh: Gütersloher Verlagshaus, 1983). The exhibition on Luther and the arts ran from 11 Nov. 1983 to 8 Jan. 1984. See Werner Hofmann (ed.), *Luther und die Folgen für die Kunst* (Munich: Prestel-Verlag, 1983).

162. Daniel A. Augsburger, "The Luther Research Congress in Erfurt," *Andrews University Seminary Studies*, 22 (Spring 1984): 181–3.

163. Jan Herman Brinks, "Luther and the German State," *Heythrop Journal*, 39 (1998): 12.

164. Hans Süssmuth, "Luther 1983 in beiden deutschen Staaten," in Hans Süssmuth (ed.), *Das Luther-Erbe in Deutschland: Vermittlung zwischen Wissenschaft und Öffentlichkeit* (Düsseldorf: Droste Verlag, 1985), 37.

165. Ibid.

166. Quoted Ibid. 39.

167. *Martin Luther und die Reformation in Deutschland*, 5.

168. "Ansprache anlässlich der Ausstellung 'Martin Luther und die Reformation in Deutschland' in Nürnberg" (24 June 1983), <http://helmut-ohl.kas.de/index.php?menu_sel=17&menu_sel2=&menu_sel3=&menu_sel4=&msg=2275> (accessed June 2014).

169. See Mátá Millisits, "Jubilee of the Reformers and the Reformation," tr. Anita Polgári, "Reformed Church in Hungary" (18 Feb. 2014), <http://reformatus. hu/mutat/jubilee-of-the-reformers-and-the-reformation> (accessed June 2014).

170. Ellen S. Erbes, "A Quincentennial Celebration in Uppsala, Sweden and a Glimpse of Swedish Church History," *Andrews University Seminary Studies,* 22 (Spring 1984): 173–5.

171. Valentine Maltby, "A Report on Some Significant Conferences of the Luther Quincentennial Year in the United States," *Andrews University Seminary Studies,* 22 (Spring 1984): 165–71.

172. Merle Severy, "The World of Martin Luther," *National Geographic Magazine,* 164 (Oct. 1983): 428–63.

173. Kenneth A. Briggs, "Luther's Role in Christianity Evaluated on 500th Birthday," *New York Times* (8 Nov. 1983).

174. Nati Krivatsy, *Martin Luther (1483–1546): A Jubilee Exhibition at the Folger Shakespeare Library* (Washington, DC: Folger Shakespeare Library, 1983).

175. Briggs, "Luther's Role in Christianity."

176. Actually Congar, one of the founding fathers of Catholic ecumenism, published in 1983 *Martin Luther, sa foi, sa réforme: Études de théologie historique* (Paris: Editions du Cerf, 1983). Surprisingly, this work has never been translated into English.

177. Kenneth A. Strand, "A Brief Biographical Survey: Books on Luther Appearing in America during 1983 and 1984," *Andrews University Seminary Studies,* 22 (Spring 1984): 157–64.

178. See the text at <http://www.prounione.urbe.it/dia-int/l-rc/doc/e_l-rc_luther. html> (accessed June 2014).

179. The *chiesa evangelica lutherana* or *Christuskirche* (Church of Christ) was begun in 1911 and completed in 1922 as a worship site for the small community of Lutherans in Rome. The first known Lutheran service to occur in Rome was in 1817, for the third centenary of the Reformation, held in the private lodgings of the Prussian Embassy's secretary; a few years later a chapel was set up in the Embassy premises at the Palazzo Caffarelli. See <http://www.romeartlover.it/Alchiese.html#A> (accessed June 2014).

180. Quoted material in this paragraph is taken from Radano, *Lutheran and Catholic Reconciliation on Justification,* 70–1, 74–5. Cf. Henry Kamm, "Pope Praises Luther in an Appeal for Unity on Protestant Anniversary," *New York Times* (6 Nov. 1983).

Conclusion: 2017?

Life must be lived forwards but can only be understood
backwards

(Søren Kierkegaard)

So when you are offering your gift at the altar, if you remember
that your brother or sister has something against you, leave your
gift there before the altar and go; first be reconciled to your
brother or sister, and then come and offer your gift.

(Matthew 5: 23–4)

31 October 2017 focuses the mind, again, on the increasingly distant
events in sixteenth-century Saxony, and their far-flung, protean off-
spring: Protestantism. Allow me, then, to return to a question first
posed in the introduction: given its great complexity and its many
trajectories of influence and interpretation, how ought one to commemorate the Reformation 500 years after the fact; how should one,
in other words, *not just remember the Reformation, but remember it rightly*? The
difficulty of answering the question does not appear to be inhibiting
the attempt to do so. I shall sketch, therefore, several projects of
remembrance under way today before concluding with some final
ruminations of my own.

As one might expect, Germany has led the way as 2017 draws near.
In the early 2000s, government officials, scholars, and representatives
of the German Evangelical Church (EKD) came together to launch
"Luther 2017: 500 Years of the Reformation," an ambitious ten-year
project, beginning in 2008 (Luther first arrived in Wittenberg in 1508)
and culminating in 2017. One year was not enough to grapple with
the impact of the Reformation, organizers reasoned, and so the
"Luther Decade" model was adopted. Each year leading up to 2017
has had a separate theme, focusing on a significant aspect of the

Reformation and its influence. In 2017, a dizzying array of conferences, concerts, and symposia will take place.[1] In its literature and in
a short film "On the Way to the Reformation Jubilee," the architects
of "Luther 2017" make fairly sweeping claims of a causal relationship
between Luther's actions and the emergence of various modern
goods such as literacy, tolerance, education, freedom, and the social
welfare state.[2]

The opportunities that the centenary afforded for religious pilgrimage and tourism have not been lost on businesses or on the German
National Tourist Board. On websites and in glossy brochures, the
latter makes the following appeal:

> The Reformation had a profound effect not only on theology and the
> church but also on culture, science, business, politics, language and
> education. It left hardly a sphere of life untouched. On 31 October
> 2017 it will be 500 years since Martin Luther nailed his theses to that
> church door. Ahead of the anniversary in 2017, you can already
> discover the history of the Reformation on eight routes running right
> across Germany.... [B]arrier-free travel, an excellent tourism infra-
> structure and transport links by road and rail to all destinations, will
> make your visit to the Luther sites—and to Germany—an experience
> to remember. Welcome to Germany, the birthplace of Martin Luther.[3]

If the opportunities afforded by the jubilee have been clear-cut to the
tourist industry, scholars have been less certain of what to do about
2017.[4] Even the terminology—"celebrate" or "commemorate" or
"remember"—has been the subject of much debate and disagree-
ment. In 2011, in a special issue of the estimable *Berliner Theologische
Zeitschrift*, the editors recognized the problem straightforwardly, titling
the volume *Ratlos vor dem Reformationsjubiläum 2017?*, which might be
rendered freely in English as "Clueless in Light of the Reformation
Jubilee in 2017."[5] One contributor, perhaps only partly joking, has
vowed to leave Germany for the whole of 2017!

Many voices in this volume, and elsewhere, have criticized
Germany's commemorative efforts for being too focused on Luther
and Germany, too beholden to political and economic interests, and,
concomitantly, for insufficiently recognizing the pre- or transnational
character of the Reformation and the global scope of Protestantism
today. With other factors, such criticism helped spawn "Refo500," a

multi-year commemorative, networking project, seated in the Netherlands. With over one hundred partners worldwide, Refo500 attempts to be self-consciously global in its scope and operates in a more scholarly idiom than "Luther Decade," even if it wants to mediate knowledge about the sixteenth century beyond the scholarly guilds. Refo500 describes its mission as helping people "make a connection between items from the time of the Reformation and our time, between then and now, between people and Reformation history." And under "goal" on its website, it indicates that "on the occasion of the 500th anniversary of the Reformation, Refo500 wants to reach a wide audience by giving broad attention to the meaning of the Reformation."[6]

The Reformation, of course, tore Western Christianity asunder. It should not surprise, therefore, that in our age, after the ecumenical movement and the Second Vatican Council, commemorative efforts aimed at 2017—picking up on threads from 1967 and 1983—should have questions of Christian unity as a focus. Exactly what kind of focus depends on a host of institutional, theological, national, and geographical factors. But priority of place in this respect must be assigned to the Catholic Church and the Lutheran World Federation's 2013 joint project, "From Conflict to Communion: Lutheran–Catholic Common Commemoration of the Reformation in 2017." Drawing inspiration from their history-making *Joint Declaration on the Doctrine of Justification* (1999), these two imposing church bodies regard 2017 as an opportunity to deplore past divisions, engage in self-criticism for opportunities lost, and strive for greater understanding and unity in the future. As Karlheinz Diez (Auxiliary Catholic Bishop of Fulda, Germany) and Eero Huovien (Lutheran Bishop Emeritus of Helsinki, Finland) have evocatively sized up the opportunity:

> In 2017, Catholic and Lutheran Christians will most fittingly look back on events that occurred 500 years earlier by putting the Gospel of Jesus Christ at the center. The gospel should be celebrated and communicated to the people of our time so that the world may believe that God gives Himself to human beings and calls us into communion with Himself and His church. Herein lies the basis for our joy in our common faith.... The true unity of the church can only exist as unity in the truth of the gospel of Jesus Christ. The fact that the struggle for this truth in the sixteenth century led to the loss of unity in Western

Christendom belongs to the dark pages of church history. In 2017, we must confess openly that we have been guilty before Christ of damaging the unity of the church. This commemorative year presents us with two challenges: the purification of memories and healing of memories, and the restoration of Christian unity in accordance with the truth of the gospel of Jesus Christ.[7]

Germany's Luther 2017 Decade, Refo500, and "From Conflict to Communion," are but three of the many commemorative efforts marching restively toward 31 October 2017. At the time this book went to press, numerous others were in the works in practically all parts of the world touched by Protestantism.[8]

Having canvassed many past commemorations in this book, what concluding reflections are in order in light of this impending milestone, which all too soon itself will become part of the historical record? Permit me to organize my final thoughts under two headings: the ethical and the ecumenical. Admittedly, the latter is an explicitly theological category, intended mainly for those, such as myself, who identify with the Christian message or at least are sympathetic to it. Still, I hope my reflections on the subject might profit those who do not identify as such; so eavesdropping is encouraged, even welcomed.

The Ethical

The upcoming commemoration of the Reformation like commemorations in general raises a host of complex moral questions concerning the relationship of the present to the past, the living to the dead. In his engaging book *The Ethics of Memory*, the Israeli scholar Avishai Margalit has asked: "Are we obligated to remember people and events from the past? If we are, what is the nature of this obligation? . . . Who are the 'we' who may be obligated: the collective 'we,' or some distributive sense of 'we' that puts the obligation to remember on each and every member of the collective?"[9] With respect to the latter question, it would seem that in 2017 the "we" is multiple "communities of memory": Lutherans certainly, other sorts of Protestants, Christians in general, followed still by other groups: scholars of the Reformation era, people who live in countries shaped by Protestantism, and, finally, any educated person interested in expanding their historical and religious literacy. The "we," in fact, amounts to a veritable "come one, come all" and "come, let us reason together."

For all parties, the quincentennial moment provides impetus to reflect on how deeper currents of history—and their interpretations—affect our lives. Too often in our presentist, media-saturated world, appeals to "history" mean going back only as far as, say, the fall of the Berlin Wall or the end of World War II. By contrast, considering the Reformation's many trajectories of influence, and the wide range of meanings given to Protestantism, helps us acknowledge the purchase of the remote past on our lives. It shows how seemingly distant ideas and events continue to shape not only our social reality but even the lenses through which we experience and make sense of this reality. Knowledge of this kind, like historical knowledge in general, as the great Swiss historian Jacob Burckhardt once wrote, "is not only a right and a duty; it is also a supreme need..., our very freedom in the awareness of universal bondage and the stream of necessities."[10]

Unfortunately, however, the past that most extensively envelops us, that molds and structures our identities and experience, is often the most difficult to see and the easiest to distort. An avoidable conclusion of the preceding inquiry is the realization that past commemorations have been heavily shaped—*conditioned* is perhaps not too strong a word—by the milieu in which they took place. All too often, historical actors have unwittingly disfigured the Reformation by pressing it into the service of myriad ideologies, ambitions, aspirations, and interests. This realization need not lead us to resigned historical fatalism, however. Rather, it should help us see both the Reformation and its memory as enmeshed in great historical complexity and contingency. And this, in turn, should encourage a measure of interpretative humility or what Nicholas of Cusa famously called "learned ignorance," the chastened circumspection that study, reflection, and an awareness of our limitations can supply.[11] One should, therefore, resist the temptation to wax oracular in 2017, to make blanket, unqualified assertions about the meaning of Protestantism or to invoke the Reformation as a catch-all causal agent to expain this or that, positive or negative, development in the modern world. The historical complexities involved are simply too immense.

In fact, we might do better to learn to smile at such sweeping invocations of the Reformation. In his Pulitzer prize-winning book

A Confederacy of Dunces, John Kennedy Toole profiles the memorable character Ignatius Reilly, who contemns the entire modern world. Reilly "often bloated," writes Toole, "while lying on his bed in the morning considering the unfortunate turn that events [in world history] had taken since the Reformation."[12] We could just as easily imagine Ignatiuses of a Pollyanna sort, and we have glimpsed some in this study, who regard the Reformation as the spigot from which all modern goods flow. Both deserve a gentle smile and a question or distinction intended to steer the conversation in a more nuanced direction.

While knowledge of past jubilees should prod us to think harder about the sixteenth century, it should also embolden us to ask searching questions about exactly what historical forces and circumstances in our own day merit considering in 2017. What should be in our field of vision as we size up this quincentennial moment? Too many things come to mind to catalog exhaustively, but permit me to suggest four worth considering.

First, as inhabitants of a consumerist, market-driven civilization, we should pay close attention to the economic interests in play in light of 2017. Persons and events of historical importance, of course, have long attracted commercial interests. And this in itself is not blameworthy. Still, due diligence is required to perceive when commercial interests dovetail with high-minded educational/religious interests to promote the common good and when they—as is often the case— descend into opportunism, greed, and kitsch. A few years ago the German artist Ottmar Hörl pointedly raised such questions when he cast several hundred "Luther Dwarves" (in red, green, blue, and black colors) and exhibited them on the central town square of Wittenberg.[13] Because of Hörl's plans to sell the one-meter figures after the exhibition, one local theologian likened his project to "the tasteless selling of indulgences." (Strong words in Wittenberg!) Furthermore, the tourist industry, and its various adjuncts and beneficiaries, merits moral scrutiny in 2017. Both those who pay for and those who stand to profit from commemoration play an outsized role in shaping social memory, and as such they can sometimes succumb to the temptation to silence inconvenient truths about the past and/or distort by oversimplification topics of great complexity.[14]

Second, and happily, a rich pluralism in present-day Reformation studies, abetted by the digitization of countless Reformation-era works and documents, promises positively to affect commemorative efforts. According to the historian Euan Cameron, "The last few years have seen a formidable diversification of interests in . . . Reformation history"; the field now is "diffuse, fecund, and unpredictable" and "multi-dimensional as never before."[15] While much of this scholarship might not make its way to more public and religious celebrations, the sheer volume of the scholarship and the plurality of outlooks—not to mention possibilities of dissemination no longer restricted to scholarly articles and books, but available on websites and other media platforms—holds much promise, and potentially provides some degree of immunity from brazenly ideological or monetary interests and the proclivity to simplify.

Third, with all due respect to Max Weber's notion of "disenchantment," we live in a churningly religious world, at once similar and dissimilar to the world of the sixteenth century.[16] What used to be known as the "secularization thesis"—the view that modernity led necessarily to the irreligion in society—appears now woefully inadequate as a social-scientific paradigm to explain the contemporary world.[17] What is more, we live in an age that has witnessed the resurgence of religiously inspired violence, most prominently but not only within militant branches of Islam.[18] In light of 2017, many, therefore, have understandably asked if Europe's protracted struggle with confessional polemics and violence after the Reformation—the so-called "Age of Religious Wars"—offers lessons about and possible remedies for global conflicts today. I will let those with greater competence on the contemporary scene to draw sharper conclusions, but the parallel realities present rich opportunities to pose insightful questions and make connections between past and present.

On a related point, greater awareness today of global religious pluralism has also inspired scholarship on Western Christians' views of non-Christian faiths. One need only mention Luther's harsh views of Muslims and Jews to grasp the dark history behind contemporary religious frictions and misunderstandings.[19] These unsavory aspects of the Reformation—what today would be called Islamophobia and anti-Semitism—certainly deserve attention in 2017. At the same time, one hopes that such attention does not lead to reductionist interpretations (e.g., "Luther to Hitler"), in which sixteenth-century figures are read only through the prism of their most offensive words.

What is more, awareness of the persecution of religious minorities such as the Anabaptists in the sixteenth century ought to help sensitize us to the waves of persecution that we have witnessed in our own time, not least directed against Christians.

Fourth, awareness of the globalization of Protestantism has already and certainly ought to inform interpretations of the Reformation's legacy in 2017. Since the last centennial jubilee in 1917, the global landscape of Christianity in general and Protestantism in particular has undergone a fundamental transformation. In 1910 an estimated 11 percent of the world's Protestants lived outside of Europe and North America; today that figure stands at over 73 percent.[20] In the twentieth century, writes the scholar of world Christianity Dana L. Robert, "a massive cultural and geographic shift away from Europeans and their descendents toward people of the Southern Hemisphere" has taken place, due both to missionary efforts and to local patterns of indigenization.[21] Whether dominant patterns of Global South Christianity are discernably "Protestant" or warrant other adjectives (Pentecostal, evangelical, revivalist, charismatic?) has been and will continue to be a lively topic for discussion in 2017 and beyond.

At the same time, "mainline" forms of Protestantism—Presbyterianism, Methodism, Lutheranism, and more—have also benefitted from global expansion, even if they have generally witnessed numerical decline in the West. More Lutherans worship on Sunday in a handful of African countries than in all of the traditional Lutheran state-church societies of northern Europe combined.[22] It should have come as no surprise that the Lutheran World Federation chose Namibia (today a Lutheran majority country!) in late October/early November of 2015 to hold its first conference "marking the beginning of the core period leading up to the Reformation Anniversary [in 2017]." The Federation sized up the moment as follows: "Reformation ideas and insights moved from an originally purely European context to interacting with diverse contexts all over the world. In order truly to capture this wide diversity of contexts, the conference takes place in the global South and offers the possibility to engage with contextual insights from around the world."[23] Such lines also invite the question of what the future holds for Europe's own religious identity 500 years after the Reformation.

To be sure, many other considerations should inform commemorations in 2017, but sensitivity to commercial interests, awareness of the pluralistic scope of Reformation studies, cognizance of the insufficiency of the "secularization thesis" as an explanatory paradigm of modernity, and knowledge of the globalization of Protestantism and Christianity in general in our age, should be among the topics that receive attention once 31 October 2017 is past. Together, they hold potential to help us reflect on and remember the Reformation rightly.

The Ecumenical

Any Christian body or institution interested in commemorating the Reformation in 2017 must reckon with the far-reaching implications of the ecumenical movement of the twentieth-century and the Second Vatican Council, along with Pope John Paul II's historic encyclical on ecumenism, *Ut Unum Sint* (1995). The commemorations of 1967 and 1983, as we have seen, began to focus attention on ecumenical concerns. The topic is of vital importance for Christianity today— and especially to Protestants, who, sadly, have made an art form of sowing divisions—for the imperative of unity flows directly from the Christian Gospel and is regularly traced to Christ's own words in the book of John: "I do not ask for these only, but also for those who will believe in me through their word, that they may all be one, just as you, Father, are in me, and I in you, that they also may be in us, so that the world may believe that you have sent me" (John 17: 20–1). What is more, fraternal relations among Christians, scripture and church tradition hold, ought to be a model for human cooperation and good will in general.

Sadly, Christian practice has seldom lived up to Christian principle on this score, and, in fact, the latter has often gravely contradicted the former. But remembrance of the Reformation in 2017 might provide the impetus for narrowing the gap between the two, if the right conciliatory habits of heart and mind are cultivated. Permit me to suggest a few lines of inquiry that might work toward such ends.

In 2017, it is *theologically* important to think of the Reformation in historical terms and not in theological ones alone. As the best scholarship on the sixteenth century makes clear, the Reformation— or, the Reformation*s*, as is increasingly preferred—occurred as a bewilderingly complex, confusing set of historical events, not as a check-list of doctrinal principles that dropped from the sky after 1517. Multiple problems come from looking at the Reformation era strictly from a doctrinal or theological standpoint. They include a temptation for partisans to regard the conclusions and condemnations from this era as timeless and above criticism. They also encourage over-simplified stories of this period's place in church history that conveniently lends credence to one's own religious standpoint. By contrast, an honest appraisal of the contingency and messiness, the unexpected sources and ironic outcomes, of the Reformation—something too often overlooked in past commemorations—might help one step back, gain perspective, and regard the conclusions of this era as important, to be sure, but not necessarily set in stone.

Attention to the historical accidents of the Reformation—particularly attention to the fact that many of the condemnations and doctrinal statements of this era, whether Protestant or Catholic, issued from a highly propagandistic, polemical, and political atmosphere—has been one of the key factors allowing for significant ecumenical progress in recent years. With a more sensitive approach to history, divided Christians today have been creating areas of common ground where none seemed to exist beforehand. Taking stock together and repenting of painful memories, not historical ignorance or affected amnesia, marks out the royal, arduous road toward unity, according to John Paul II in *Ut unum sint*:

> [T]he commitment to ecumenism must be based upon the conversion of hearts and upon prayer, which will also lead to the *necessary purification of past memories*. With the grace of the Holy Spirit, the Lord's disciples, inspired by love, by the power of the truth and by a sincere desire for mutual forgiveness and reconciliation, are called to *re-examine together their painful past* and the hurt which that past regrettably continues to provoke even today.... All together, they are invited by the ever fresh power of the Gospel to acknowledge...the mistakes made and the contingent factors at work at the origins of their deplorable divisions. *What is needed is a calm, clear-sighted and truthful vision of things,* a vision enlivened by divine mercy and capable of freeing people's minds and of inspiring in everyone a renewed willingness, precisely with a view to proclaiming the Gospel to the men and women of every people and nation.[24]

For a concrete example of what this might entail, one might consider the path laid down by the Lutheran–Mennonite dialogue, whose first-ever, jointly written history of Lutheran–Anabaptist relations in the sixteenth century paved the way for a public declaration of repentance and request for forgiveness on the part of the Lutheran World Federation in 2010, which was met with a full declaration of forgiveness on the part of the Mennonite World Conference. As the Lutheran–Mennonite joint report movingly recorded: "The past cannot be changed, but we can change the way the past is remembered in the present. This is our hope. Reconciliation does not only look back into the past; rather it looks into a common future."[25]

The prospects of one's imminent death, Samuel Johnson famously said, "wonderfully concentrates the mind." The same might be said of preparing for, reflecting on, and observing major commemorative dates. To be sure, there is something naggingly arbitrary about large centennial numbers such as 500. But why not make a virtue of necessity? Insofar as they have the capacity to focus attention on the past that is inevitably constitutive of our present, marking them has the potential to encourage historical knowledge, foster reflection and self-examination, and—with respect to painful and divisive memories—perhaps change for the better "the way the past is remembered in the present."

Sadly, however, as this inquiry has shown, this potential has not always been realized at past jubilees and centennials, and, instead, partisan, xenophobic, and narrowly time-bound concerns have often prevailed. True enough. But the past is not necessarily prologue to the present, and, therefore, equipped with retrospective insight and chastened expectations, one might be forgiven for hoping that this time around things will be different.

Notes

1. See <http://www.luther2017.de>.
2. One may view the film "Auf dem Weg zum Reformationsjubiläum" at <http://www.luther2017.de/en/2017/reformationsjubilaeum/film-auf-dem-weg-zum-reformationsjubilaeum/film-auf-dem-weg-zum-reformation sjubilaeum>.
3. "Luther 2017: 500 Years since the Reformation," travel brochure available online at <www.germany.travel>.
4. On Reformation-related tourism, see also <http://www.luther500festival.com>.

5. See *Ratlos vor dem Reformationsjubiläum 2017?*, *Berliner Theologische Zeitschrift*, 28 (2011).

6. See Refo500's website at <http://www.refo500.nl>.

7. See *From Conflict to Communion: Lutheran–Catholic Common Commemoration of the Reformation in 2017: Report of the Lutheran-Roman Catholic Commission on Unity* (Leipzig: Evangelische Verlagsanstalt/Paderborn: Bonifatus, 2013), 7.

8. And many are very explicitly religious. The Lutheran Church Missouri Synod (LCMS) in the US, for example, has adopted as its motto for 2017: "Reformation 2017: It's *Still* All About Jesus." See <http://blogs.lcms.org/2015/reformation-2017> (accessed June 2015).

9. Avishai Margalit, *The Ethics of Memory* (Cambridge, MA: Harvard University Press, 2002), 7.

10. Jacob Burckhardt, *Reflections on History*, tr. M. D. Hottinger (Indianapolis, IN: Liberty Fund, 1979), 40.

11. On this theme, see James L. Heft et al. (eds), *Learned Ignorance: Intellectual Humility among Jews, Christians, and Muslims* (Oxford: OUP, 2011).

12. John Kennedy Toole, *A Confederacy of Dunces* (New York: Grove Press, 1980), 41.

13. Stefan Locke, "Wittenberg und die 500 Zwerge," *Frankfurter Allgemeine Zeitung* (25 Apr. 2010): 58.

14. Michel-Rolph Trouillot, *Silencing the Past: Power and the Production of History* (Boston: Beacon, 1995).

15. Euan Cameron, "Nearly 500 Years and Still Counting: The Reformation in Recent Scholarship and Debates," *Expository Times,* 126 (2014): 1–14. This is a brief and very informative survey of recent scholarship.

16. John Micklethwait and Adrian Wooldridge, *God is Back: How the Global Revival of Faith is Changing the World* (New York: Penguin Press, 2009). For a forceful defense of a Weberian point of view, see Carlos Eire, "Incombustible Weber: How the Protestant Reformation Really Disenchanted the World," in Andreas Sterk and Nina Caputo (eds), *Faithful Narratives: Historians, Religions, and the Challenge of Objectivity* (Ithaca, NY: Cornell University Press, 2014), 132–48.

17. See Peter Berger (ed.), *The Desecularization of the World* (Grand Rapids, MI: Eerdmans, 1999), 1–18.

18. Jonathan Sacks, *Not in God's Name: Confronting Religious Violence* (New York: Schocken Books, 2015).

19. See Eric W. Gritch, *Luther's Anti-Semitism: Against his Better Judgment* (Grand Rapids, MI: Eerdmans, 2012); Gregory J. Miller, "Wars of Religion and Religion in War: Luther and the 16th-Century Islamic Advance in Europe," *Seminary Ridge Review,* 9 (2007): 38–59; and Adam Francisco, *Martin Luther and Islam: A Study in Sixteenth-Century Polemics and Apologetics* (Leiden: Brill, 2007).

20. Mark A. Noll, *Protestantism: A Very Short History* (New York: OUP, 2011), 8.

21. Dana L. Robert, "Shifting Southward: Global Christianity since 1945," *International Bulletin of Missionary Research,* 24 (2000): 50.

22. On Lutheran demographics worldwide, see Todd Johnson and Kenneth R. Ross (eds), *Atlas of Global Christianity* (Edinburgh: Edinburgh University Press, 2010), 70, 90, 98, and Nathan Smart, *Atlas of the World's Religions* (New York: OUP, 1999), 166–7.

23. "Reformation in Global Perspective: Interactions between Theology, Politics, and Economics," prospectus of the International Conference, 28 Oct.–1 Nov. 2015, Windhoek, Namibia, located at <https://www.lutheranworld.org/sites/default/files/DTPW-Reformation_in_Global_Perspective_Windhoek_October_2015.pdf> (accessed June 2015).

24. *Ut unum sint* at <https://w2.vatican.va/content/john-paul-ii/en/encyclicals/documents/hf_jp-ii_enc_25051995_ut-unum-sint.html> (accessed June 2015, emphases added).

25. See Lutheran–Mennonite International Study Commission, *Healing Memories: Reconciling in Christ:* (Lutheran World Federation/Mennonite World Conference, 2010), 108. I am grateful to Sarah Hinlicky Wilson for underscoring to me the significance of this dialogue and document. For deeper engagement with the issues that such an enterprise entails, see Jeffrey N. Blusten, *Forgiveness and Remembrance: Remembering Wrongdoing in Personal and Public Life* (Oxford: OUP, 2014).

Select Bibliography

Ahlstrom, Syndey E. *A Religious History of the American People*. New Haven: Yale University Press, 1972.

Altgeld, Wolfgang. *Katholizismus, Protestantismus, Judentum: Über religiös begründete Gegensätze und nationalreligiöse Ideen in der Geschichte des deutschen Nationalismus*. Mainz: Matthias-Grünewald, 1992.

Anderson, Benedict. *Imagined Communities: Reflections on the Origins and Spread of Nationalism*, rev. edn. London: Verso, 2006.

Anderson, Stewart. "Martin Luther in Primetime: Television Fiction and Cultural Memory Construction in Cold War Germany." *View: Journal of European Television, History, and Culture*, 3 (2012): 22–6.

Asmussen, Hans. "Muss Luther nach Nürnberg?" *Nordwestdeutsche Hefte*, 11 (1947): 31–7.

Assmann, Jan. "Collective Memory and Cultural Identity." *New German Critique*, 65 (1995): 125–33.

Augustana Tract Society. *Luther-Kalender: Jubel-Ret 1883*. Rock Island, IL: Augustana Tract Society, 1883.

Baeumer, Max L. "Lutherfeiern und ihre politische Manipulation." In Reinhold Grimm and Jost Hermand (eds), *Deutsche Feiern*, 46–61. Wiesbaden: Akademische Verlagsgesellschaft Athenaion, 1977.

Bagchi, David, and David C. Steinmetz, eds. *The Cambridge Companion to Reformation Theology*. Cambridge: Cambridge University Press, 2004.

Barnes, Robin Bruce. *Prophecy and Gnosis: Apocalypticism in the Wake of the Lutheran Reformation*. Stanford, CA: Stanford University Press, 1988.

Bartel, Horst, et al. "Thesen über Martin Luther: Zum 500. Geburtstag." *Zeitschrift für Geschichtswissenschaft*, 11 (1982): 879–93.

Barth, Karl. *Protestant Theology in Nineteenth Century America: Its Background and History*. London: SCM Press, 1972.

Bartol, Cyrus Augustus. *Martin Luther*. Boston: Office of the Unitarian Review, 1883.

Bennett, J. M. R. "The British Luther Commemoration of 1883–1884 in European Context." *Historical Journal*, 58 (2015): 543–64.

Berg, Gunnar and Hans-Hermann Hartwich, eds. *Martin-Luther Universität von der Gründung bis zur Neugestaltung nach zwei Diktaturen*. Opladen: Leske & Budrich, 1994.

Berger, Peter, ed. *The Desecularization of the World: Resurgent Religion and World Politics*. Grand Rapids, MI: Eerdmans, 1999.

Biermann-Rau, Sibylle. *An Luthers Geburtstag brannten die Synagogen*. Stuttgart: Calwer Verlag, 2012.

Billington, Ray Allen. *The Protestant Crusade, 1800–1860: A Study in the Origins of American Nativism.* New York: Macmillan, 1938.

Blackbourn, David, and Geoff Eley. *The Peculiarities of German History.* Oxford: Oxford University Press, 1984.

Blusten, Jeffrey N. *Forgiveness and Remembrance: Remembering Wrongdoing in Personal and Public Life.* Oxford: Oxford University Press, 2014.

Bouyer, Louis. *The Spirit and Forms of Protestantism.* Princeton: Scepter Publishers, 1956.

Brady, Thomas A. *German Histories in the Age of the Reformation, 1400–1650.* Cambridge: Cambridge University Press, 2009.

Brakelmann, Günter, ed. *Der Deutsche Protestantismus im Epochenjahr 1917.* Wittenberg: Luther-Verlag, 1974.

Brandenburg, Erich. *Martin Luther als Vorkämpfer deutschen Geistes: Eine Rede zur 400-jährigen Jubelfeier der Reformation.* Leipzig: Quelle & Meyer, 1917.

Bräuer, Siegfried. "Das Lutherjubiläum 1933 und die deutschen Universitäten." *Theologische Literaturzeitung,* 108 (1983): 641–62.

Bräuer, Siegfried. *Martin Luther in marxistischer Sicht von 1945 bis zum Beginn der achtziger Jahre.* Berlin: Evangelische Verlagsanstalt, 1983.

Brinks, Jan Herman. "Luther and the German State." *Heythrop Journal,* 39 (1998): 1–17.

Burder, Henry Forster. *The Reformation Commemorated; A Discourse Delivered at the Meeting-House, St. Thomas's Square, Hackney, December 28th, 1817.* London, 1818.

Burleigh, Michael. *Earthly Powers: The Clash of Religion and Politics in Europe, from the French Revolution to the Great War.* New York: HarperCollins, 2005.

Cameron, Euan. "Nearly 500 Years and Still Counting: The Reformation in Recent Scholarship and Debates." *Expository Times,* 126 (2014): 1–14.

Carpenter, Joel A. *Revive Us Again: the Reawakening of American Fundamentalism.* New York: Oxford University Press, 1997.

Chadwick, Owen. *The Christian Church in the Cold War.* New York: Penguin Books, 1992.

Christian Century. "What has Protestantism Accomplished." 25 Oct. 1917: 5.

Clark, Christopher. "Confessional Policy and the Limits of State Action: Frederick William III and the Prussian Church Union 1817–1840." *Historical Journal,* 39 (1996): 985–1004.

Commemoration of the Four Hundredth Anniversary of the Birth of Martin Luther by the Massachusetts Historical Society, November 10, 1883 (Boston, 1883).

Congar, Yves. "Church Reform and Luther's Reformation, 1517–1967." *Lutheran World,* 14 (1967): 351–9.

Connerton, Paul. *How Societies Remember.* Cambridge: Cambridge University Press, 1989.

Conrad, Paul. *Die Reformation und das deutsche Volk: Festschrift zur Jahrhundertfeier der Reformation.* Berlin: Mittler & Sohn, 1917.

Corcoran, James Andrew. "Martin Luther and his American Worshipers." *American Catholic Quarterly Review,* 9 (1884): 527–76.

Cordes, Harm. *Hilaria evangelica academia: Das Reformationsjubiläum von 1717 an den deutschen lutherischen Universitäten.* Göttingen: Vandenhoeck & Ruprecht, 2006.

Croll, P. C., ed. *Tributes to the Memory of Luther.* Philadelphia, 1884.

Crouter, Richard. *Friedrich Schleiermacher: Between Enlightenment and Romanticism.* Cambridge and New York: Cambridge University Press, 2005.

Cyprian, Ernst Salomon. *Hilaria Evangelica.* Gotha: M. G. Weidmann, 1719.

Delgado, Mariano, Volker Leppin, and David Neuhold. *Ringen um Die Wahrheit: Gewissenskonflikte in Der Christentumsgeschichte.* Fribourg: Academic Press; Stuttgart: W. Kohlhammer GmbH, 2011.

Dibelius, Otto. *Das Königliche Predigerseminar zu Wittenberg: 1817–1819.* Berlin-Lichterfelde: E. Runge, 1918.

Dickens, A. G., and John Tonkin. *The Reformation in Historical Thought.* Cambridge, MA: Harvard University Press, 1985.

Dillenberger, John. *Protestant Thought and Natural Science.* London: Collins, 1961.

Dillenberger, John, and Claude Welch. *Protestant Christianity Interpreted through its Development.* New York: Charles Scribner's Sons, 1954.

Duding, Dieter, Peter Friedemann, and Paul Münch. *Öffentliche Festkultur: Politische Feste in Deutschland von der Aufklärung bis zum Ersten Weltkrieg.* Reinbek bei Hamburg: Rowohlt, 1988.

Düfel, Hans. "Das Luther-Jubiläum 1883." *Zeitschrift für Kirchengeschichte*, 95 (1984): 1–94.

Eade, J. C., ed. *Romantic Nationalism in Europe.* Canberra: Humanities Research Centre, 1983.

Eich, Friedrich, ed. *Gedenkblätter zur Erinnerung und Enthüllungsfeier des Lutherdenkmals in Worms.* Worms, 1868.

Eisenstadt, S. N., ed. *The Protestant Ethic and Modernization: A Comparative View.* New York: Basic Books, 1968.

Elliger, Walter, ed. *Die evangelische Kirche der Union: Ihre Vorgeschichte und Geschichte.* Witten: Luther-Verlag, 1967.

Elliger, Walter. "Zum Thema Luther und Thomas Müntzer." *Luther Jahrbuch*, 34 (1967): 90–116.

Engeman, Thomas S., and Michael P. Zuckert, eds. *Protestantism and the American Founding.* Notre Dame, IN: University of Notre Dame Press, 2004.

Erbes, Ellen S. "A Quincentennial Celebration in Uppsala, Sweden and a Glimpse of Swedish Church History." *Andrews University Seminary Studies*, 22 (Spring 1984): 173–80.

Ericksen, Robert P. "The Luther Anniversary and the Year 1933 in the Mirror of U.S. Church Press Reports." *Kirchliche Zeitgeschichte*, 26 (2013): 319–34.

Evangelical Alliance Martin Luther: Celebration of the Evangelical Alliance of the United States, of the 400th Anniversary of the Birthday of Martin Luther, October 13th, 1883. New York, 1883.

Flügel, Wolfgang. "'Ein feste Burg ist unser Gott': Luther im Weltkrieg des Reformationsjubiläum 1917." *Dresdner Hefte*, 1919 (2014): 59–68.

Flügel, Wolfgang, and Stefan Dornheim. "Die Universität als Jubliäumsmultiplikator in der Frühen Neuzeit." *Jahrbuch für Universitätsgeschichte,* 9 (2006): 51–70.

Francisco, Adam. *Martin Luther and Islam: A Study in Sixteenth-Century Polemics and Apologetics.* Leiden: Brill, 2007.

Friedrich, G., ed. *Chronik der dritten Jubelfeier der Reformation in Frankfurt am Main.* Frankfurt am Main, 1817.

Fuhrmann, Rainer. *Das Reformationsjubiläum 1817: Martin Luther und die Reformation im Urteil der Protestantlischen Festpredigt des Jahres 1817.* Bonn: V+V Sofortdruck, 1973.

Fulbrook, Mary. *Anatomy of a Dictatorship: Inside the GDR, 1949–1989.* Oxford: Oxford University Press, 1995.

Fulbrook, Mary. *The People's State: East German Society from Hitler to Honecker.* New Haven: Yale University Press, 2005.

Gerrish, B. A. *The Old Protestantism and the New: Essays on the Reformation Heritage.* Chicago: University of Chicago Press, 1982.

Gillis, John R., ed. *Commemorations: The Politics of National Identity.* Princeton: Princeton University Press, 1994.

Graebner, August Lawrence. *Dr. Martin Luther, Lebensbild des Reformators den Glaubensgenossen in America gezeichnet.* Milwaukee, WI, 1883.

Gregory, Brad S. *The Unintended Reformation: How a Religious Revolution Secularized Society.* Cambridge, MA: Belknap Press of Harvard University Press, 2012.

Greschat, Martin. "Reformationsjubiläum 1917: Exempel einer fragwürdigen Symbiose von Politik und Theologie." *Wissenschaft und Praxis in Kirche und Gesellschaft,* 61 (1972): 419–29.

Grisar, Hartmann. "Die Literatur des Lutherjubiläums 1917: Ein Bild des heutigen Protestantismus." *Zeitschrift für katholische Theologie,* 42 (1918): 591–628, 785–814.

Gritch, Eric W. *Luther's Anti-Semitism: Against his Better Judgment.* Grand Rapids, MI: Eerdmans, 2012.

Gunsaulus, Frank Wakeley. *Martin Luther and the Morning Hour in Europe: Two Lectures Delivered at the University of Chicago, October 16 and 17, 1917.* Chicago: University of Chicago Press, 1917.

Hans, Julius. *Das Unvergängliche in Luther und seinem Werk.* Augsburg: J. A. Schlosser, 1883.

Harms, Klaus. *Das sind die 95 Theses, Oder, Streitsätze Dr. Luthers Theuren Andenkens.* Kiel: Academischen Buchhandlung, 1817.

Harms, Wolfgang. *Illustrierte Flugblätter aus den Jahrhunderten der Reformation und der Glaubenkämpfe 24 Juli bis Oktober 1983: Kunstsammlung der Veste Coburg.* Coburg: Kunstsammlung der Veste Coburg, 1983.

Harms, Wolfgang and Michael Schilling eds. *Deutsche Illustrierte Flugblätter des 16. und 17. Jahrhunderts,* ii. Tübingen: Niemeyer, 1997.

Harnack, Adolf von. *Martin Luther in seiner Bedeutung für die Geschichte der Wissenschaft und Bildung.* Giessen: Alfred Töpelmann, 1911.

Harnack, Adolf von. *Martin Luther und die Grundlegung der Reformation*. Berlin: Wiedmannsche Buchhandlung, 1917.

Harrison, Peter. *The Bible, Protestantism, and the Rise of Natural Science*. Cambridge: Cambridge University Press, 1998.

Hatch, Nathan O. *The Democratization of American Christianity*. New Haven: Yale University Press, 1989.

Hecker, Isaac Thomas. "Luther and the Diet of Worms." *The Catholic World*, 38 (1883): 145–61.

Heron, Alasdair. *A Century of Protestant Theology*. Philadelphia: Westminster Press, 1980.

Heschel, Susannah. *The Aryan Jesus: Christian Theologians and the Bible in Nazi Germany*. Princeton: Princeton University Press, 2008.

Hillerbrand, Hans, ed. *The Encyclopedia of Protestantism*, 4 vols. New York: Routledge, 2004.

Hoffmann, Stephen P. "The GDR, Luther, and the German Question." *Review of Politics*, 48 (1986): 246–63.

Hoffmeister, Hermann. *Luther und Bismarck als Grundpfeiler unserer Nationalgröße*. Berlin, 1883.

Hollinger, David A. *After Cloven Tongues of Fire: Protestant Liberalism in Modern American History*. Princeton: Princeton University Press, 2013.

Hoover, Arlie J. *The Gospel of Nationalism: German Patriotic Preaching from Napoleon to Versailles*. Stuttgart: F. Steiner, 1986.

Horst, Stephan. "Das evangelisch-Jubelfest in der Vergangenheit." *Deutsch-Evangelisch—Monatsblätter für den gesamten deutschen Protestantismus*, 8 (1917): 2–12.

Howard, Thomas Albert. *Religion and the Rise of Historicism: W. M. L. de Wette, Jacob Burckhardt, and the Theological Origins of Nineteenth-Century Historical Consciousness*. Cambridge: Cambridge University Press, 2000.

Howard, Thomas Albert. *Protestant Theology and the Making of the Modern German University*. Oxford: Oxford University Press, 2006.

Hsia, R. Po-Chi, ed. *A Companion to the Reformation World*. Oxford: Blackwell, 2004.

Hübner, Hans, and Burchard Thaler. *Festchrift anlässlich des 150. Jahrestages der Vereinigung der Universitäten Wittenberg und Halle*. Halle: Martin-Luther-Universität Halle-Wittenberg, 1967.

Hutchison, William R. *The Modernist Impulse in American Protestantism*. Cambridge, MA: Harvard University Press, 1976.

Iggers, Georg G. *The German Conception of History: The National Tradition of Historical Thought from Herder to the Present*, rev. edn. Middletown, CT: Wesleyan University Press, 1983.

Iggers, Georg G. "Historicism: The History and Meaning of the Term." *Journal of the History of Ideas*, 56 (Jan. 1995): 129–52.

Iserloh, Erwin. "Luthers Thesenanschlag: Tatsache oder Legende?" *Trierer Theologische Zeitschrift*, 70 (1961): 303–12.

Iserloh, Erwin. *Luther zwischen Reform und Reformation: Der Thesenanschlag fand nicht statt*. Münster: Aschendorff, 1962.

Jenkins, Philip. *The Next Christendom: The Coming of Global Christianity*. New York: Oxford University Press, 2002.

Jenkins, Philip. *The Great and Holy War: How World War I Became a Religious Crusade*. New York: HarperOne, 2014.

Johnston, A. *The Protestant Reformation in Europe*. New York: Longman, 1991.

Kadai, Heino O., ed. *Accents in Luther's Theology: Essays in Commemoration of the 450th Anniversary of the Reformation*. St Louis, MO: Concordia Publishing House, 1967.

Kaelber, Lutz, ed. *The Protestant Ethic Turns 100: Essays on the Centenary of the Weber Thesis*. Boulder, CO: Paradigm Publishers, 2005.

Kastner, Ruth. *Geistlicher Rauffhandel: Form und Function der Illustrierten Flugbläter zum Reformationsjubiläum 1617 in ihrem Historischen und Publizistichen Kontext*. Frankfurt am Main and Bern: Peter Lang, 1982.

Kastner, Ruth. "The Reformer and the Reformation Anniversaries." *History Today*, 33 (1983): 22–6.

Keil, Robert. *Die Burschenschaftlichen Wartburgfeste von 1817 und 1867*. Jena: Mauke's Verlag (H. Dufft), 1868.

Keyser, Friedrich, ed. *Reformations Almanach für Luthers Verehrer: Auf das Evangelische Jubeljahr, 1817–1821*. Erfurt: G. A. Keysers Buchhandlung, 1817–21.

Kreussler, Heinrich Gottlieb. *Martin Luthers Andenken im Münzen nebst Lebebsbeschreibungen Merkwürdigen Zeitgenossen Desselben: Mit 47 Kupfern un der Ansicht Wittenbergs un Eisenachs zu Luthers Zeit*. Leipzig: B. Fleischer, 1818.

Krivatsy, Nati. *Martin Luther (1483–1546): A Jubilee Exhibition at the Folger Shakespeare Library*. Washington, DC: Folger Shakespeare Library, 1983.

Kühn, Hugo. *Das Wartburgfest am 18 Oktober 1817, mit Einem Anhang: Die Feier des Dritten Evangelischen Jubelfestes auf der Wartburg*. Weimar: A. Duneker, 1913.

Küster, Volker, ed. *Reshaping Protestantism in a Global Context*. Berlin: Lit Verlag, 2009.

Landry, Stan. *Ecumenism, Memory, and German Nationalism, 1817–1917*. Syracuse, NY: Syracuse University Press, 2014.

Lau, Franz. "Die gegenwärtige Diskussion um Luthers Thesenanschlag." *Luther-Jahrbuch*, 34 (1967): 11–59.

Laube, Stefan, and Karl-Heinz Fix, eds. *Lutherinszenierung und Reformationserinnerung*. Leipzig: Evangelische Verlagsanstalt, 2002.

Lehmann, Hartmut. *Martin Luther in the American Imagination*. Munich: Wilhelm Fink Verlag, 1988.

Lehmann, Hartmut. *Luthergedächtnis 1817 bis 2017*. Göttingen: Vandenhoeck & Ruprecht, 2012.

Lehmann, Karl, and Wolfhart Pannenberg, eds. *The Condemnations of the Reformation: Do they Still Divide?* Tr. Margaret Kohl. Minneapolis: Fortress Press, 1990.

Lenz, Max. *Luther und der deutsche Geist: Rede zur Reformationsfeier 1917 in Hamburg*. Hamburg: Broschek, 1917.

Loofs, Friedrich. "Die Jahrhundertfeier der Reformation an den Universitäten Wittenberg und Halle 1617, 1717, 1917." *Zeitschrift des Vereins für
Kirchengeschichte in der Provinz Sachsen,* 14 (1917): 1–68.

Lotz, David. *Ritschl and Luther: A Fresh Perspective on Albrecht Ritschl's Theology in
Light of his Luther Study.* Nashville, TN: Abingdon Press, 1974.

Lotz, David. "Albrecht Ritschl and the Unfinished Reformation." *Harvard
Theological Review,* 73 (1980): 337–72.

Lutheran-Mennonite International Study Commission. *Healing Memories: Reconciling in Christ: Report of the Lutheran-Mennonite International Study Commission.*
The Lutheran World Federation/The Mennonite World Conference,
2010.

Lutheran-Roman Catholic Commission on Unity. *From Conflict to Communion:
Lutheran-Catholic Common Commemoration of the Reformation in 2017: Report of the
Lutheran-Roman Catholic Commission on Unity.* Leipzig: Evangelische Verlag-
sanstalt/Paderborn: Bonifatus, 2013.

McCain, Paul Timothy, William H. T. Dau, and F. Bente, eds. *Concordia: The
Lutheran Confessions: A Reader's Edition of the Book of Concord.* St Louis, MO:
Concordia Publishing House, 2005.

McGovern, William. *From Luther to Hitler: The History of Fascist-Nazi Philosophy.*
Boston: Houghton Mifflin, 1941.

McGrath, Alister E. *Christianity's Dangerous Idea: The Protestant Revolution.* New
York: HarperOne, 2007.

McGrath, Alister E., and Darren E. Marks, eds. *The Blackwell Companion of
Protestantism.* Oxford: Blackwell, 2004.

McNeill, Thomas. "The Interpretation of Protestantism during the Past
Quarter-Century." *Journal of Religion,* 6 (1926): 504–25.

Maltby, William, and Valentine C. Hubbs. "A Report on Some Significant
Conferences of the Luther Quincentennial Year in the United States."
Andrews University Seminary Studies, 22 (Spring 1984): 165–71.

Margalit, Avishai. *The Ethics of Memory.* Cambridge, MA: Harvard University
Press, 2002.

Marsch, Angelika. *Bilder zur Augsburger Konfession und ihren Jubiläen.* Weissen-
horn: Anton H. Konrad Verlag, 1980.

Marsh, Charles. *Strange Glory: A Life of Dietrich Bonhoeffer.* New York: Alfred
A. Knopf, 2014.

Martin, David. *Tongues of Fire: The Explosion of Protestantism in Latin America.*
Oxford: Blackwell, 1990.

Martin, David. *Pentecostalism: The World their Parish.* Oxford: Blackwell, 2002.

Marty, Martin. *The Protestant Voice in American Pluralism.* Athens, GA: University
of Georgia Press, 2004.

Maser, Peter. *"Mit Luther alles in Butter?": Das Lutherjahr 1983 im Spiegel ausgewählter Akten.* Berlin: Metropol Verlag, 2013.

Matheson, Peter Clarkson. "Luther and Hitler: A Controversy Reviewed."
Journal of Ecumenical Studies, 173 (1980): 445–53.

168   *Select Bibliography*

Mau, Rudolf. "Luthers 500. Geburtstag: Feiern ohne zu Rühmen: Beobachtungen zum Lutherjubiläum 1983 in der DDR." *Theologische Literaturzeitung,* 138 (Oct. 2013): 1045–58.

Mayer-Kulenkampf, Ilse. "Rankes Lutherverhältnis, dargestellt nach dem Lutherfragment von 1817." *Historische Zeitschrift,* 72 (1951): 65–99.

Meding, Wichmann von. "Das Wartburgfest im Rahmen des Reformationsjubliäums 1817." *Zeitschrift für Kirchengeschichte,* 96 (1985): 204–36.

Meding, Wichmann von. *Kirchenverbesserung: Die Deutschen Reformationspredigten des Jahres 1817.* Bielefeld: Luther-Verlag, 1986.

Megill, Allan. *Historical Knowledge, Historical Error: A Contemporary Guide to Practice.* Chicago: University of Chicago Press, 2007.

Meinecke, Friedrich. *Historism: The Rise of a New Historical Outlook.* Tr. J. E. Anderson. New York: Herder & Herder, 1972.

Merton, Robert K. *Science, Technology and Society in Seventeenth-Century England.* New York: Harper Torchbooks, 1970.

Moeller, Bernd, ed. *Luther in der Neuzeit: Wissenschaftliches Symposion des Vereins für Reformationsgeschichte.* Gütersloh: G. Mohn, 1983.

Möller, Wilhelm. *Rede am Luther-Jubiläum den 10. November in der Aula der Christian-Albrechts-Universität.* Kiel, 1883.

Mork, Gordon R. "Martin Luther's Left Turn: The Changing Picture of Luther in East German Historiography." *History Teacher,* 16 (1983): 585–95.

Müller, Winfried, ed. *Das historische Jubiläum. Genese, Ordungsleistung und Inszenierungsgeschichte eines institutionellen Mechanismus.* Münster: LIT Verlag, 2004.

Neill, Stephen. *A History of Christian Missions.* New York: Penguin, 1986.

Niebuhr, H. Richard. "Protestantism." In *Encyclopedia of the Social Sciences,* xii, ed. E. R. A. Seligman, 571–5. New York: Macmillan Co., 1935.

Nipperdey, Thomas. "Nationalidee und Nationaldenkmal im 19. Jahrhundert in Deutschland." *Historische Zeitschrift,* 206 (1968): 529–85.

Nipperdey, Thomas. *Germany from Napoleon to Bismarck, 1800–1866.* Tr. Daniel Nolan. Princeton: Princeton University Press, 1983.

Nirenberg, David. *Anti-Judaism: The Western Tradition.* New York: W. W. Norton, 2013.

Noll, Mark A. *American Evangelicalism: An Introduction.* Oxford: Blackwell, 2001.

Noll, Mark A. *America's God: From Jonathan Edwards to Abraham Lincoln.* Oxford: Oxford University Press, 2002.

Noll, Mark A., ed. *Confessions and Catechisms of the Reformation.* Vancouver: Regent College Publishing, 2004.

Noll, Mark A. *Protestantism: A Very Short Introduction.* New York: Oxford University Press, 2011.

Noll, Mark A., and Carolyn Nystrom. *Is the Reformation Over?* Grand Rapids, MI: Baker Academic, 2005.

Nora, Pierre. *Realms of Memory: Rethinking the French Past.* 3 vols. Tr. Arthur Goldhammer. New York: Columbia: University, 1996–8.

Nytroe, Sarah K. "The American Reformation Quadricentennial, 1917." *Lutheran Quarterly,* 26 (2012): 57–82.

Oberman, Heiko. "The Nationalist Conscription of Martin Luther." In Heiko Oberman (ed,), *The Impact of the Reformation: Essays*, 69–78. Grand Rapids, MI: Eerdmans, 1994.

Oehmig, Stefan. *700 Jahre Wittenberg: Stadt, Universität, Reformation.* Weimar: H. Böhlaus Nachfolger Weimar, 1995.

Olick, Jeffrey K., Vered Vinitzky-Seroussi, and Daniel Levy, eds. *The Collective Memory Reader*. Oxford: Oxford University Press, 2011.

O'Malley, John. *What Happened at Vatican II*. Cambridge, MA: Belknap Press of Harvard University Press, 2008.

Osterhammel, Jürgen. *The Transformation of the World: A Global History of the Nineteenth Century*. Tr. Patrick Camiller. Princeton: Princeton University Press, 2014.

Pass, John Roger. *The German Political Broadsheet, 1600–1700*. Wiesbaden: O. Harrassowitz, 1985.

Pauck, Wilhelm. *The Heritage of the Reformation*, 2nd edn. New York: Oxford University Press, 1968.

Pelikan, J., ed. *Interpreters of the Reformer: Essays in Honor of Wilhelm Paulk*. Philadelphia: Fortress Press, 1968.

Pelikan, J. *Reformation of Church and Dogma (1300–1700)*. Chicago: University of Chicago Press, 1984.

Pond, Elizabeth. "Martin Luther Lauded by East Germany." *Christian Science Monitor*, 17 June 1980.

Pöschel, Philipp Friedrich. *Zwei Predigten am dritten Saekularfeste der Reformation: als am 31. October 1817*. Nuremberg, 1817.

Probst, Christopher J. *Demonizing the Jews: Luther and the Protestant Church in Nazi Germany*. Bloomington, IN: Indiana University Press, 2012.

Radano, John A. *Lutheran and Catholic Reconciliation on Justification: A Chronology of the Holy See's Contributions, 1961–1999, to a New Relationship between Lutherans and Catholics and to Steps Leading to the* Joint Declaration on the Doctrine of Justification. Grand Rapids, MI: Eerdmans, 2009.

Rausch, David A., and Carl Hermann Voss. *Protestantism: Its Modern Meaning*. Philadelphia: Fortress Press, 1987.

Reichelt, Silvio. *Die Reformationsfeier zu Wittenberg 1917*. Wittenberg: Max Senf, 1918.

Reuter, Johann Gottlieb. *Fünf Predigten zu und bei der Secularfeier der Kirchenreformation 1817 gehalten*. Bayreuth, 1817.

Ricoeur, Paul. *Memory, History, Forgetting*. Tr. Kathleen Blamey and David Pellauer. Chicago: University of Chicago Press, 2004.

Ringer, Fritz K. *The Decline of the German Mandarins: The German Academic Community, 1890–1933*. Cambridge, MA: Harvard University Press, 1969.

Ringshausen, Gerhard. "Das 450. Reformationsjubliäum 1967 in West und Ost." *Kirchliche Zeitsgeschichte*, 26 (2013): 373–99.

Robert, Dana. "Shifting Southward: Global Christianity since 1945." *International Bulletin of Missionary Research*, 24(2) (2000): 50–8.

Robertson, H. M. *Aspects of the Rise of Economic Individualism: A Critique of Max Weber and his School*. Cambridge: Cambridge University Press, 1933.

Rouse, Ruth, and Stephen Charles Neill, eds. *A History of the Ecumenical Movement, 1517–1948.* Philadelphia: Westminster Press, 1954.

Roy, Martin. *Luther in der DDR: Zum Wandel des Lutherbildes in der DDR-Geschichtsschreibung: mit einer dokumentarischen Reproduktion.* Bochum: Verlag Dieter Winkler, 2000.

Rupp, Gordon. *Martin Luther: Hitler's Cause or Cure?* London: Lutterworth Press, 1945.

Schaeffer, D. F. *Historical Address Commemorative of the Blessed Reformation Commenced by Dr. Martin Luther on the 31st of October A. D. 1517 Delivered in the Lutheran Church at Frederickstown on the 31st of October 1817.* Frederickstown, MD, 1818.

Schilling, Heinz. *Konfessionalisierung und Staatsinteressen.* Paderborn: Schöningh, 2007.

Schnabel, Franz. *Deutsche Geschichte im neunzehnten Jahrhundert: Die protestantischen Kirchen in Deutschland.* Freiburg im Breisgau: Herder, 1965.

Schnell, Hugo. *Martin Luther und die Reformation auf Münzen und Medaillen.* Munich: Klinkhardt & Biermann, 1983.

Schönstädt, Hans-Jürgen. *Antichrist, Weltheilsgeschehen und Gottes Werkzeug: Römische Kirche, Reformation und Luther im Spiegel des Reformationsjubiläums 1617.* Wiesbaden: Steiner, 1978.

Schönstadt, Hans-Jürgen, "Das Reformationsjubiläum 1617: Geschichtliche Herkunft und geistige Prägung." *Zeitschrift für Kirchengeschichte,* 93 (1982): 5–57.

Schönstadt, Hans-Jürgen. "Das Reformationsjubiläum 1717: Beiträge zur Geschichte seiner Entstehung im Spiegel landesherrlicher Verordnungen." *Zeitschrift für Kirchengeschichte,* 93 (1982): 58–118.

Schorn-Schütte, Luise, ed. *125 Jahre Verein Reformationsgeschichte.* Heidelberg: Gütersloh, 2008.

Schudson, Michael. "The Past in the Present versus the Present in the Past." *Communication,* 11 (1989): 105–13.

Schulin, Ernst. "Luther's Position in German History and Historical Writing." Tr. U. Watson. *Australian Journal of Politics and Religion,* 20 (1984): 85–98.

Scribner, Robert. *Popular Culture and Popular Movements in Reformation Germany.* London: Hambledon Press, 1987.

Seiss, Joseph Augustus. *Luther and the Reformation: The Life-Springs of our Liberties.* Philadelphia, 1884.

Sheehan, James J. *German History, 1770–1866.* Oxford Clarendon Press, 1989.

Sheeleigh, Matthias. *Luther: A Song-Tribute, on the Four Hundredth Anniversary of his Birth.* Philadelphia, 1883.

Skowronek, Alfons ed. *Martin Luther in ökumenischer Reflexion.* Warsaw: Akademia Teologii Katholickiej, 1984.

Smith, Enoch. *Martin Luther: A Memorial Volume for Schools and Families.* Allentown, PA, 1883.

Smith, Helmut Walser. *German Nationalism and Religious Conflict: Culture, Ideology, Politics, 1870–1914.* Princeton: Princeton University Press, 1995.

Smith, Preserved. "English Opinion of Luther." *Harvard Theological Review*, 2 (1917): 129–58.

Spitz, Lewis W. *The Reformation: Basic Interpretations*. Lexington, MA: D. C. Heath & Co., 1972.

Spitz, Lewis W. "The State of Reformation Research." *Concordia Journal*, 4 (1978): 6–15.

Stange, Douglas C. "A Marxist De-Lutheranization of the German Reformation." *Concordia Theological Monthly*, 38 (1967): 596–600.

Steinmetz, Max, and Gerhard Brendler, eds. *Weltwirkung der Reformation: Internationales Symposium anläßlich der 450-Jahr-Feier der Reformation in Wittenberg vom 24. Bis 26. Oktober 1967*. Berlin: Deutscher Verlag der Wissenschaften, 1969.

Stephenson, Barry. *Performing the Reformation: Public Ritual in the City of Luther*. Oxford: Oxford University Press, 2010.

Stern, Leo, and Max Steinmetz, eds. *450 Jahre Reformation*. Berlin: Deutscher Verlag der Wissenschaften, 1967.

Strand, Kenneth A. "A Brief Biographical Survey: Books on Luther Appearing in America during 1983 and 1984." *Andrews University Seminary Studies*, 22 (Spring 1984): 157–64.

Strom, Jonathan, Hartmut Lemann, and James Van Horn Melton, eds. *Pietism in Germany and North America, 1680–1820*. Farnham: Ashgate, 2009.

Stroud, Dean G., ed. *Preaching in Hitler's Shadow: Sermons of Resistance in the Third Reich*. Grand Rapids, MI: Eerdmans, 2013.

Süssmuth, Hans, ed. *Das Luther-Erbe in Deutschland: Vermittlung zwischen Wissenschaft und Öffentlichkeit*. Düsseldorf: Droste Verlag, 1985.

Swatos William H., and Lutz Kaelber, eds. *The Protestant Ethics Turns 100: Essays on the Centenary of the Weber Thesis*. Boulder, CO: Paradigm Publishers, 2005.

Tanner, Klaus, and Jörg Ulrich, eds. *Spurenlese. Reformationsvergegenwärtigung als Standortbestimmung, 1717–1983*. Leipzig: Evangelsiche Verlagsanstalt, 2012.

Thurston, Herbert. *The Holy Year of Jubilee*. New York: AMS Press, 1980.

Tillich, Paul. *The Protestant Era*. Chicago: University of Chicago Press, 1948.

Tischer, J. F. W. *The Life, Deeds, and Opinions of Dr. Martin Luther*. Tr. John Kortz. Hudson, NY, 1818.

Traupe, Gert. *Protestantismus und sozialer Wandel: Zur Transformation von Religion in einer multikulturellen Gesellschaft*. Münster: LIT, 1999.

Treitschke, Heinrich von. *Historische und politische Aufsätze*, iv. Leipzig: Verlag von S. Hirzel, 1897.

Troeltsch, Ernst. *Die Bedeutung des Protestantismus für die Entstehung der modernen Welt*. Munich: R. Oldenbourg, 1911.

Troeltsch, Ernst. *Protestantism and Progress: A Historical Study of the Relation of Protestantism to the Modern World*. Tr. W. Montgomery. Boston: Beacon Press, 1958.

Trouillot, Michel-Rolph. *Silencing the Past: Power and the Production of History*. Boston: Beacon, 1995.

Ullman, Ernst. *Von der Macht der Bilder: Beiträge des C.I.H.A.-Kolloquiums "Kunst und Reformation."* Leipzig: E. A. Seemann, 1983.

Vereb, Jerome-Michael. *"Because he was a German": Cardinal Bea and the Origins of the Roman Catholic Engagement with the Ecumenical Movement.* Grand Rapids, MI: Eerdmans, 2006.

Vinke, Rainer, ed. *Lutherforschung im 20. Jahrhundert: Rückblick, Bilanz, Ausblick.* Mainz: Verlag Philipp von Zabern, 2004.

Volf, Miroslav. *The End of Memory: Remembering Rightly in a Violent World.* Grand Rapids, MI: Eerdmans, 2006.

Walinski-Kiehl, Robert. "History, Politics, and East German Film: The Thomas Müntzer (1956) Socialist Epic." *Central European History,* 39 (2006): 30–55.

Wallmann, Johannes. "Karl Holl und seine Schule." *Zeitschrift für Theologie und Kirche,* 4 (1978): 1–33.

Walls, Andrew. *The Missionary Movement in Christian History.* Maryknoll, NY: Orbis, 1996.

Ward, William. *The Reformation from Popery Commemorated: A Discourse Delivered in the Independent Meeting House, Stowmarket, November 9, 1817.* Stowmarket, 1817.

Weber, Max. *The Protestant Ethic and the Spirit of Capitalism.* London: G. Allen & Unwin, 1930.

Welch, Claude. *Protestant Thought in the Nineteenth Century,* 2 vols. New Haven: Yale University Press, 1972.

Wendebourg, Dorothea. "Die Reformationsjubiläen des 19. Jahrhunderts." *Zeitschrift für Theologie und Kirche,* 108 (2011): 270–335.

Wentz, Abdel Ross. *Martin Luther in the Changing Light of Four Centuries.* Gettysburg: Gettysburg Complier Print, 1917.

Wenz, Philipp Jacob. *Die Kirchenverbesserung des 16. Jahrhunderts.* Emden: Gedruckt bei Wittwe Hyner, 1819.

Werdermann, Hermann. *Martin Luther und Adolf Hitler: Ein geschichtlicher Vergleich.* Gnadenfrei in Schlesien: Gnadenfrei, 1935, 2nd edn. 1937.

Wessel, Klaus. *Das Wartburgfest der Deutschen Burschenschaft am 18 Oktober 1817.* Eisenach: Röth, 1954.

Wiener, Peter F. *Martin Luther: Hitler's Spiritual Ancestor.* London: Hutchinson & Co., 1945.

Willebrands, Johannes Cardinal, ed. *Mandatum unitatis: Beiträge zur Ökumene.* Paderborn: Bonifatius, 1989.

Willkomm, Martin. *Luther als Vater seiner Kinder.* Zwickau: Johannes Herrmann, 1917.

Winckler, Lutz. *Martin Luther als Bürger und Patriot: Das Reformationsjubiläum von 1817 und der politische Protestantismus des Wartburgfestes.* Lübeck: Matthiesen Verlag, 1969.

Wuthnow, Robert. *Boundless Faith: The Global Outreach of American Churches.* Berkeley, CA: University of California Press, 2009.

Zeeden, E. W. *Martin Luther und die Reformation im Urteil des deutschen Luthertums: Dokumente zur inneren Entwicklung des deutschen Protestantismus von Luthers Tode bis zum Beginn der Goethezeit*, ii. Freiburg im Bresigau: Herder, 1952.

Zum Luther-Jubiläum: Bibliographie der Luther-Literatur des Jahres 1883. Frankfurt am Main: Verlag der Schriften-Niederlage, 1883.

Index